Nationalism in a Global Era

Despite predictions forecasting the demise of the nation-state in the global era, the nation persists as an important source of identity, community and collective memory for most of the world's population. This book explores the nation and nation-state's continuing relevance despite the pressures of globalization and related forces.

Nationalism in a Global Era makes a unique contribution to the literature on nations and nationalism by examining not where nations came from, but by looking at why, despite myriad threats, they continue as a vibrant and strong social cohesive. More than simply a corrective to the many scholarly but premature epitaphs for the nation-state, this text sets out to explain the continued health of nations despite looming threats. The contributors include leading experts in the field such as Anthony D. Smith, William Safran and Edward A. Tiryakian, as well as younger scholars. A variety of approaches ranging from theoretical to empirical and historical to sociological are used to uncover the reasons why nations continue to remain vital in the global age. Featuring case studies on Ireland, Thailand, Poland, the Baltic States, Croatia and Jordan, the book will be of great interest to students and researchers of international politics, sociology, nationalism and ethnicity.

Mitchell Young is completing a Ph.D. in Government at the London School of Economics and Political Science, UK. **Eric Zuelow** is Assistant Professor of European and World History at West Liberty State College, West Virginia, USA. **Andreas Sturm** recently gained a Ph.D. in Government from the London School of Economics and Political Science, UK.

Nationalism and ethnicity/Routledge studies in nationalism and ethnicity

Series Editor: William Safran
University of Colorado at Boulder

This series draws attention to some of the most exciting issues in current world political debate: nation-building, autonomy and self-determination; ethnic identity, conflict and accommodation; pluralism, multiculturalism and the politics of language; ethnonationalism, irredentism and separatism; and immigration, naturalization and citizenship. The series includes monographs as well as edited volumes and, through the use of case studies and comparative analyses, will bring together some of the best work found in the field.

Nationalism and ethnicity

Ethnicity and Citizenship
The Canadian case
Edited by Jean Laponce and William Safran

Nationalism and Ethnoregional Identities in China
Edited by William Safran

Identity and Territorial Autonomy in Plural Societies
Edited by William Safran and Ramon Maíz

Ideology, Legitimacy and the New State
Yugoslavia, Serbia and Croatia
Siniša Malešević

Diasporas and Ethnic Migrants
Germany, Israel and Russia in comparative perspective
Rainer Munz and Rainer Ohliger

Ethnic Groups in Motion
Economic competition and migration in multiethnic states
Milica Z. Bookman

Post-Cold War Identity Politics
Northern and Baltic experiences
Edited by Marko Lehti and David J. Smith

Welfare, Ethnicity and Altruism
New findings and evolutionary theory
Edited by Frank Salter

Routledge studies in nationalism and ethnicity

Ethnic Violence and the Societal Security Dilemma
Paul Roe

Nationalism in a Global Era
The persistence of nations
Edited by Mitchell Young, Eric Zuelow and Andreas Sturm

Nationalism in a Global Era

The persistence of nations

Edited by Mitchell Young, Eric Zuelow
and Andreas Sturm

Routledge
Taylor & Francis Group

LONDON AND NEW YORK

First published 2007
by Routledge
2 Park Square, Milton Park, Abingdon, Oxon OX14 4RN

Simultaneously published in the USA and Canada
by Routledge
270 Madison Ave, New York, NY 10016

Routledge is an imprint of the Taylor & Francis Group, an informa business

© 2007 Selection and editorial matter, Mitchell Young, Eric Zuelow
and Andreas Sturm; individual chapters, the contributors

Typeset in Garamond by Wearset Ltd, Boldon, Tyne and Wear
Printed and bound in Great Britain by TJI Digital, Padstow, Cornwall

British Library Cataloguing in Publication Data
A catalogue record for this book is available from the British Library

Library of Congress Cataloguing in Publication Data
A catalog record has been requested for this book

ISBN10: 0-415-41405-9 (hbk)
ISBN10: 0-203-96351-7 (ebk)

ISBN13: 978-0-415-41405-0 (hbk)
ISBN13: 978-0-203-96351-7 (ebk)

Contents

Illustrations

Notes on contributors

Gabriella Elgenius is a Research Fellow and Lecturer at Oxford University. Her Ph.D. dissertation, *Expressions of Nationhood: National Symbols and Ceremonies in Contemporary Europe*, is to be published in 2007. Her recent written work has appeared in the *British Social Attitudes Report*, and *Nations and Nationalism*.

Mark A. Jubulis is Associate Professor and Chair of the Department of History, Political Science, and Legal Studies at Gannon University Erie, Pennsylvania. He is the author of *Nationalism and Democratic Transition: The Politics of Citizenship and Language in Post-Soviet Latvia* (2001).

Stefanie Nanes is Assistant Professor at the Department of Political Science, Hofstra University Hempstead, NY. She is the author of "Fighting Honor Crimes: Evidence of Civil Society in Jordan" (*Middle East Journal*, 57(1).

William Safran is Professor Emeritus of Political Science at the University of Colorado, Boulder. He has written widely on comparative and French politics, ethnicity and nationalism. Among his more recent books are *Identity and Territorial Autonomy in Plural Societies* (2000), *The French Polity* (6th edn, 2002), *The Secular and the Sacred: Nation, Religion, and Politics* (2003), and *Language, Ethnicity, and the State* (2005).

Anthony D. Smith is Professor Emeritus of Ethnicity and Nationalism at the London School of Economics. His previous publications include *Theories of Nationalism* (1971, 1983), *The Ethnic Origin of Nations* (1986), *National Identity* (1991), *Nations and Nationalism in a Global Era* (1995), *Nationalism and Modernism* (1998) and *Chosen People* (2004).

Andreas Sturm recently received his Ph.D. from the London School of Economics. He is the author of *Die Handels- und Agrarpolitik Thailands von 1767 bis 1932* [*The Commercial and Agrarian Policy of Thailand from 1767 to 1932*] (1997).

Edward A. Tiryakian is Professor of Sociology at Duke University, North Carolina. He has written widely on themes such as national identity, modernity, and sociological theory and has taught at Duke, Princeton and Harvard universities, as well as at the Free University of Berlin, the Institut d'Etudes Politiques in Paris and Concordia University in Montreal.

Christopher S. Wilson is a Visiting Instructor in the Faculty of Art, Design and Architecture at Bilkent University, Ankara, Turkey and a Ph.D. candidate at the Middle East Technical University, Ankara. He is currently writing a dissertation examining the five architectural constructions that have been used to house the dead body of Mustafa Kemal Atatürk.

Mitchell Young is completing a Ph.D. at the London School of Economics, having worked in the intelligence field in the Balkans. His written work has appeared in *Millennium*, *Nations and Nationalism* and *Studies in Ethnicity and Nationalism*.

Geneviève Zubrzycki is Assistant Professor of Sociology at the University of Michigan-Ann Arbor. She is the author of *The Crosses of Auschwitz: Nationalism and Religion in Post-Communist Poland* (2006).

Eric Zuelow is Assistant Professor of European and World History at West Liberty State College, West Virginia and creator/editor of *The Nationalism Project* nationalismproject.org. He is currently preparing his first book, *Making Ireland Irish: Tourism and National Identity since the Irish Civil War*, for publication.

Acknowledgments

As with all books, more debts have been incurred in the development of this project than can possibly be acknowledged in the short space available. The book would not have been possible without the Association for the Study of Ethnicity and Nationalism (ASEN), founded in 1990 by research students and academics at the London School of Economics and Political Science (LSE). As part of its activities, ASEN organizes an annual conference to discuss and debate a wide variety of questions about nationalism, nation and national identity; this book has emerged from the 2004 conference entitled "When is the Nation?". The editors would like to thank the organizers of that event, Dr Gordana Uzelac and Dr Atsuko Ichijo, for their cooperation, support and assistance with this publication. We are grateful to the volume's contributors for their chapters and for their patience during the long process of compiling the manuscript. Professor William Safran, both a contributor and the editor of the Routledge Studies in Nationalism and Ethnicity series, deserves special recognition. His comments and advice were invaluable. Heidi Bagtazo and Harriet Brinton of Routledge were exceedingly helpful in getting this project off the ground and answering the questions of relatively novice editors as the work progressed.

Each of us has incurred personal debts along the way. Zuelow would like to thank Catherine M. Burns. Sturm would like to thank Dr Klairung Amratisha. Young thanks his parents William and Joan, whose encouragement and hospitality made the completion of this project a lighter task. Finally, the editors are grateful to Professor Anthony D. Smith – also a contributor – whose work was celebrated at the "When is the Nation?" conference and whose scholarship serves as the inspiration for this volume.

1 The owl's early flight

Globalization and nationalism, an introduction

Eric Zuelow, Mitchell Young and Andreas Sturm

It is not impossible that nationalism will decline with the decline of the nation-state, without which being English or Irish or Jewish, or a combination of these, is only one way in which people describe their identity among many others which they use for this purpose, as occasion demands. It would be absurd to claim that this day is already near. However, I hope it can at least be envisaged. After all, the very fact that historians are at least beginning to make some progress in the study and analysis of nations and nationalism suggests that, as so often, the phenomenon is past its peak. The owl of Minerva which brings wisdom, said Hegel, flies out at dusk. It is a good sign that it is now circling round nations and nationalism.

(Hobsbawm 1990: 192)

The owl has been busy since Eric Hobsbawm made the above comment in 1990. Today, in 2006, scholars share knowledge in at least four journals dedicated to nations and nationalism (and countless other publications that touch on the subject); academic presses are replete with nationalism-related monographs/collections; and scholarly nationalism studies associations offer an intellectual community for those interested in national identity. Just as Hobsbawm predicted the evolution of a more global sense of identity, now scholars make use of a truly global medium, the internet, to communicate about an identity that is supposed to be on the wane.

What has all of this study taught us? Hobsbawm's decline of the nation-state thesis still has its supporters, even adherents who go much farther than Hobsbawm himself was willing to go. Arjun Appadurai, for example, suggests "we need to think ourselves beyond the nation" because the modern nation-state is in "a serious crisis" brought on by transnational conditions. Globalization has "de-territorialized" the nation and created post-national *citoyens du monde* (Appadurai 1996). Appadurai is not alone in this view. Jonathan Rosenbaum and Janet Staiger (among others) point to the demise of national cinema as but one sign of growing homogenization (Williams 2002: 217–48). Others have coined new phrases, Disneyfication, McDonaldization, and even Coca-Colonization, to illustrate the submergence of national distinctiveness in a sea of Americanized global-culture.

Public intellectuals present this erosion of both the state as a political-legal body and the nation as a cultural community as inevitable. Harvard economist Richard N. Cooper has written that population increase, growth in per capita income, and greater capacity in computation and communication will lead to "increased international mobility among firms and individuals, reducing economic and ultimately cultural differences among different parts of the globe" (Cooper 1997). Influential columnist Thomas L. Friedman quotes the equally influential writer Fouad Ajami, saying the market will "empower common men and women" to fulfill desires that might include "strip malls along every street and Taco Bells on every corner . . . even though in the short run that will steamroll their local and national cultures" (Friedman 1999: 241).

Despite these pronouncements, many examples suggest that nations, national identity, and nationalism persist. The following cases can stand for others. In 1999, Scotland and Wales were granted devolved parliaments – the result of long nationalist campaigns – and the countries' respective nationalist parties, the Scottish National Party and Plaid Cymru in Wales, attained official opposition status in these new bodies. In response, English nationalists formed the English Defence Force, the English National Party and the English Democrats in order to secure a devolved *English* parliament. At virtually the same time, across the Irish Sea, Sinn Féin and the Democratic Unionist Party, both "nationalist" in the scholarly sense though advocating diametrically opposed versions of Ulster identity, emerged as the leading political parties in Northern Ireland. The Palestinian nationalist group Hamas won a 58-seat majority in the Palestinian legislative elections held in January 2006. Volunteers (or vigilantes, depending on one's view) seeking to limit illegal immigration into the United States have adopted a traditional American symbol of resistance, the Minuteman. While the Basque separatist organization ETA announced a permanent ceasefire in March 2006, it did so largely because the Madrid train bombings altered the political landscape, not because the group had abandoned nationalist aspirations. And finally, on a more banal level, no national community in the world acknowledges the demise of its national distinctiveness – each still believes itself unique and continues to point toward an assortment of exceptional national characteristics, traditions and places. Even the adoption of the Euro, sometimes depicted as a sign of diminishing national distinctiveness in Europe, prominently features the national symbols of member states on both coin and paper currency. In short, this time at least, the owl of Minerva may have decided to stretch its wings at noon rather than dusk and the story of early twenty-first-century nation-states appears to be one of persistence, not decline.

Nationalism in a Global Era: The Persistence of Nations provides an interdisciplinary and varied exploration of why nations have continued to be vibrant and strong social cohesives. More than simply a corrective to the work of scholarly eulogists intent on writing a premature epitaph for the nation-state, this collection sets out to explain the continued health of nations despite looming threats. Contributors adopt a variety of approaches ranging from theoretical to empirical and historical to sociological, in order to uncover both the reasons why nations continue to remain vital and the mechanisms that help perpetuate them.

The present volume is divided into three parts. The first offers three theoretical approaches toward understanding the persistence of nations. The second examines how celebrations, monuments and even tourism, said by many to be a harbinger of the demise of national identity, help nations remain relevant. The final part addresses both the threats to modern national identities and nation-states as well as the response to these threats.

Theoretical approaches

Few subjects in the social sciences and humanities have spawned anything like the copious theories and debates found in nationalism studies – a fact that reflects both the booming scholarly interest in and the complex nature of each. Since the early 1980s. scholarly discourse has been dominated by the view that nations are a product of modernity, created by nationalist elites to mobilize and unify diverse populations. The main proponents of this view are ubiquitous in scholarly discourse – Hobsbawm, Karl Deutsch, Ernest Gellner and Benedict Anderson. Yet the dominant orthodoxy is not without challengers. Anthony D. Smith and his supporters, for example, doubt that intelligentsias could form nations *ex nihilo*. For Smith nations are the product of almost primordial *ethnie*: assorted traditions, historical experiences, language and other common socio-cultural antecedents. This alternate model, called ethno-symbolism, promises an understanding both of why particular nations were formed and why nationalisms possess distinctive features and content. According to Smith, nations existed during the premodern age and continued to develop over an extended period of time. Nationalism, however, is a product of modernity that used preexisting *ethnie* to form a strong emotional connection between people and nation. By providing nations with a longer and more coherent genealogy, Smith placed nations and nationalism onto a broader historical canvas while drawing attention to the importance of emotion for the mobilization of nationalist sentiment.

As the authors in Part I of this volume show, Smith's ethno-symbolist view provides a means for understanding the persistence of nations; because nations have deep roots, they carry with them tremendous emotional appeal. While an emerging "global culture" might seem significant, the reality is that it poses a minimal threat to the nation precisely because people have a deep loyalty and affection for their national communities.

Smith himself opens the first section by examining the extent to which globalization is diminishing national identity in Western and Central Europe. He concludes that nation-states, both as political bodies and cultural communities, have come under considerable stress. Among other issues, nation-states are threatened by immigration, the loss of common national myths, pan-Europeanization and increasing economic integration. Today, states must avidly debate the question "who is 'us'" while at the same time developing a polemics of multiculturalism and multiethnic state membership. Local populations must defend national laws against European directives. Preservationists must be forever vigilant in guarding "national" heritage – whether buildings or the countryside – against "international" developers and those not tuned into the national soul. For Smith, however, these threats and the spirited response to them is clear indication that "the nation" as a social-psychological phenomenon is far from dead.

This "persistence of the nation" is accompanied by what Smith sees as a growing alienation from the state on the part of many publics in Western Europe. Public dissatisfaction with state responses to perceived threats to the "national" community may contribute to a future decoupling of "the state" and "the nation" even in the old, established states of Western Europe. Here, the hidden "dominant ethnicity" may reemerge under the pressures of globalization. As Smith puts it, "the mingling of different cultures and religions in a harsher political climate has once again returned the dominant *ethnie* to its ethnic moorings amid moral panics..."

William Safran picks up where Smith leaves off by providing an extended exploration of the territorialization, deterritorialization, and reterroritorialization of the nation. To this end, he examines three diasporic *ethnie*: Armenians, Sikhs and Jews. Safran begins by discussing the concept of "homeland" which may exist with or without an independent state. He notes that the homeland is often the location of centers of religious worship – indeed this is true of all three of his cases. The diasporic nation "differs from a diaspora *ethnie* in that it territorializes and politicizes the 'myth-symbol complex.'" Diaspora *ethnies* are an early and continuing example of globalization as they constitute "part of a trans-border, and often highly organized, global communication network; many of their institutions are transnational, and they use a language that is disseminated far below an intellectual elite or a church hierarchy and far beyond the confines of their host countries."

Of course, diasporas have played an important part in gaining or regaining the *political* independence of the homeland. Safran points to the mobilizing effect that diasporas can have on fellow members of their *ethnie* residing in the "homeland." Certainly the Sikh, Armenian and Jewish diasporic *ethnie* have played a role in the attempts to gain political status for the cultural and religious homeland. This echoes the findings of Meredith L. Weiss (2006) that diasporic communities matter when such a "population has resources and motivation to contribute."

In his chapter Tiryakian, asks an important question: "When is the nation no longer?" Modernist academics tend to equate nation-states with nation; therefore, in the case of the disappearance of such a state, Yugoslavia and apartheid South Africa, for example, it is assumed that the nation disappears as well. Tiryakian rejects this approach by distinguishing between the two entities. He strengthens Anthony Smith's argument that nations can persist over long periods of time by showing that nations can survive even in a submerged state. Reviving such nations in later periods means that some nations could emerge from multiple beginnings and be resilient to change. Central in this process of remaining a nation is that critical segments of the population still view themselves as members of that nation's societal community.

Memory and the persistence of nations

Diasporic communities rely heavily on an idealized memory of the homeland, just as nations rely on specific, romanticized memories of the past. Indeed, the relationship between nations and memory has been clear since at least 1882 when Ernest Renan famously suggested: "Forgetting, I would even go so far as to say historical error, is a crucial factor in the creation of a nation" (Renan 1996: 45). Nationalists remember only what is helpful to their cause. Scottish nationalists remember Robert Bruce's stunning upset against the English at Bannockburn in 1314 while the great king's tendency to change sides frequently is forgotten (Barrow 1988). Americans celebrate a mythology of manifest destiny and the settlement of uninhabited space while forgetting the reality of indigenously occupied place. One simply cannot separate "collective memory" from national identity.

During the past 20 years, scholars from across disciplines recognized the importance of group memory and turned their attention to the nature of the memory process (Halbwachs 1992; Connerton 1989), the subjects remembered (Eley 1988; Rousso 1991), and the tools of remembrance (Koshar 1998, 2000; Young 1993). Memory scholars have also endeavored to historicize group memory. Most famously, Pierre Nora (1989) contends that prior to the nineteenth century, memory was absolutely central to society (*mileux de mémoire*), while today memory must be connected to specific places of memory (*lieux de mémoire*). John R. Gillis (1994) offers a slightly different view which features three overlapping phases: "the pre-national (before the eighteenth century), the national (from the American and French Revolutions to the 1960s), and the present, post-national phase" (1994: 5). Each phase was different from the last, but in all cases, identity, memory and politics were closely connected (1994: 3–5).

This connection between politics, identity and memory rests at the very heart of memory studies because modern politics gains legitimacy from a remembered past while forwarding contemporary agendas. Commemoration of the Holocaust is particularly instructive. During the Cold War, Holocaust memory in the Soviet sphere was dominated by the idea that the Holocaust was a result of Western imperialism – a threat that must be forever guarded against. Meanwhile, in the West, the Holocaust was explained as a result of totalitarianism, once exemplified by Fascism, then by Soviet Communism, but always to be guarded against (Huener 2003; Young 1993). In both cases, political regimes and political ideologies were bolstered by self-definition as the polar opposite of evil.

The contributors to the second part of *Nationalism in a Global Era* build on these debates by placing particular emphasis on the role played by memory in assuring the persistence of nations; just as the two Germanys used Holocaust memory to meet new demands, so too do nations recast the past in the face of global challenges. Toward this end, the authors pay particular attention to *who* is both behind and involved in the shaping of collective memory, whether that be elites, average citizens, or some combination of the two.

Gabriella Elgenius begins the section with a comparative discussion of national celebrations and commemorations, focusing specifically on Bastille Day (France), Constitution Day (Norway), and Remembrance Sunday (Britain). Building on two assumptions, that national days represent an expression of nationhood and that their status illustrates the continued popularity of the nation, Elgenius argues that national holidays help to sanctify the nation, setting the national liturgy apart from the mundane of the everyday. National days represent secular religious practice that helps perpetuate the symbolism of the nation in much the same way as the Catholic mass or other religious ceremony does for the faithful. As Elgenius notes, national days can be powerful tools that bind past, present and future generations together.

Elgenius is careful to point out that the three holidays that she has chosen for study differ in form and therefore suggest variance in the relative importance of various social groups. Britain's Remembrance Sunday, for example, celebrates Britain's war dead and therefore resembles a national funeral with full military honors. Average Britons can watch the parade and lay flowers but do not themselves march past the Cenotaph in Whitehall. In contrast, Norway's Constitution Day features a children's parade and can "best be described as a sincere and joyful national celebration marked by flag-waving, national music, national dress (*bunad*), parades, speeches, church services and the laying of wreaths at war memorials" – it is, in other words, a more grassroots experience involving far more of the population. On the one hand, memory work is predominately carried out by the state as the masses watch, while on the other the action of commemorating the past is far more grassroots, even if the state plays a significant role as well.

Whereas Elgenius suggests but does not emphasize the importance of place to successful memory work, Christopher Wilson offers an extended exploration of the role of place in Turkish national memory by examining both the creation and uses of Anıtkabir, Mustafa Kemal Atatürk's mausoleum complex at Ankara. Wilson begins by placing the construction of the various buildings into historical context and exploring how particular design elements were chosen to create a history for the modern Turkish people that at once forgot the Ottoman Empire while looking back further to classical and even preclassical origins. Of course, the story of Anıtkabir does not end with its design and construction. One cannot assume, following a popular Hollywood movie, that "if you build it, they will come" – it is necessary to continually ensure relevance through the development and perpetual re-enactment of a commemorative liturgy. Wilson explores how Anıtkabir is variously used by the state to celebrate the nation *and* by protest groups anxious that the site serve to nationalize various political issues – a variety of groups, in other words, are given a chance to participate in the perennial (re-)construction of the nation. By using the site, whether for protest or national celebration, Anıtkabir is at once reaffirmed as the symbolic soul of the Turkish *ethnie* while also lending this symbolic resonance to whatever group performs memory work at the site.

In his chapter, Andreas Sturm also recognizes the importance of place by tracing the development of Thai memory sites from the mid-nineteenth century to the present. For Sturm, the commemorative process is less about cross-societal creation and more about the combination of "mainstream elite groups" involved in an active process of contesting the precise definition and composition of the nation. The result of this process is a constant "reinterpretation and adaptation" of the nation, producing "distinguishably different nationalisms" over time and allowing the Thai nation the crucial malleability needed to persist despite global threats. Sturm identifies three distinct competing nationalisms over the course of his study – monarchical, political/statist and royal – and he illustrates how and why they developed, peaked and gradually changed form to meet developing needs: a process that is likely to continue into the foreseeable future.

Geneviève Zubrzycki also addresses the role of place, liturgy and the question of who is remembering in her chapter about the commemorative conflict at Auschwitz, perhaps the most widely known Holocaust site. She describes how, in the summer and fall of 1998, self-defined "Poles-Catholics" erected hundreds of crosses outside the former Nazi death camp at Auschwitz. According to Zubrzycki, this act soon spawned a "war of the crosses" which "materialized and crystallized, within a single site and series of events, social conflicts regarding the role of Catholicism in defining Polishness, the place of religion and the Church in the new polity, and the role of anti-Semitism in the construction and affirmation of Polish national identity" – in short, the crosses served as a trigger for dialogue about the nature of Polishness. In contrast to Sturm's discussion of Thai nationalism, the characters in Zubrzycki's narrative seem to represent regular Polish citizens rather than elites. Indeed, far from following the path proscribed by elite institutions – the Episcopate of Poland, for example – her subjects actively resisted top–down authority. The crosses themselves serve as a testament to competing ideas about the nature of Polishness because each featured an affixed message from the individual or organization responsible for erecting it. For Zubrzycki, this is significant because the act of debating the relationship between Polishness and Catholicism served to "resacralize the national." Over time, the cross was first secularized, made a symbol of Poland as the Christ of Nations, and then resacralized to create a national religion of Polishness. This process of transforming popular perception of the cross helped Poland to weather both the various partitions of the country as well as the transformation from Communism to democracy.

For Eric Zuelow, the process of shaping and reshaping the nation is neither a top–down nor a bottom–up process – it is both. Zuelow claims that nations are perpetually "re-imagined through an ongoing exchange of ideas" that occurs across society; the challenge is to uncover how this process actually functions. Toward this end, Zuelow proposes that national dialogue takes place at specific points that he terms "nexus" where debate and discussion is inspired by historically contingent triggers such as economic programs, hot-button political issues, commemorative activity or even artistic works. Zuelow opts to examine the role that tourism development played in post-Civil War Ireland and he illustrates that Irish men and women, from across society, were faced with developing a vision of Ireland that would be acceptable to all audiences.

While globalization theorists often suggest that tourism undermines national identity by deterritorializing both hosts and guests, Zuelow suggests that tourism plays a far different role in the story of nations and nationalism. He argues that tourism forced the Irish people, broadly defined, to determine how to present Irish history, redevelop the Irish countryside to erase a legacy of poverty, and create traditions that would be widely acceptable as attractions – traditions which both reflected the "new Ireland" while also looking backward to a (newly created) historical narrative of unity and joy. In other words, tourism forced the host community to both ask and answer the question: "Who do we think we are?" Ultimately Zuelow uses the case of Irish tourism development to challenge the usual top–down narrative of national development (Hobsbawm and Ranger 1983) as well as the bottom–up approach exemplified by Partha Chatterjee (1993: 3–13) and others.

Threat, response, re-emergence

The chapters by Elgenius, Wilson, Sturm, Zubrzycki and Zuelow show that the intersubjective community that is the nation remains an important social phenomenon. Yet the globalization theorists are surely right that the close linking of state and nation, something of an ideal for the last century and a half, faces serious challenges. First, according to globalization theorists, trends in technology and economics, even demographics are eroding the importance of the state. This position crosses the political spectrum, although the "right" and "left" of the globalization continuum place emphasis on slightly different factors. On the one hand, for those on the "right," adherents to the so-called "Washington Consensus," ever-freer markets will lead to an era of increasing prosperity. As this happens, national governments will lose control over economic policy at the same time that the distinctiveness of national cultures, everything from clothing to film, will likewise disappear. On the other hand, those on the "left" draw attention to an ever-thicker web of international law and international organizations. Unsurprisingly, as the chaos of international relations is brought under control, old assumptions "that sovereignty is an indivisible, illimitable, exclusive and perpetual form of public power – entrenched within an individual state" are now defunct (Held 2004: 139). The forces of internationalism have irreparably breached the nation-state: the global age has come.

Yet it would be a mistake to underestimate the power of the concept of "nation" and its ability to mobilize a population. Self-defined nations have faced challenges equal to that of the current era of globalization. The spread of totalitarian regimes during the first half of the twentieth century, for example, turned many former nation-states into stateless nations, but failed to eliminate the underlying desire for national sovereignty. Then, even as globalization was supposedly poised to end the age of nations altogether, these same groups gave rise to a revivification of cultural nationhood that, in turn, spawned a reemergence of former nation-states. As noted earlier, nationalist movements in both the former Soviet sphere and in places like Scotland, Wales, Catalonia, northern Italy, Quebec and Flanders suggest something quite different than the demise of nations and the drive for statehood.

Of course, it is the ex-socialist world where the renaissance of national identity as social and political phenomenon has been most pronounced. Mark Jubulis's account of the national revival in the Baltic republics, and its role in the breakup of the Soviet Union, shows how these small states reemerged after decades under Soviet domination. Jubulis first critiques the prevailing institutional accounts of the role of nationalism in the breakup of the Soviet Union, making a convincing case that the institutional arrangements of the Soviet Union did not create a sense of national identity. Rather, it was in the Baltics – nations that had begun to develop a sense of national identity in the nineteenth century and that achieved statehoods in the aftermath of World War I – where national movements were the strongest. These movements used traditional cultural resources to mobilize the population with the goal of forming a sovereign state. Only the political apparatus of the state could protect the national *cultures* of these lands, lands faced with pressures, such as large-scale migration, similar to those many nation-states face today. The national revivals were focused almost from the beginning on regaining sovereignty, the only hope for national survival.

In his chapter on another country in the former Communist space, Mitchell Young examines linguistic nationalism and language reform in Croatia. The case is important because the newly independent Republic of Croatia is certainly heavily subject to the pressures of globalization and its regional variant, Europeanization. Croatia's governments have expressly stated their desire to join both the EU and NATO – i.e. to be fully integrated into the West. Yet, at the same time, the country has tried to establish an identity separate from its Yugoslav past. Language is a particularly important part of this program as many Croatians feel that their language was submerged in the ill-fated attempt to merge with the Serbs – both politically and linguistically. Establishing a national identity, even a linguistic identity, in a global era is a tricky business. The rights of language minorities must be respected: governments must not appear too nationalistic. Young makes the case that Croatia has used indirect actions – particularly funding – to support various institutions in their effort to build a linguistic identity for the new Republic. He shows that even informatics, one of the technical phenomena supposedly eroding national identity, can become sites of national identity-building as new nations apply technology to their own languages and improve them for use in the twentieth century.

Croatia and the Baltic states could all claim a state tradition built on a formalized culture dating back at least to the nineteenth century. Jordan had fewer cultural resources to work with. Stefanie Nanes's contribution explores the persistence of that state and its evolution toward a national identity, despite severe challenges. Nanes shows how even newly formed states can build a durable national identity while apparently lacking deep roots.

Nanes makes the case that Jordanian national identity is based firmly on a preexisting tribal identity, an identity that in turn is tied to Islam. This Islamic connection is not synonymous with recent conceptions of Islamist politics, rather it is a long-term connection based on the Hashemite dynasty and its traditional role in guarding Muslim holy places. Modern Jordanian national identity draws the tribes together as supporters of the monarchy, which in turn is symbolically connected to Islam. This evolution has obscured earlier attempts at building a pan-Arab nationalism – largely an elite and intellectual effort. Jordanian national identity has also flourished despite challenges, particularly the demographic impact of Palestinian Arabs who remain outside the system of tribal affiliation. Nanes's case shows that a firm national identity can become rooted despite the lack of a historical state structure – if such an identity is based on traditional ethnic components.

In all three cases, the Baltics, Croatia and Jordan, a sovereign nation has come into existence despite the threats inherent in the current globalized age. The Baltic states and Croatia survived the attempt of an earlier universalizing ideology to minimize national differences, especially as a motivation for *political* action. However, members of the *nations* of these ex-Communist polities found that the *political* apparatus of the nation-state was necessary to protect the national *cultural* community. Emerging as independent actors in a globalizing world, they will have to confront a perhaps more serious threat: the leveling force of the free-market economy promoted by "right" globalization theorists. Jordan, on the other hand, faces a less benign threat. The upheavals of the Middle East have meant the growth of another universalizing ideology, that of Islamic fundamentalism. While it remains to be seen whether its more traditional connection with Islam – via the tribes and the Hashemite dynasty – can survive in the region's current travails, Nanes's chapter seems to indicate a qualified "yes."

Conclusion

None of the contributors to this volume doubts that national identity and modern nation-states face challenges, but together they present a clear response to those who believe the owl of Minerva left its branch at dusk; it has only just turned noon. Each of the cases presented here, whether it be England, France, Ireland, Thailand, Turkey, Croatia, the Baltic states, Jordan, or even diasporic communities such as the Sikhs, Jews or Armenians, suggests that nations are flexible groupings, deeply rooted in both a real and imagined past, and that they are capable of adapting to myriad threats – including globalization.

At one level, the threat of globalization to cultural and even political nationalism is mostly limited – as Smith notes in his chapter – to the West (i.e. Europe and to a lesser extent North America). The studies of Thailand and Turkey clearly show that national identity rooted in strong leadership figures remains a powerful phenomenon in many places. On the periphery of Europe, the nations that emerged from behind the Iron Curtain are often wholeheartedly enthusiastic about a European Union that offers opportunities for trade and migration. However, in all of these new republics significant segments of the population have sought and continue to seek a strong national identity – whether through establishing the titular nation's clear political dominance as in the Baltics, reconnection with "historic" Western roots as in Croatia, or commemoration of the nation's suffering and redemption as in Poland. Nor are these phenomena limited to the "new Europe;" as Elgenius shows, national days of remembrance and celebration continue to be popular expressions of identity in the long-established states of "old Europe."

It is difficult to identify equally popular celebrations of the greatest "post-national" project, the European Union. Indeed there is conflict over the very idea of European identity, as shown in Tiryakian's discussion of the controversy over mention of religion in the European constitution. While the early builders of the European community may have had in mind a European identity based on pre-national Catholic Europe (Smith 1995: 129), it is an open question whether that sentiment reigns in Brussels today. Efforts at top–down creation of a European identity notably lack the sort of popular celebrations Elgenius's chapter details. It may be that Europe can be built on commitment to a minimal set of rights and duties – commonly called constitutional democracy or constitutional patriotism (Habermas 2001). However, the lack of ritual, celebration and memory would indicate – at least to the ethno-symbolist – that post-national Europe has a long way to go in creating a political and cultural community that is nearly as effective as the nation-state.

What of the legal, economic and technological factors supposedly consigning the nation-state to oblivion? European funding certainly had a part in creating the "Celtic Tiger" and turning many Irish men and women into enthusiasts for Europe. As Zuelow shows, however, efforts at economic improvement via a heavily "global" sector – tourism – have reached back to portray a specific image of the homeland, while the very campaign of improvement has served to reinforce collective identity. The globalization of communication networks has increased the ability of diaspora *ethnie* to organize in response to events of importance to their nation. These diasporic networks are sophisticated and effective at using "global" technology to create institutions and mobilize co-ethnics in far-flung places, as Safran shows. There could be no better case illustrating this ability than Zubrzycki's depiction of the "War of the Crosses" at Auschwitz, a controversy that eventually involved Jewish organizations worldwide. The case of Croatian language reform illustrates that communications technology can cut two ways; preparing the "national" language for the information age also becomes an effort at building national identity. The response of the Croatian government to some of the legal aspects of globalization and Europeanization – in the form of granting concessions to language minorities – does show that efforts at global governance have some effect. Yet such concessions are often grudging and mechanisms have been put in place to counteract their practical effect. Furthermore, as Anthony Smith points out in his chapter, the growth of such transnational legal regimes has every chance of creating a national backlash. Neither economic integration, nor the communications technology revolution, nor the growth of international legal institutions has spelled the end of national identity; on the contrary they have often reinforced it.

Perhaps what is most surprising is the eagerness of so many to begin eulogizing nations, not the persistence of nations. The history of nations and nationalism *is* one of evolution and persistence. Hobsbawm himself has shown that European nations changed form during the period between 1870 and 1918, adjusting themselves to the realities of a rapidly changing world (Hobsbawm 1990: 101–30). Likewise, as Billig (1995) has shown, nations easily change to become "hot" or "banal" as circumstances warrant. This flexibility is itself a tremendously powerful thing that should not be ignored by scholars; indeed, any significant understanding of nations, nationalism and national identity requires it be acknowledged and explained. This book hopes to draw attention both to the need for scholarly exploration of the flexibility of nations, as well as to suggest a variety of approaches toward understanding the persistence of nations, despite threats such as globalization.

References

Appadurai, A. (1996) "Sovereignty without Territoriality: Notes for a Postnational Geography," in P. Yaeger (ed.) *The Geography of Identity*, Ann Arbor: University of Michigan Press.

Barrow, G.W.S. (1988) *Robert Bruce and the Community of the Realm of Scotland*, Edinburgh: Edinburgh University Press.

Billig, M. (1995) *Banal Nationalism*, London: Sage Publications.

Chatterjee, P. (1993) *The Nation and Its Fragments: Colonial and Postcolonial Histories*, Princeton: Princeton University Press.

Connerton, C. (1989) *How Societies Remember*, Cambridge and New York: Cambridge University Press.

Cooper, R.N. (1997) "States, Citizens and Markets in the 21st Century," in T. Courchene (ed.) *The Nation State in a Global/Information Era: Policy Challenges*, Kingston, Ont.: John Deutsch Institute, Queen's University.

Eley, G. (1988) "Nazism, Politics and the Image of the Past: Thoughts on the West German Historikerstreit," *Past and Present*, 121: 171–208.

Friedman, T.L. (1999) *The Lexus and the Olive Tree*, New York: Farrar, Strauss, and Giroux.

Gellner, E. (1983) *Nations and Nationalism*, Ithaca: Cornell University Press.

Gillis, J.R. (ed.) (1994) *Commemorations: The Politics of National Identity*, Princeton: Princeton University Press.

Habermas, J. (2001) "Constitutional Democracy: A Paradoxical Union of Contradictory Principles?" *Political Theory*, 29(6): 766–81.

Halbwachs, M. (1992) *On Collective Memory*, Chicago: University of Chicago Press.

Held, D. (2004) *Global Covenant: The Social Democratic Alternative to the Washington Consensus*, London: Polity Press.

Hobsbawm, E.J. (1990) *Nations and Nationalism since 1780*, Cambridge: Cambridge University Press.

Hobsbawm, E.J. and Ranger, T. (1983) *The Invention of Tradition*, Cambridge and New York: Cambridge University Press.

Huener, J. (2003) *Auschwitz, Poland, and the Politics of Commemoration, 1945–1979*, Athens: Ohio University Press.

Koshar, R. (1998) *Germany's Transient Past: Preservation and National Memory in Twentieth Century Germany*, Chapel Hill: University of North Carolina Press.

—— (2000) *From Monuments to Traces: Artifacts of German Memory, 1870–1990*, Berkeley and Los Angeles: University of California Press.

Mosse, G.L. (1975) *The Nationalization of the Masses: Political Symbolism and Mass Movements in Germany from the Napoleonic Wars through the Third Reich*, Ithaca and London: Cornell University Press.

Nora, P. (1989). "Between Memory and History: *Les Lieux de Mémoire*," *Representations*, 26: 7–25.

Renan, E. (1996) "What Is a Nation?" in G. Eley and R.G. Suny (eds) *Becoming National: A Reader*, New York and Oxford: Oxford University Press.

Rousso, H. (1991) *The Vichy Syndrome: History and Memory in France since 1944*, Cambridge: Harvard University Press.

Smith, A.D. (1995) *Nations and Nationalism in a Global Era*, Cambridge: Polity Press.

Weiss, M. (2006) "Globalization and Ethnonationalist Movements," in D.R. Cameron, G. Ranis and A. Zinn (eds) *Globalization and Self-Determination: Is the Nation-State under Siege?*, London: Routledge.

Williams, A. (ed.) (2002) *Film and Nationalism*, New Brunswick and London: Rutgers University Press.

Young, J. (1993) *The Texture of Memory: Holocaust Memorials and Meaning*, New Haven: Yale University Press.

Part I

Theoretical approaches

2 Nations in decline?

The erosion and persistence of modern national identities

Anthony D. Smith

The longevity of nations has long exercised a fascination for scholars and public alike. For many people, nations and national states are part and parcel of the modern world, their comforting presence, durability and future continuity not seriously in doubt. Yet, over a century ago, Ernest Renan foresaw the likely supersession of nations by a European federation, though not in his epoch. Marx and Engels too looked to the transcendence of 'national narrow-mindedness' by the restless energy of international capitalism. In the last century, Karl Deutsch envisaged the subordination of nations to wider continental and regional political communities, while Ernest Gellner, as part of his debunking of nationalist myths, projected a future without nationalism (though not without nations) once the great hump of industrialisation had been surmounted and an affluent modernity attained (Renan 1882; Marx and Engels 1959; Deutsch *et al.* 1957; Gellner 1983).

The massive acceleration of globalising trends – of economic interdependence, total militarisation, mass migration, global communications and the diffusion of consumerism – has only confirmed these scholarly analyses, and increased the gulf between them and popular perceptions. For many theorists, the sheer magnitude of these changes portends the demise of nations, national states and nationalism, and the deterritorialisation of nations. For Eric Hobsbawm, the global trends which override national boundaries have altogether relegated nations and nationalism to a secondary role; no longer a 'major vector' of history, they have become mere complicating factors, their recent revival largely reactions of popular fear and loathing in the face of massive uprooting and the withering of family ties – a view that is echoed by Immanuel Wallerstein's description of nationalism as the 'nervous tic' of capitalism. A variant of this view sees nationalisms decoupled from nation-states; the decline of the latter as a result of global economic forces, according to Mathew Horsman and Andrew Marshall, does not entail the demise of nationalism. On the contrary, its proliferation betokens widespread new attachments to a variety of forms of the 'nation', including regional-continental (European) and provincial-ethnic forms (Hobsbawm 1992: ch. 6; Horsman and Marshall 1994: 84–6, 179).

Equally appealing for many scholars has been the notion that we are entering into a 'post-national order' in what is essentially a 'post-modern epoch'. Here the argument is directed less at national states than to the hybridisation of national identities. At the European level, Yasemin Soysal hypothesises a post-national order on the basis of immigrants acquiring universal rights outside national citizenship, even though these rights and benefits continue to be organised and administered by the respective national states. More generally, theorists of 'postmodern' society like Homi Bhabha posit identity change as an inevitable consequence of mass migration and the influx of culturally diverse economic migrants, asylum-seekers and ex-colonials into more affluent Western societies, challenging the pedagogic narratives proclaimed by the national state and the education system of the dominant majority. What remain of the 'nation' are the diverse cultures of the varied groups that have come to compose an increasingly multicultural West (Soysal 1994; Bhabha 1990).

Defining the nation

That nations and national identities have been subject to huge pressures and have undergone considerable transformations, few would contest. The question is whether, as a result of such pressures and changes, people have become more or less attached to their nations, and more or less wedded to a vibrant sense of national identity; conversely, whether such national identities appear increasingly obsolete compared to the continental and global alternatives on offer. Elsewhere, I have argued that a global culture, in whatever form, appears culturally fragmented, historically shallow and affectively neutral, by comparison with the emotive, easily intelligible and vibrant national cultures with which the vast majority of human beings have become familiar; and much the same still applies, *mutatis mutandis*, to regional continental communities and identities like the European Union. But, even if the alternatives on offer are as yet pale and unappealing to most people, the degree of popular attachments to nations and the corresponding strength of a sense of national identity, are still very much open questions. It is this issue that I wish to explore (Smith 1995: chs 1, 5).

First, some ground-clearing. To assess such attachments, we need to have a clear idea of their object. Unfortunately, agreed definitions of the concepts of 'nation' and 'national identity' are notoriously elusive, nor is there any consensus over the meanings to be attributed to terms like 'nationalism' and 'national sentiment'. Yet, no progress is possible without some attempt at defining key terms of our discourse. In this spirit, I offer the following methodological and substantive assumptions.

1   The terms 'nation' and 'national identity' need to be separated analytically from that of the 'state', even in the case of composite state-nations like Great Britain. This means that the much-vaunted 'decline of the state' in a post-modern epoch is not the same as a decline of nations;

analytically, these are quite separate issues. At the same time, substantively, as we shall see, the national state is heavily involved in the question of the decline or persistence of nations.

2 In the same way, terms like 'nation' and national identity' need to be sharply distinguished from 'nationalism', seen as an ideology and movement, or ideological movement. They also need to be separated from 'national sentiments' which have not been ideologised or politically organised. Again, the decline of the one does not entail that of the other. For all that, as we shall see, nationalism plays a key role in the decline or persistence of nations.[1]

3 Terms like 'nation' and 'national identity' operate on different levels. Abstractly, they refer to conceptual categories and ideal types. In this sense, the concept of the *nation* may be defined in ideal-typical terms as a named and self-defined human community whose members cultivate shared myths, symbols, values and memories, reside in and are attached to an historic homeland, create and disseminate a distinctive public culture, and observe common laws and customs. In practice, of course, particular instances of the 'nation' approximate in greater or lesser degree to this ideal-type. Similarly, *national identity* as a category may be defined as the continuous reproduction, reinterpretation and transmission of a pattern of symbols, values, memories, myths and traditions that compose the distinctive heritage of a nation, and the identification of individuals with the cultural elements of that heritage.

4 At the same time, on a more concrete level, these terms refer to intersubjective realities, which over time are constituted in people's minds as well as institutionally as objective, communal realities. That is to say, the term 'nation' may also refer to historical communities born of specific social processes operating and combining over the long term. So that nations and national identities operate simultaneously on two levels: as subjects of meaning and discourse, and as powerful communities for their members and in their consequences. Being historical, nations and national identities are always subject to change and their contents to contestation. Yet, in defining boundaries and shaping the course of collective action, they appear no less real and durable than do states or social classes.[2]

5 *Nationalism*, too, can be analysed on more than one level. Ideal-typically, we are speaking of an ideological movement for attaining and maintaining autonomy, unity and identity on behalf of a human population, some of whose members deem it to constitute an actual or potential 'nation'. Though there are several types of nationalist ideology and many varieties of movement, the ideal-type serves to demarcate nationalist from other kinds of ideological movement, as well as from national sentiments. At the same time, nationalisms, like nations, are historical phenomena generated by distinct social and cultural processes, taking many forms, both between and within particular communities and cultures (Smith 2001: ch. 1).

6   The formation of nations may be traced to the development of certain social processes and sources, and their combination over time. These help to shape human population categories and communities into approximations of the ideal-type of the nation. Of course, in practice, a variety of factors are involved in the development of these social processes and sources. But analysis of their development makes it possible to chart the movement of communities away from, as well as towards, the ideal-type of the nation, and hence to gauge the 'decline' of nations through the method of negation, that is, by observing and analysing the erosion of the sources and processes which underpin both individual nations and a 'world of nations'.

Processes of nation formation

Our main proposition is that the bases of nations as historical intersubjective realities are to be sought in key social processes and in cultural resources that are felt to be sacred. These *social* processes are of a general, transhistorical nature. Yet there is nothing determinate about them. As social processes, their development is often intermittent and reversible, depending as they do on human actions and interpretations. The development and combination of these social processes, and hence the formation of nations, though not in principle confined to particular historical epochs, are likely to occur only in specific historical circumstances. The processes in question include:

1   *self-definition*: the social process of naming and defining by self and others of a community constituting 'us' in contrast to 'them', outsiders who are dissimilar and unfamiliar;
2   *myth-and-memory-making*; the cultivation of myths, symbols, memories and traditions, and their dissemination by specialists to the members of the community;
3   *territorialisation*: residence in, and the growth of memories and attachments to an historic homeland, and the identification of the members with its landscapes;
4   *public culture*: the formation of a distinctive public culture, and its dissemination, usually by elites, through public rituals, codes and education;
5   *law-making*: the observance of shared ancestral customs, and the establishment and diffusion by elites of common laws and legal codes to the members of the community.

The cultural resources are more specific. They are, in fact, specialised developments from the more general processes, but they add a quality of awe and sanctity, which gives them a binding, religious dimension; and in this way, they serve as 'sacred foundations' of national identity. They include:

1   *myths of origins and ancestry*, including various tales often of descent from heroic or godlike ancestors, associated with founding events, such as the tales of Abraham, Romulus and Remus, or Clovis;

2   *myths of election*: a belief in the group's mission or covenant entrusted to it by the deity, and hence its conditional privilege and separate destiny;

3   *collective attachments to sacred ancestral homelands*, and a sense of intimacy with, and devotion to, sanctified landscapes;

4   *myth-memories of golden ages*: memories of heroic ages and sacred pasts, on the part of later generations of members, together with a desire to emulate its heroes and heroines;

5   *ideals of sacrifice and destiny*: commemoration and celebration by the members of a community of the glorious dead who inspire the living and help to regenerate the nation.

Apart from adding an aura of sanctity and veneration, these cultural resources crystallise certain aspects of the general processes, and illustrate the importance of subjective elements of will, devotion and belief. The first resource, for example, translates the development of self-definition into readily intelligible myths of origin, descent and foundation; and thereby provides both explanation and legitimation for the existence of the ethnic or the national community. The second, myths of ethnic election, are perhaps the most influential and dynamic of the general processes of myth-and-memory cultivation, conferring on the *ethnie* or nation divine protection and blessing, and singling it out for a special task or mission. The third, a shared sense of intimacy and devotion to sacred landscapes is but one, albeit the most intensive and poignant, aspect of the wider process of territorialisation of memories and attachments. Fourth, myth-memories of one or more golden ages, with their appeal to heroic and harmonious social orders and polities in the communal past, present an idealised image of a distinctive and original public culture, a mirror of the 'true soul' of the community, to be emulated and perhaps surpassed. However, ideals of heroic sacrifice to attain the nation's true destiny are related to the liturgies and rituals of a distinctive public culture, rather than to legal codes or law and custom, though law too can be sanctified, to become The Law (Torah, Shariah) of a community of the faithful, who may also be identified with one or more *ethnies* or nations.[3]

The main point here is that, because they are closely related to the general processes, a nation's cultural resources can be used to assess the persistence or erosion of national identity. As a general proposition, we may say that the more of these resources present in a community, and the more carefully they are cultivated, the more we may expect to find a strong, vibrant and enduring, though never static, sense of national identity. Conversely, the less of these resources to be found in a given community, and the less cherished and venerated they are, the more attenuated and intermittent a community's sense of national identity is likely to be. However, it is not sufficient to confine our enquiry to the strength or otherwise of these cultural resources. We need to see how far their development or attenuation mirrors that of the general social processes themselves, through whose combination nations are formed (Smith 2003).

Self-definition

Before proceeding, we need to define the limits of the enquiry. Here I am concerned with the persistence or erosion of nations in the West, and more particularly in the well-established nations and national states of Western and Central Europe. Outside the West, we are confronted with very different conditions and national phenomena, particularly in the old societies but new states of Africa and Asia, where the flames of nationalism are often kindled by violent ethnic conflicts. Here, nations and national identities may be in the making, or threatened with secession and irredentism. To these 'hot' nationalisms, the following reflections hardly apply (See Billig 1995).

Turning to the West, can we justly claim that national self-definitions have been eroded or transcended, or that the process of self-designation has been reversed in recent decades? At first glance, such a claim is not unfounded. Who now seriously believes that the Saxons are 'our ancestors', i.e. of the present-day English, or that Clovis's baptism was the true foundation of 'France'? Do present-day Germans still trace their ancestry to the virtuous barbarians depicted by Tacitus in his *Germania*, or the Dutch to the equally courageous and freedom-loving Batavii? And, even if these myths of origin are half-believed, do they retain any of their former importance?[4]

It is fact doubtful whether, even in the Victorian epoch, these myths possessed much significance, since knowledge and interest in them was likely to have been confined to an educated stratum. Rather, their importance lay elsewhere, as expressions of something more profound and widely diffused: a sense of what distinguishes 'us' from 'them'. The real question concerns, not myths of origin, but the persistence of this sense of collective self and its associated national sentiments.

And here, there is evidence that this sense has, if anything, experienced a revival, largely but not only as a response to recent high levels of immigration to European countries. It is not just their rates, but the differences in the culture and religion of many immigrants that has sparked intense controversy and violence. The hostile reactions to Muslim immigrants in parts of France, capitalised on by the radical right of Le Pen and others, the negative responses to 'Asians' in parts of England, associated with the racism of the British National Party, German popular responses to Turks and Vietnamese migrants, opposition in southern Italy to illegal Albanian immigration, Czech prejudice against the Roma, Greeks against Turks, and recently the equally hostile sentiments and violence witnessed in the Netherlands, are just some examples of a trend that has strengthened the sense of national identity and culture in Western and Central Europe, as the marginalisation and persecution of Jews had done so over the centuries. The debates over immigration and asylum-seekers in Britain and other countries have only served to reinforce widespread commitments to ways of life characteristic of particular nations, and to spur new policies on citizenship and new assertions of national identity (Cesarani and Fulbrook 1996; Triandafyllidou 2001, esp. chs 4–5).

Equally important for national self-definition have been the current debates about 'multiculturalism', notably in education, and the need to balance freedom of choice with a measure of cultural community and political solidarity. Undoubtedly, the extent and nature of immigration has led to some radical reinterpretations, notably the notion of an increasing 'hybridisation' of national identity. But these ideas have not completely superseded earlier traditions, particularly among the older generation. There may well be, as Homi Bhabha claims, a considerable gulf between received 'pedagogic' traditions of 'the nation' and everyday 'performative' practices leading to 'hybrid' identities in some cities. But, despite growing awareness of and tolerance towards other faiths and cultures, these practices and ideas have been assimilated into a new, more flexible, but still strong and vigorous national culture and sense of collective identity – as witnessed for example in the adverse reactions to the recent description of Britain as a 'community of communities' by a group of social and political theorists (Bhabha 1990).[5]

Finally, we may note the continued use of 'we', 'us' and 'our' to refer to the nation's identity, landscapes or achievements. This is especially marked in sport, where 'we' are opposed to 'them', 'our' national opponents. But, as Billig (1995) has demonstrated, it can apply equally in fields as diverse as the economy, education, political systems and weather reports, indicating the resilience and engrained nature of 'banal nationalism'.

Cultivation of myths, memories and symbols

Turning to the cultivation of national myths, memories, symbols and values, and more especially to the veneration accorded to them, can we find evidence of considerable indifference and obsolescence among most citizens? Or are we again dealing mainly with the different perceptions of successive generations?

Take the question of national memories. What is striking is the loss of a single 'national story', the growth of multiple histories, and, for many younger people, the irrelevance of much of what was long held to be important and sacred about the 'national past'. In France, for over a century, that past was transmitted through the textbook of the Third Republic written by Ernest Lavisse, and disseminated in every school across the country by a monolithic educational system. Only in the 1980s was the predominance of this official national history challenged, and room made for other interpretations. In Britain, too, a lively 'history debate' in the 1980s, and the rise of 'empathetic' history in a more child-centred education system, has rendered the old nationalist traditions transmitted through various texts obsolete. The new history curriculum, with its emphasis on the twentieth-century dictators and contemporary history, has also eroded the younger generation's knowledge and sense of a 'linear', national history from the Anglo-Saxons to Dunkirk. This conflicts with that sense of a sacred national past to which the older generation remains wedded (See Citron 1988; Samuel 1989: Vol. I; Gardiner 1990).

Symbols, too, have been reinterpreted or rendered secondary, if not obsolete. National flags and anthems still evoke respect and loyalty among older generations, but are often felt to lack meaning and relevance among a younger generation impatient of the paraphernalia of an outdated nationalism. But, though anthems may be regarded as burdensome, and are played less often than before, flags, as Billig (1995) has explained, constitute an unseen part of the nation's landscape, often fluttering unnoticed on buildings, and helping to underpin a sense of national unity and national difference from others.

There is a similar paradox with regard to 'national myths'. On the one hand, many such myths have been discounted and debunked, especially those relating to the nation's presumed early history, or their interpretation has been heavily revised. On the other hand, the central myth of ethnic election remains more or less intact, if sometimes tacit. Of course, it has been heavily secularised in the West over the last two centuries. No longer the deity, but history has chosen 'us' to be the bearer of special or even of universal values. 'Ours' is a unique destiny embodied in a mission to bring virtue, liberty, equality or pluralism to a benighted humanity. The British boast the 'Mother of Parliaments' and 'fair play'; the Dutch see their society as a model of tolerance; the French trumpet their nation as the exporter of liberty and equality; the Greeks claim their land as the fount of democracy. For all that, these beliefs are accorded a quasi-religious veneration, being regularly invoked by politicians and press alike, with comparisons drawn from fields as divergent as economic statistics, educational attainment, and success in sports, to bolster the nation's morale. It is, of course, difficult to gauge how widely these myths are believed by their respective populations, but constant repetition, especially in times of crisis, helps to reinforce a sense of unique national identity, if not one of outright nationalism.[6]

Territorialisation

We are often told that globalisation has rendered all borders porous and that trade, currency flows, military technology and mass communications have deterritorialised nations. Since territory is so central to nations and nationalism, we might expect, if this were the case, to witness the rapid erosion of nations and nationalisms.

Now, though economic exchange was already global a century ago, it is undoubtedly true that technologies, goods, currencies, services and personnel cross borders today much more freely and to a much greater degree, and that international capitalist institutions and transnational agencies have created an unprecedented degree of economic interdependence. But does this signify a 'deterritorialisation' of Western nations? Institutionally, the national state in Europe, while retaining formal control, may have lost some of its economic functions, notably in the context of the European Union, but the idea that the national state has become 'powerless' seems far-fetched. Indeed, it has been argued that European integration has helped to rescue and strengthen the national state. Clearly, it has to date done little to prevent unilateral foreign policy and military initiatives by the stronger national states. Certainly, the internal powers of the state over its territories, resources and citizens have been greatly augmented by new developments in such fields as research and technology, demography, health and genetics; with the result that the national state has penetrated the lives of its citizens in respect of domains as varied as those of criminal justice, education, transport, housing and the environment (Gowan and Anderson 1997: esp. chs 1–2; Smith 1995: chs 4–5).

The environment has provided particularly fertile soil for debate and contestation. The many battles between powerful commercial developers, on the one hand, and environmentalists and heritage preservation groups, on the other, are evidence of the importance of 'our' ethnoscapes and natural habitats to many citizens. Subjectively, these conflicts help to focus public attention on the natural beauty and cultural heritage of local landscapes and thereby to renationalise the idea of safeguarding and cultivating the homeland. In this way, existing national attachments to poetic landscapes are rekindled and deepened. Alternatively, new architectural and communications developments may become a source of national pride and evidence of national achievement, as with the spectacular recent aqueduct built across the Tarn gorge in the French Midi, whose feat of engineering was recently praised by President Chirac as the work of a 'conquering nation'. Mass tourism, too, directs attention to national differences in scenic and architectural heritages, and thus to the cultural diversity of territorial homelands so beloved of nationalists, even where its commercial consequences may endanger those very specificities.[7]

The fact is that the territorialisation of attachments and memories has developed over a long period and stabilised nations in so much of Europe. As a result, even within an ever closer European Union, it is unlikely to be unravelled or bypassed in the foreseeable future. Despite the increased mobility of many segments of national populations, generations of attachments to specifically national rural and urban landscapes, reinforced by the 'tourist gaze', are not in immediate danger of being eroded, even if the sanctity accorded the land and some of its holy sites has been somewhat attenuated.

Public culture

A key element of the ideal-type of the nation is the formation and dissemination to the members of a distinctive public culture, including linguistic
codes, an education system, public rituals and an official 'ethno-history' – a
set of traditions about the communal past held by the members of the
nation and handed down the generations. Here, I shall confine my discussion
to the ideal of the golden age, a key aspect of such ethnohistories, and to
some of the nation's public rites and ceremonies. The evidence for the persistence of an ideal of the golden age or ages, is patchy. Most European nations
can look back to one or more such ages – the Spanish and Dutch golden
ages, the English Elizabethan age, the Scots Enlightenment, the era of Celtic
Christianity in Ireland, the Grand Siècle and the Napoleonic age, the Italian
Renaissance, the eras of the Hohenstauffen and the Romantics, the Viking
age, the era of the Kalevala, Periclean Athens and Byzantium, and so on.
The question, however, is whether these ages still retain their aura of veneration, and continue to exert any influence on people's perceptions and actions
(Hosking and Schopflin 1997).

Take the question of history curricula. The decline of 'national history'
teaching, that is, of the introduction of children and students to a linear
exposition and panorama of the nation's history/ies, would suggest growing
ignorance of, and detachment from, these ages of heroism and creativity
among the younger generation. Indeed, the very ideal of heroism has been
repudiated in some quarters – if only to resurface in the domain of sport and
physical and mental endurance. Yet, again, among older generations there is
still much admiration for heroic figures like de Gaulle and Churchill, and
the Second World War years still evoke the powerful emotions of a dark
and awesome age of courage and fortitude. Creativity and genius in the arts
and sciences, on the other hand, continue to attract respect and emulation,
though its great figures are often detached from their 'national' historical
contexts. Hence, the mixed reception accorded today to national ideals of
the golden age, and a certain waning of the former veneration for such ages
and their heroes and heroines (See Citron 1988; Gardiner 1990).

It is otherwise with the collective rituals of a public culture. Granted,
some national holidays pass with little mass enthusiasm; others are celebrated with panache and gravity, and executed with choreographic precision.
Typical are the flags, bands and massed regiments of Bastille Day in Paris,
with its ceremonies beside the Tomb of the Unknown Warrior at the Arc de
Triomphe and its procession down to the Place de la Concorde, matched by
a host of festivities across the land, recalling the birth of Republican France.
Across the Channel, the solemn funeral marches, bands and wreaths of
poppies laid at the foot of the Cenotaph in London's Whitehall, during the
annual Remembrance Day ceremony, commemorate the massive sacrifice of
life in the two World Wars, as well as a host of other twentieth-century conflicts – ceremonies that find parallels in Italy, Poland, Russia, Israel and

Australia. In all these cases, it is the nation itself – its history, struggles, losses, regeneration and destiny – that is celebrated and remade. In these public rituals, a sense of national identity is powerfully evoked, also among younger generations, even if there is perhaps less willingness to 'die for the nation' than among the generations raised before the two world wars.[8]

Laws and customs

Greater doubts surround the final defining process, the dissemination of shared laws and customs across the nation. On the one hand, as we saw, the state is increasingly active in the regulation of every aspect of social life, preserving, homogenising and protecting the nation, and legislating for every section of the community and for every contingency.

Conversely, public responses, carried through electoral and party preferences, and proclaimed through the national media, appear to accord with the basic assumptions of a shared rule of law, and thereby reinforce a sense of national identity.

Nevertheless, this apparent symmetry and harmony is threatened on a number of fronts. The first is the growing gulf between successive governments, and more broadly the national state, and its citizens. Instead of binding the nation together, the institutions of state, acting in the name of the nation, are often in danger of alienating the public. The spate of legislative 'interference' in family and social life, instead of reinforcing unity among citizens, often divides and weakens national ties. A second danger stems from the heterogeneity of the citizenry consequent on massive immigration. The attempt to legislate for different cultural, ethnic and religious groups has provoked periodic division and hostility, thereby weakening national cohesion, if not national consciousness. Finally, there is the growing fear of economic and political absorption of individual nations and their states in wider blocs of nations, notably the European Union, and a consequent loss of national identity and freedom of collective action through the legal 'interference' of supranational institutions in the national legislative process. Here, the unity sought by nationalists in terms of shared law and custom is in danger of being replaced by the regulative homogeneity ('harmonisation') pursued by 'distant Eurocrats'.[9]

Despite these dangers, the dissemination of national laws and customs, and the continual refinement of common laws and shared legal institutions, are likely to continue to underpin a sense of common national identity. The 'threat' of a pan-European harmonisation may even strengthen this process of 'nationness', and encourage citizens to emphasise their different legal institutions and lawcodes, particularly where 'state' and 'nation' are closely intertwined.

The role of the national state and nationalism

By now, it must be clear that the separation of 'state' and 'nation', while analytically necessary, must be qualified in practice. At many points in the previous analysis, we see that the national state underpins, regulates and protects the life of the nation. This is obvious enough in the case of territorialisation, and it applies, with some qualifications, to the dissemination of common laws and customs. But the state is also heavily involved in the formation and dissemination of a distinctive public culture. Although other institutions like churches and armies can forge and spread public cultures, the most common vehicle of inclusion has been the state, and especially the national state, i.e. one that is legitimated by nationalism and seeks to protect or create one or more nations.

This is perhaps most readily seen in the way that state action either establishes public rituals or overlays private initiatives. This is what occurred in the runup to the celebrations of the 600th anniversary commemoration of the foundation of Switzerland, recalling the *Bundesbrief* of 1291 between the three forest cantons (Uri, Schwyz and Unterwalden) on the Rutli meadow on Lake Lucerne. A similar overlay occurred in Britain after the First World War, when the ceremonies at the unveiling of the Cenotaph and the commemoration of the Glorious Dead which had been initiated by the British Legion were combined with public rituals presided over by the royal family and state, religious and military dignitaries. And, in most other European nations, the state organises these public ceremonies, with or without the assistance of veterans' associations (See Kreis 1991; Mosse 1975: chs 3–4; 1990).

What of the role of nationalism itself? Has its influence diminished and its force abated? Leaving aside those parts of Europe like the Balkans, where 'hot' nationalisms have all too recently left their mark, can we not reasonably claim that most European national states are free of the ideological movement of nationalism, having attained to that state of affluent modernity that Ernest Gellner envisaged?

To answer this, we need to distinguish between two kinds of nationalism, that of non-state nations incorporated in historic national states like the Scots, Basques and Catalans, and the nationalism of the dominant *ethnie* or nation in national states, like the English and Castilians in a multinational United Kingdom and Spain. Nationalism, the ideological movement, is still a vital source of popular perception and action among non-state nations, even if a majority of 'the people' do not opt for outright independence and state sovereignty. Nations like Scotland, Catalonia and Euzkadi have attained a high degree of autonomy and unity, and their identity has been well established for centuries. Undoubtedly, a nationalism that is at once ethnocultural and political, and is based on a long-established homeland, provides a strong ideological framework for the self-definitions, public culture and many of the laws and customs of the nation, as well as for its cultivation of separate national myths, memories and symbols. In these cases, it has proved possible to 'revive' the nation on the basis of prior ethnic identities, but still remain within the wider orbit of a multinational state (See Guibernau 1999).

What of the dominant *ethnie* nations? Can we discern a weakening of their earlier nationalisms in an era of ever closer European union? Here, the evidence is more fragmented and contradictory. On the one hand, having attained their cultural and political goals long ago, dominant *ethnie* nations have no need of the ideological movement of nationalism. Many Europeans feel a measure of shame, even guilt, at the horrors perpetrated in the two World Wars, and attribute their cause to a 'nationalism' that they are happy to repudiate and condemn. For these people, the nation is not only passé, it has lost whatever iconic status it once possessed, and needs to be swept away in the new post-modern era of cosmopolitan Europeanism. On the other hand, nationalism's ideals have been fully institutionalised and the national sentiments which it fed have permeated the citizenries. In this sense, national*ism* has done its work well. It has helped to forge nations on the basis of preexisting ethnic ties and communities, unite their populations around the national ideal, and hasten the process of national identification on the part of 'the people'.

For dominant *ethnies*, a more inclusive territorial and political nationalism helps to sustain their position, while appearing to avoid too obvious an ethnic bias in the maintenance of old-new nations. That this has not prevented serious ethnic cleavages and antagonisms is evidence of the persistence of a prior ethnic nationalism beneath a civic overlay. Even in France, the home and prototype of the civic, republican nation, anti-Semitism, anti-Islamism and racism have exposed the ethnic foundations of a cultural-linguistic nationalism that undergirded the revolutionary commitment to secularism, liberty and equality. Elsewhere, as we saw, the mingling of different cultures and religions in a harsher political climate has once again returned the dominant *ethnie* to its ethnic moorings amid moral panics and heightened competition for the nation's resources, producing a xenophobic ethnic nationalism which sometimes verges on culturalist racism.[10]

Conclusion

In a brief survey, it is hardly possible to do justice to many facets of the problem of the persistence or erosion of nations and national identities in contemporary Western Europe. While nationalism in its strong form has clearly abated for the dominant *ethnie* nations, it remains a powerful force among non-state nations. Moreover, its goals and outlook have been firmly entrenched in the institutions of the international system and of the national state which, despite a loss of some functions in a global economy, has increased its internal regulative powers and penetration of society. And despite the disparagement of nationalism in many quarters, the national sentiments which it encouraged, and the national identities which it helped to delineate, remain pervasive and resilient, even when they are reinterpreted and renewed by successive generations.

What *has* diminished, to some extent, in post-1945 Europe is the sanctity which surrounded the nation in former times. The main reason for this is the enlargement of the 'profane' sphere of materialism, consumerism and rational calculation at the expense of the 'sacred' domain. This erosion of the sacred has led to widespread scepticism about myths of origin, the traditional national history, memories of golden ages and some, though not all, national ceremonies. This is particularly marked among the younger generation (and may therefore be transient). On the other hand, most people remain strongly attached to their homelands and their poetic landscapes; they are still wedded to some version, albeit secularised, of a myth of national election; and they accord honour to those who sacrificed their lives for the nation, even when they disagree with government policies which necessitated the sacrifice. More generally, the fundamental social processes that have created nations have also helped to stabilise the nations of Western Europe to a considerable degree. Processes of self-definition, the cultivation of myths, symbols, memories and traditions, territorialisation of memories and attachments, and the spread of public culture are well entrenched, and may even have been revitalised by globalisation and its perceived threats. Even the processes of making and disseminating national laws and customs have not yet been seriously undermined by the growth of the regulatory powers of the European Union or world bodies, despite the many anxieties expressed on this score.

Moreover, new factors have renewed national bonds, including economic interdependence, mass communications and migration. If war was formerly the focus and 'test' of nations, today it is immigration that fulfils this function. Under the impact of culturally diverse waves of immigrants, national identities are being redefined and reshaped. Yet, through this very process they are also being strengthened, as the members of nations reflect upon and argue among themselves about the meaning and role of their national identities. In this sense, as self-reflexive and self-celebrating communities, nations and nationalism are still very much alive.

Notes

1 For the problems of defining key terms like 'nation' and 'nationalism', see Deutsch (1966: ch. 1), Connor (1994: ch. 4) and Smith (2001: ch. 1).

2 For Brubaker (1996), nations should be seen as social practices, political forms and contingent events; the analyst must not accept the reifying process of the participants, which turns nations into fixed, enduring, substantial collectivities. Once again, the social scientist sees (and sees through) what the participants cannot see, the contingency and fluidity of national 'constructs'. See on this, Smith (1998: 76–7).

3 The subject of the religious background of nationalism is a large one; see especially Mosse (1975), O'Brien (1988), Hastings (1997) and Smith (2003).

4 On the English, see Johnson (1995); for the French case, see Citron (1988) and the special number on Clovis of *Notre Histoire* (1996); on the Germans, see Geary (2002: ch. 1) and Scales (2000); and for the Batavians, see Gorski (2000).

5 For the debates over the 'Parekh Report' (*Runneymede Trust: The Future of Multi-Ethnic Britain: The Parekh Report*, London: Profile Books, 2000), and the balance to be struck between individual rights, cultural differences and national solidarity, see the discussion in Kumar (2003: 256–62).

6 On myths of ethnic election, see the essays in *Nations and Nationalism* (1999) and Smith (2003: chs 3–5).

7 On territory and nation, see Hooson (1994); on heritage, tourism and national identity, see Boswell and Evans (2002: Part II).

8 For these rituals of sacrifice, see Mosse (1975, 1990); Kapferer (1988); and Smith (2003: ch. 9).

9 The issue of identity cards affords a good example of such 'interference' in citizen liberties, emerging recently, albeit in quite different ways, in Greece and Britain. For the fears of European regulation, see Delanty (1995).

10 See the recent volume on dominant *ethnies*, edited by Kaufmann (2004).

References

Bhabha, H. (ed.) (1990) *Nation and Narration*, London and New York: Routledge.

Billig, M. (1995) *Banal Nationalism*, London: Sage.

Boswell, D. and Evans, J. (eds) (2002) *Representing the Nation: A Reader*, London: Routledge.

Brubaker, R. (1996) *Nationalism Reframed*, Cambridge: Cambridge University Press.

Cesarani, D. and Fulbrook, M. (eds) (1996) *Citizenship, Nationality and Migration in Europe*, London: Routledge.

Citron, S. (1988) *Le Mythe National*, Paris: Presses Ouvriers.

Connor, W. (1994) *Ethno-nationalism: The Quest for Understanding*, Princeton: Princeton University Press.

Delanty, G. (1995) *Inventing Europe*, Basingstoke: Macmilllan.

Deutsch, K. (1966) *Nationalism and Social Communication*, New York: MIT Press.

Deutsch, K., Burrell, S. and Kann, R.A. (1957) *Political Community and the North Atlantic Area*, Princeton: Princeton University Press.

Gardiner, J. (ed.) (1990) *The History Debate*, London: Collins and Brown.

Geary, P. (2002) *The Myth of Nation: The Medieval Origins of Europe*, Princeton and Oxford: Princeton University Press.

Gellner, E. (1983) *Nations and Nationalism*, Oxford: Blackwell.

Gorski, P. (2000) 'The Mosaic Moment: An Early Modernist Critique of Modernist Theories of Nationalism', *American Journal of Sociology*, 105: 1428–68.

Gowan, P. and Anderson, P. (eds) (1997) *The Question of Europe*, London and New York: Verso.

Guibernau, M. (1999) *Nations without States*, Cambridge: Polity Press.

Hastings, A. (1997) *The Construction of Nationhood: Ethnicity, Religion and Nationalism*, Cambridge: Cambridge University Press.

Hobsbawm, E. (1992) *Nations and Nationalism since 1780*, Cambridge: Cambridge University Press.

Hooson, D. (ed.) (1994) *Geography and National Identity*, Cambridge, MA and Oxford: Blackwell.

Horsman, M. and Marshall, A. (1994) *After the Nation State: Citizens, Tribalism and the New World Disorder*, London: HarperCollins.

Hosking, G. and Schöpflin, G. (eds) (1997) *Myths and Nationhood*, New York: Routledge.

Johnson, L. (1995) 'Imagining Communities, Medieval and Modern', in S. Forde, L. Johnson and A. Murray (eds) *Concepts of National Identity in the Middle Ages*, Leeds: School of English, University of Leeds, 1–19.

Kapferer, B. (1998) *Legends of People, Myths of State: Violence, Intolerance and Political Culture in Sri Lanka and Australia*, Washington, DC: Smithsonian Institution.

Kaufmann, E. (ed.) (2004) *Rethinking Ethnicity: Majority Groups and Dominant Minorities*, London: Routledge.

Kreis, J. (1991) *Der Mythos von 1291: Zur Entstehung des Schweizerischen Nationalfeiertags*, Basel: Friedrich Reinhardt Verlag.

Kumar, K. (2003) *The Making of English National Identity*, Cambridge: Cambridge University Press.

Mark, K. and Engels, F. (1959) *Basic Writings on Politics and Philosophy*, L.S. Feuer (ed.), New York: Anchor Books, Doubleday & Company.

Mosse, G. (1975) *The Nationalisation of the Masses*, Ithaca, NY: Cornell University Press.

—— (2000) *Fallen Soldiers: Reshaping the Memory of the World Wars*, Oxford: Oxford University Press.

Nations and Nationalism (1999) *Chosen Peoples* (Special Issue) 5(3).

Notre Histoire (1996) *Clovis: La Naissance de France* (Special Issue) 132 (April 1996).

O'Brien, C.C. (1988) *God-Land: Reflections on Religion and Nationalism*, Cambridge MA: Harvard University Press.

Renan, E. (1882 [1996] 'What Is a Nation?', Lecture, Sorbonne, Paris, 11 March, in G. Eley and R.G. Suny (eds) *Becoming National: A Reader*, Oxford: Oxford University Press: 41–55.

Samuel, R. (ed.) (1989) *Patriotism, The Making and Unmaking of British National Identity*, London: Routledge.

Scales, L. (2000) 'Identifying "France" and "Germany": Medieval Nation-Making in Some Recent Publications', *Bulletin of International Medieval Research*, 6: 23–46.

Smith, A.D. (1995) *Nations and Nationalism in a Global Era*, Cambridge: Polity Press.

—— (1998) *Nationalism and Modernism: A Critical Survey of Recent Theories of Nations and Nationalism*, London and New York: Routledge.

—— (2001) *Nationalism: Theory, Ideology, History*, Cambridge: Polity Press.

—— (2003) *Chosen Peoples: Sacred Sources of National Identity*, Oxford: Oxford University Press.

Soysal, Y. (1994) *Limits of Citizenship: Migrants and Post-National Membership in Europe*, Chicago, IL: Chicago University Press.

Triandafyllidou, A. (2001) *Immigrants and National Identity in Europe*, London and New York: Routledge.

3   Comparing visions of the nation

The role of ethnicity, religion and diaspora nationalism in Armenian, Jewish and Sikh relations to the homeland

William Safran

Diasporas and homelands

Nationalisms, like nations, are not constructed *ex nihilo*. The rise and mobilization of national collective identity – aiming at the politicization of that identity and, ultimately, the building or rebuilding of a "nation-state" – is based on a number of cultural and symbolic elements or ethnosymbols, among which the following are most frequently listed: religion, territory and the collective memory of major events (Smith 2001: 23).

No single theory of ethnicity, nationalism and nation-building is suitable for all situations. We can, however, contribute to further study by exploring nation-building in comparable cases and assessing the weight of symbols and ascriptive variables in the shaping of ethnonational identity. It is the contention of this study that there are clear differences between diaspora and homeland communities with respect to the relative importance of these elements, and, more specifically, that religion is the most important one in the diaspora, and territory in the homeland.

Three specific *ethnies* are examined: those of the Armenians, Jews and Sikhs. These have been chosen because of their commonalities. In all of them, religion, kinship, language, territory and historical memory play a role. Their collective identities are based to a significant extent on the consciousness of having originated in a specific land; they are marked by the existence of ramified diasporas; they have experienced oppression and statelessness; and they have been engaged in a quest extending over many generations to gain or regain political control over their homelands.

Diasporas maintain their connections with the homeland whether its independent statehood has been in existence for long or has been recently regained. These connections not only provide a degree of autonomy, but they also help to assuage problems such as discrimination, alienation, and the internalization of negative stereotypes held by the majority in the host country. Many members of the diaspora attribute these problems to their lack of legitimacy, and they want to gain self-respect by embracing a "hyphenated" status that would link their own identities with a "homeland" that enjoys a positive image (Tatla 1999: 201).[1]

From a distance the homeland is often easier to imagine in a more pleasant way than from inside the homeland itself. Thus, diaspora Armenians had a romantic vision of the homeland as a sort of paradise consisting of verdant fields and flowing streams (T.T. Minassian 2002). For Jews in the diaspora, especially in Eastern Europe, the Holy Land – and later, Israel – was a place of orange groves, kibbutzim and self-reliant pioneers. This explains the iconic character of Yerevan to diaspora Armenians and the Israelocentrism of many American and Western European Jews.

The ethnic identity described above is a symbolic one because it does not necessarily inform the quotidian behavior of a person. It is considered irrational insofar as it is not guided by considerations of concrete gain. Sometimes, to be sure, ethnicity is not merely symbolic, as in the case of persons who stand out as being different from the rest of society in a given hostland because of a physical marker such as skin color or behavioral marker such as dress. Such differences, as well as numerous ethnic symbols mentioned above, constitute the rallying points around which people mobilize. Yet in the majority of cases, ethnic identification is voluntary and can be periodically set aside.[2]

Diasporas are not the same as "state-nations."[3] The former are *trans-statal* ethnonations, whereas the latter contain *transethnic* elements clustered around what Anthony Smith has called a "core *ethnie*." Both diaspora and core *ethnies* share a number of symbols, which include language, customs, rites, food, artifacts, narratives and myths, including the myth of common descent. Most, if not all, of these symbols originated in the homeland.

A nation differs from a diaspora *ethnie* in that it territorializes and politicizes the "myth-symbol complex" (Smith 1986: 15) that it shares with the diaspora. In so doing it may incorporate the symbols of other *ethnies* or it may suppress them. There is an open question: are ethnosymbols in the diaspora more pristine than in the homeland? On the one hand, *ethnies* in the diaspora may be more isolated from their immediate political surroundings and have fewer political constraints than they have in a homeland whose nationalism has become "civic" and which is preoccupied with practical tasks; on the other hand, ethnic symbols in diaspora have become more syncretic under the influence of surrounding hostland culture, whereas in the homeland such symbols enjoy special protection.

Ethnic diasporas are communities that are not fully absorbed into the modern nation – whether ethnic or civic – as defined in terms of the majorities in their respective host societies. As such, they are more determined to preserve their particular identities than immigrants *tout court*, and they have equipped themselves with various means for doing so. It is perhaps the failure of diasporas to dissolve that has led John Breuilly to regard them as pre-political and pre-modern and as "[having] little in the way of institutional embodiment beyond the local level" and to argue that their identities are expressed in a language that is important only to a narrow cultural elite (Breuilly 1996: 150). In fact, however, diaspora *ethnies* are far from local; they are part of a transborder, and often highly organized, global communication network; many of their institutions are transnational, and they use a language that is disseminated far below an intellectual elite or a church hierarchy and far beyond the confines of their host countries (Walker 1998: 541). It is difficult to pinpoint the basic communicative elements in this network. At one time, language played a major role, but with the global dominance of English and the decline of the use of the homeland language among diaspora ethnics and the homogenization and massification of popular culture, religion may be the only thing left standing. It is, however, a secularized religion, dominated not by theology or scholarship, but by physical ethnosymbols.

Therefore, diasporas are almost ideal-typical intermediaries between *ethnie* and nation. The array of ethnic symbols listed above as well as notions of "sacred territory" have served the diaspora's own purposes as well as the purpose of state-(re)building. In the latter process, diasporas have been leading actors. They have done the advance work of the modern "nation-state" in institutionalizing and codifying ethnic symbols to a significant degree. In the absence (and anticipation) of a restored nation-state, diasporas have been functioning as cultural storage chambers in the sense that they are more autonomous both with respect to the dominant hostland culture and the homeland (which may be under the political control of an authoritarian regime or a foreign power).[4] As Gurmat Singh Aulakh, a leader of the Sikh diaspora in the United States, put it (in 1999),

> The Indian government's true intention is to annihilate the Sikh religion ... [At least] the Sikh diaspora is free. India can't threaten them, torture them, or violate their dignity and rights. They are the ones who will provide leadership to the [community of believers].[5]

The belief that the diaspora is needed to preserve the nation in case the homeland is attacked by neighbors and its people threatened with annihilation is not unique to the Sikhs. The destruction of Israel is the daily fear of diaspora Jews, many of whom feel that Jews are safer outside Israel than in it. In their view, the diaspora constitutes a sort of demographic sanctuary.

Although the homeland is normally regarded as the origin of the diaspora, it is not the only cultural locus of the ethnonational community. The Jews, Armenians and Sikhs each have two cultural and religious centers – the homeland and the diaspora – and these complement one another. The reciprocal nature of the relationship is manifested in the widespread belief among Armenians that there are "two poles of the Armenian nation, which are Armenia and the diaspora" (Hovanessian 2000: 93) and in the notion of the "centrality of the Jewish people," which replaced the traditional Zionist insistence on the "centrality of Israel" a few years after its founding

(Beilin 2000: 59; Walinsky 1981: 68–9). In the case of the Jews, the homeland–diaspora linkage is reflected in the Law of Return, and in the case of the Armenians, not only in a right to return but also in a bill introduced in Yerevan in 1995, which granted Armenian citizenship to diaspora Armenians (Hovanessian 2000: 87, 103); and in both cases, in the existence of transnational organizations. After the restoration of independence in 1991, Armenia's relationship with the diaspora was restructured; at a meeting in Yerevan of 1,200 delegates from all over the diaspora, it was decided to create juridically defined coordinating agencies (ibid.: 102).[6] Recently, some Israelis have even proposed the establishment of a second parliamentary chamber in their country to represent the interests of the diaspora.

The diaspora is not merely a subaltern or extension of the homeland, but it is also a site for the cultural creation of symbols that are subsequently exported to the homeland. That includes ethnoreligious practices (e.g. non-Orthodox forms of Jewish worship, *Landsmannschaften*, ethnically specific synagogues) introduced to Israel, and even aspects of quasi-religious syncretism, such as the celebration of Christmas (as a secular holiday) – a pattern analogous to the observance of Hindu festivities by Sikhs, especially outside Punjab. Imports have also included elements of language, such as Yiddish idioms, which resulted in Hebrew back-formations or were taken over wholesale (though in translation) by Israeli Hebrew (Safran 2005).

Brian Axel's statement that "diaspora has produced the homeland" (Axel 2001: 199) need not be taken literally, if only because the Chinese, Greek, Polish and Cuban homelands have continued to exist independently of diasporas and have preceded them. Nevertheless, diasporas have helped to mobilize *stateless* homeland peoples toward achieving political independence. In this process religion and historical memory have played crucial roles. It is in that sense that one can accept Lord Acton's remark that "exile is the nursery of nationality" (cited in Anderson 1992: 4). The nurturing role has included not only the preservation of the homeland culture (adapted to hostland conditions) and diplomatic support, but also the activities of political formations oriented primarily to the concerns of the homeland, such as Zionist parties in prewar Poland; the Armenian Revolutionary (Dashnak) Federation in France and Greece; and a variety of pro-Israel organizations in the United States.

An independent Jewish state was conceived by Theodor Herzl in the diaspora half a century before it materialized; and it was from the diaspora – the Armenian National Congress meeting in Tbilisi – that Armenia was declared independent on May 28, 1918 (an anniversary was still celebrated by the Armenian Revolutionary Federation even after 1920, when Armenian independence came to an end). As in the case of the state of Israel, the construction of the post-Soviet Armenian Republic would have been more difficult without the efforts of the diaspora. Diasporas, however, are often unable to help, as attested by the Kurdish, Tibetan and Sikh diasporas. Khalistan was declared an independent state by diaspora Sikhs, meeting in the Panthic Committee in 1987 – but this was no more than a symbolic act.

The factor of religion

Whereas the older nationalisms were imbued with religion (Hastings 1997) the modern nationalisms of the Armenians, Jews and Sikhs developed in an age of secularism. Yet there has been a resurgence of religious nationalism: belief systems and systems of religion-based rituals and practices are still able to mobilize people in our secular age (Smith 1998: 227).

The role of religion must be studied in context. The relationship among ethnonationalism, territory, and religion is complex, reciprocal, and confusing. Religion was a common ingredient of ethnic or tribal nationalism; as Lewis Namier once remarked, "religion is a sixteenth-century word for nationalism" (cited by Marx 2003: 25). Whereas ethnic nationalism was not sufficiently political, most modern nationalisms are marked by a decline in the role of religion. Religions become national movements: they serve as the major instruments of nation-building for a stateless nation; but once the state is (re-)built, religion becomes less important for the homeland. In this respect, newly formed states follow the pattern of long-established ones, such as England, France and Russia, where the once solitary official churches, respectively Anglicanism, Catholicism and Eastern Orthodoxy, are no longer needed as the primary glue of national identity.

Modern nationalism tends to be secular. Modern nation-builders may invoke religion and use selective religious symbols for purposes of social and political mobilization; or, as Kedourie has argued, as an aspect of the past "in order to subvert the present," subversion in this case meaning the replacement of one (tribal or imperial) political order by another, a national one.[7] The modern nation, however, is an ideal-type. It has not been easy for modern nations to cut themselves off from their ethnoreligious moorings – as attested by Poland, Israel and Ireland, whose existence has been heavily associated with its religious past. Nor has it been easy in the most advanced secular and "civic" nations such as France and the United States. In France, which is officially committed to *laïcité*, the literary and common languages contain Christian references, and most national holidays are Catholic. (The promise made by President Chirac during the debate concerning the Islamic headscarf that a Jewish and a Muslim holy day would become part of the official calendar was quickly forgotten.)[8] In the United States, too, Christianity remains culturally dominant, as reflected, for example, in school calendars and Sunday closing laws.

If religion declines as *ethnies* turn into nations, as Anthony Smith has argued, it does not disappear among diaspora communities. Since such communities are ethnic rather than national (insofar as national is defined in political terms), ethnosymbols are still largely religious, or serve as mimetic representations of religion. This includes the use of physical, printed and ritual symbols – amulets, artifacts, books and recordings of folktales – and the celebration of ethnoreligious festivals. All these are easier than a full cultural or religious commitment involving time and effort; and so is the support of the homeland in the form of political pressure or financial contributions. The ethnosymbols connect the diaspora with the homeland in one way or another. This applies to language as well. Language may not always be necessary for state-building in the homeland itself (as the case of Ireland illustrates), but it helps to maintain a sense of community outside the homeland. In the diaspora, the pressures of the dominant hostland language are difficult to resist;[9] but to the extent that ethnonational languages – Armenian, Yiddish and the Punjabi spoken by Sikhs – continue to survive in the various hostlands, they are heavily impregnated with religious vocabulary.[10]

In the state-building efforts of the homeland, territory is a substitute for religion, but in the diaspora, ethnosymbols evoke religion and territory and are substitutes for both. To what extent does that argument apply to *ethnies* in the diaspora? Not all of them wish to make use of religious symbols to subvert the present, especially where the present is tolerant of diversity and facilitates a considerable degree of autonomy. They may, however, use religion to perpetuate the identity and communal cohesion of the diaspora; to promote solidarity with fellow ethnics globally; and to lend support to "nation-building" in the homeland. Ethnonational symbols are emphasized by diaspora elites, including those who, while nominally adhering to their respective religions and marshalling religious justifications for political mobilization in favor of the homeland, may themselves be secular. This applies to most Zionist leaders and Armenian intellectuals. It applies also to Sikh diaspora politicians (some of whom occupy official positions in the governments of their homelands), who organize campaigns and protest marches in favor of Sikh separatism in India (Singh 2000).

Homelands, too, have instrumentalized religion. In Israel, participation in religious services is not needed for Jews to affirm their membership in the national or even the Jewish community. This is also true in Armenia itself, where the church is free, but no longer needed to assert national identity. Nevertheless, despite the trend to secularization in both the homeland and the diaspora, religion continues to provide a connecting link between the two communities. No matter how secular, homeland political leaders know that the ethnonational religion enjoys a considerable degree of legitimacy in the diaspora. This explains why political leaders in Armenia (many of whom reached adulthood in a Communist context and are not guided by religious values), pay lip service to the church; and why Israeli diplomats serving abroad (to promote relations between homeland and hostland and to act as liaisons to Jewish communities) are encouraged to attend synagogue in order to show solidarity with the diaspora.

The diaspora has played a significant role in keeping alive, promoting and politicizing ethnonationalism. Diasporas often use religion and language to do this, although original-language competence has been weakening and religious sentiment has been increasingly replaced by secularism. Ethnic symbols, which function as "*mythomoteurs*,"[11] are often institutionalized. Among the Jews, they have included numerous festival observances and religious ritual objects; among Sikhs, the turban and the "five Ks" – the *kes* (hair and beard), *kara* (bracelet), *kangha* (comb), *kach* (knee-length breeches), and *kirpan* (sword) – the scabbard worn at their sides by men (to symbolize the drawing of the sword centuries ago in defense of their religion) (Ahmed 1996: 263; Axel 2001: 182); among Armenians, the *khachkar* (a representation of the carved stone crosses that dot the homeland's cemeteries and churches) and the Armenian church's instantly identifiable dome architecture, which marks not only a place to pray, but also an institution symbolizing Armenian ethnicity.

Religious symbols have served multiple purposes in homelands and diasporas. To cite the example of the Passover seder: For Orthodox Jews everywhere, the ritual, and the *Haggadah*, the accompanying narrative, has both a religious and an ethnotribal reference, as it recalls the founding of a nation. For secular Israelis it is a celebration of a national holiday; and for "emancipated" diaspora Jews, it refers to an event – the Exodus – that has universal meaning, namely, the liberation of oppressed peoples. In the Armenian diaspora, churches – often imposing edifices – may lack worshipers; yet the Church remains important even for the non-practicing, because it is the most visible institutional expression of Armenianism, and Armenians identify with it out of a sense of ethnic loyalty. (The Church's robed, instantly identifiable clergy have been the only continuously present Armenian "bureaucracy" since 301 AD). It is under church auspices that charities and other communal activities are organized. A similar purpose is fulfilled by the Sikh gurdwaras in the diaspora, which are not only places of worship but also social and educational centers as well as venues for the cultivation of the Khalistan idea (Tatla 1999: 223, 227). In diaspora, especially in the West, more and more Sikhs are only nominally Sikh; and many confine their attendance at prayer services to the holy days. This is comparable to the numerous synagogues that exist in the Jewish diaspora, which may be equally sparsely attended.

The territorial dimension: holy places and sacred spaces

The above suggests that among the ethnic symbols dealt with here, religion is the most important. It serves to hold the community together, especially in the absence of other unifiers. Religion has a number of dimensions: tribal, spiritual and spatial. The tribal dimension cannot survive forever the assimilative process at work in modern states, as ethnic symbols lose their power and relevance, a reality that has led a number of religious leaders in the diaspora to stress the spiritual aspects of their faith. Moreover, not all Jews, Sikhs and Armenians in the diaspora have been happy with the "ethnification" and politicization of their fundamentally religious communities. They argue that such a transformation detracts from the universalistic claims of their religions and threatens the protection of their communities *qua* religious ones that they enjoy in the diaspora, in particular in those host countries committed to religious liberty and pluralism. Some Sikhs have insisted that the belief of the founding gurus that "Sikhs are here to serve the interests of the entire humanity" does not accord with the idea of Khalistan (Tatla 1999: 195–6). Some Armenian theologians, to be sure, assert that Armenians are Christians like others and therefore argue that the Apostolic message can be delivered any place and in any language. Anti-Zionist Jews have opposed the founding of Israel on the grounds that it detracts from the prophetic mission of Judaism; this is true in particular of Reform Jews, who insist that the essence of Judaism is not ethnically specific and does not need a homeland of reference.

In the cases examined here, ethnonational identity is "tribal" not only because it is associated with a minority religion, itself characterized by Eric Hobsbawm as tribal. These *ethnies* are also tribal because, he argues, they have lacked a common polity and, more important, because they have "resisted" the formation of a nation-state (Hobsbawm 1992: 64). In fact, however, most diaspora ethnonations have not opposed the formation of such a state, but have just been unable to achieve it. This was true in the past of the Jews, the Armenians and the Sikhs, and it is true today of the Kurds and Parsees.

According to Hobsbawm (Hobsbawm 1992: 68), modern religions do not accord well with *modern* nationalism, because, unlike tribal religions, they aspire to be world religions and must transcend the bounds of ethnonationalism. This view reflects wishful thinking; for all religions, even globally diffused ones, are "operationalized" in ways that differ from one society to another. One reason for selective attempts of diaspora communities to de-ethnicize their respective religions and to stress their spiritual aspects is to promote easier adaptation to the hostland;[12] but such attempts have had only partial success, because de-ethnicized religions have been too "abstract" and anemic to have wide emotional appeal. Most religions, like most nation-states, have core *ethnies*. Even world religions, such as Roman Catholicism and Islam, convey their respective messages in an "ethnotribally" specific fashion. The Armenian Church is not just a branch of the world religion of Christianity, and Judaism cannot be envisaged as totally separated from its ethnocultural and territorial source. It may be true that Israel has a special role in human history, but, as the Biblical prophets insisted, that role can be best performed in the land of Israel and not in the diaspora, which is an abnormal condition (Ezekiel 20:33–8, 40, 42; Sicker 1992: 30–7).

It is difficult to disaggregate the ethnic and religious components of the ethnonational communities discussed here. It is rare (if not impossible) to find a Muslim or Jewish Armenian, a Hindu Sikh, or a Christian Jew. All adherents of Judaism are Jews, all adherents of Apostolic Christianity are Armenian, and all adherents of Sikhism are, in terms of origin, Punjabi Sikhs.

It is equally difficult to disentangle the spiritual and territorial aspects of religions, and it is almost impossible to ignore their dualism – namely that of their universalistic and particularistic dimensions. Thus Judaism has been regarded by many of its adherents – both Orthodox and Reform – as "a light unto the nations;" Christianity – whether Catholic, Evangelical, or other – as bringing salvation to all who embrace it; and Sikhism, as a religion of perfect and universal love, aimed at establishing brotherhood for the whole global community.

Most of the religions dealt with here are focused on selected ethnocommunal groups, all of which have territorial orientations. The spatial dimension is used to advance claims upon the homeland, which is regarded as sanctified soil because of its association with revelation and/or with a nation-building figure, and because it is the locus of sacred sites. This applies to the Temple Mount in Jerusalem for Jews, the Apostolic cathedral and monastery in Echmiadzin for Armenians, and the Golden Temple in Amritsar for Sikhs.

Sometimes the sacred character of a specific site is extended to territory around it and then serves as a basis for the claim of the country in which it is located, which then becomes a "holy land." The clearest case is that of the Jews. Most of the Jewish holidays observed in the diaspora, no matter how secularized, relate to the land of Israel. Thus, the three "pilgrimage" festivals focus on Jerusalem; Hanukka recalls the struggle of the Maccabees against the Syrians; the fast of the Ninth of Av commemorates the destruction of the Temple, as does the breaking of a glass during marriage rites; all synagogues in the diaspora face toward Jerusalem; and at Passover seders, which recall the exodus of the Jews from Egypt, the hope is articulated for "Next Year in Jerusalem."[13]

For the Armenian diaspora, too, the homeland is the main focal point and "*mythomoteur*" of its ethnic identity, which is evinced in collective hopes as well as religious symbols and folk arts.[14] Just as Jews pray daily for a return to Jerusalem and for the restoration of temple sacrifice, so many Armenians sing Van songs that contain geographical references and some pray for "Next Year at [Lake] Van" (G. Minassian 2002: 27),[15] and so Sikhs chant in their daily prayers that "the Khalsa [i.e. the community of the pure] shall rule." Sikhs need a state where their distinctive identity can be maintained (ibid.). As Gurmat Singh Aulakh, president of the Council of Khalistan in Washington, DC put it, "Only a free and independent Khalistan will insure that the Sikh Nation can live in peace, prosperity, and freedom" (cited by Crane 1995). Gobind Singh Ji, a prominent guru, has echoed this position, arguing that "sovereignty is a must in order for religion to survive; otherwise religion perishes."

In the Sikh case, "sovereignty" has a dual connotation. On the one hand, it refers to Khalistan, a territorially defined Sikh state; on the other hand, it refers to the well-being of the Khalsa Panth, the community of believers, specifically the adherents of a spiritual leader or guru. The territorial definition, by its very nature political, is a much more recent one, proposed in the context of the partition of India after World War II and revived in the

1970s in the diaspora. The spiritual definition can be accommodated within the existing boundaries of India. In any case, the community in terms of both definitions is focused essentially on the Punjab (Shani 2002).

The religion-based territorial focus is also found among many Jews in the diaspora, who are convinced that a full Jewish life can only be lived in a Jewish homeland, a conviction shared even by those who are themselves not religious but who realize that non-religious ethnicity cannot survive by itself. This does not necessarily mean that the homeland must be fully sovereign; rather, it must serve as a place where ethnonational culture, religion and values can be maintained and perpetuated and which, in the view of "cultural" Zionists like Ahad Ha'am, would be a source whence these values would be disseminated to the diaspora. In any case, both cultural and religious Zionists share a belief in the importance of national existence, and therefore some sort of physical presence in the homeland.

The idea of sacred space extending to a whole country does not, however, have the same importance in all cases and at all times. In the case of the Sikhs, the idea of the Punjab as a sacred land only developed in the 1940s, in reaction to the policies of the Indian government, which were viewed as impeding the free exercise of their religion (Tatla 1999: 195f). It is invoked by spokespersons of the ethnic community in their fund-raising efforts. The Jewish, Armenian and Sikh diasporas in time became rival hubs of religions regarded increasingly as polycentric in terms of hierarchies and sources of learning. Both the Armenian and Hebrew languages were modernized and standardized in the diaspora; and most of those who were involved in this process were inspired by religious considerations.[16]

In any case, the homeland serves as a focus of ethnonational orientation and identity where the notion of "return" (e.g. the Jewish *aliya* and the Armenian *nerkaght*") has played an important role. This does not mean that members of ethnic diasporas are preparing to pack up and move to their homelands. As Jivan Tabibian, the Armenian scholar, remarked: "We [Armenians] are not place bound, but we are intensely place conscious" (quoted by Viviano 2004: 40). In fact, it is often difficult to go to the homeland, or a part thereof, because it may be inaccessible. Before the Six-Day War, the Old City of Jerusalem, with its Western Wall, could be seen from a distance, but Jews could not go there. Mount Ararat, a landmark of Armenian identity, can be seen from Yerevan, but it is under Turkish rule. Yet the territorial element is more than imaginary; it is an enduring reality, in the sense that the presence of members of the ethnonational community in the homeland has continued in some fashion and that diaspora communities are in touch with it. The homeland has been most important for Sikhs – who have always been there; for Armenians, whose continuing presence in contemporary Armenia is due to the escape of this region's inhabitants from the Turkish genocide by virtue of its being part of the Russian Empire; and for Jews, small numbers of whom remained in the homeland after the various expulsions.

A physical return to the homeland, although not always easy, is at least possible today, and in all cases there have been waves of "returnees." But there is a difference between the fact and the myth of return, which has led to ambivalence. On the one hand, there are reasons for not returning, or for leaving, the homeland: for Armenians, that the homeland has become "a landscape of sadness and misery"(T.T. Minassian 2002: 72), and, more important, that it is run by leaders perpetuating the legacy of Communism; for Sikhs, that life in the Punjab is too difficult, and Sikhism has been "polluted" by the inroads of Hinduism; and for Jews, that Judaism has been denatured by an elite consisting of "Hebrew-speaking gentiles" (or, conversely, that progress is being impeded by an ultra-Orthodox and intolerant rabbinate). On the other hand, Armenians who have left the homeland are regarded as deserters and even traitors (Schwalgin 2004: 87) and for many years, Jews leaving Israel were viewed with displeasure, and those leaving a diaspora country but not completing their voyage by settling in Israel were labeled "dropouts."

Narratives as "*mythomoteurs*"

The homeland is not a totally "imagined community"; it is historical, and narratives about it are based on real events that become part of the patrimony of nation-states and serve as the identitive basis of diasporas. This applies above all to religious and national leaders such as Moses; to Guru Nanak (1469–1539), the founder of Sikhism; and to St Gregory, whose conversion (*c.*301 AD) led to the founding of the Armenian Apostolic Church and the first Christian nation.[17] These events are in each case associated with holy books, which deal with the founding of a religion, contain rules of conduct based on revelation and/or law and provide for initiation rites. In two of the cases, the scriptures (the Adi Granth and the Old Testament) set the framework for the founding of new nations as well. Some of the narratives refer to periods of glory in the homeland, such as the achievements of the Jewish kingdom under Solomon and the Maccabees' victory over the Syrians; the independent kingdom of Armenia; and the early period (1710–16 and 1765–1849) of Sikh rule in the Punjab. Others refer to major catastrophes, such as the destruction of the Second Temple in Jerusalem and the forced exile of the Jews. To reinforce and supplement such distant episodes, there are more recent events: the establishment of Israel and the Six-Day and Yom Kippur wars; the Amritsar massacres of Sikhs in 1919, the occupation of the Golden Temple in 1984, and selective incidents of Hindu domination, including persecutions;[18] and the genocide and expulsion of Armenians in the Ottoman Empire, Soviet rule, and, more recently, a major earthquake in independent Armenia. These events took place in the homeland, but they served to mark the ethnonational consciousness in the diaspora as well, especially events of a negative nature, such as the *shoah* ((Nazi) holocaust) or the earlier *hurban* (destruction of the Second Temple) for the Jews; the Armenian *yeghern* (catastrophe), the Turkish genocide; and the Sikh *ghallughara* (great destruction), the battle fought between the Sikhs and the Afghans under Ahmad Shah Durani, which cost thousands of lives. There were events of a positive nature as well, such as the so-called "golden age" of Hebrew culture in medieval Spain. Much of the Jewish diaspora literature produced at that time focused on the Holy Land, but it was not associated with political mobilization leading to the restoration of an independent homeland, because such a scenario was considered unrealistic.

The various nationalist revivals were sparked significantly by fairly recent events. The Dreyfus Affair sparked the beginning of political Zionism in Western Europe; the Holocaust transformed German Jews from "German nationals of the Mosaic faith" into "Jews in Germany," and Jews in France from "*Français d'origine israélite*" into ethnically redefined *Juifs* (Safran 1983). The massacre in Amritsar in 1984 transformed many Punjabi Sikhs from loyal citizens of India to ethnonationalists. The massacre "blurred the usual divisions between the Jat, Mazahabi, urban Khatri and Arora Sikhs and merged them into a single ethnic identity: that of a persecuted Sikh minority (Gupta 1996: 73)."[19] This is similar to what happened to the divisions between German and "Eastern" Jews, which were erased in the face of the Holocaust; and the divisions between Zionists and anti-Zionists, which diminished significantly in reaction to that event.

The above suggests that exogenous factors are an important part of the ethnonationalist narrative. Zionist mobilization in the diaspora was heavily influenced by hostility to the Jewish state; the political activities of the Armenian diaspora (including terrorism) were responses to the betrayal of Armenian hopes for an independent state after World War I and to the denial of the genocide by Republican Turkey; the nationalism of the Sikhs grew in the wake of what they perceived to be international indifference to their political aspirations and betrayals by the great powers. Another exogenous factor is the ethnonationalism of neighboring or competing countries or communities, which functions as a contagion. Punjabi Sikh nationalism was a response to Muslim and Hindu nationalisms. The Armenians' Revolutionary Federation (Dashnak), founded in neighboring Georgia in 1890, was strongly influenced by Russian revolutionary intellectuals.

Furthermore, there is a contextual factor: events, often unforeseen, may provide opportunity structures to facilitate the politicization of ethnonations. The breakup of the Ottoman Empire helped to advance practical Zionism; the decolonization of India and the creation of a multiethnic and multireligious federal state marked by internal conflict opened up possibilities for the Sikhs; and the collapse of the Soviet Union made possible the creation of an independent Armenia, a development that, in turn, made communication between the diaspora and the homeland much easier. In other cases, such as those of the Kurds and Tibetans, the geostrategic context has made it impossible for diasporas to promote homeland independence.

The narratives of each of the ethnonations discussed here have been used by them to further their political aspirations. It is difficult to separate the theological, ideological and historical elements of these narratives. The sacred writings (and/or their subsequent textual interpretations) of all three ethnonations are used not only to buttress claims upon their homeland territories, but also to explain their diaspora conditions. The Old Testament is replete with references to exile as the consequence of sins committed by the community. As for the Armenians

> there is no single Armenian text that testifies to an early understanding of diaspora as divine punishment. But there is a strong tradition, certainly established by the 11th century, when diasporization began in earnest, that shows that Armenians had a general tendency to attribute their miseries to God as punishments for their sins. Lamentations penned on the occasion of major massacres after cities fell to the Seljuk Turks . . . attest to that.[20]

It is curious that the Armenians have used the term *gaghut*, from the Hebrew *galut*, to refer to their exile (Tölölyan 2005) The Jewish case is unique, however in the sense that, unlike the Armenian and the other diasporas dealt with here, there is a theological justification for the diaspora condition embraced by *outsiders*, i.e. eternal wandering as punishment for deicide. Secular Jews, like secular Armenians and Sikhs, have preferred to use a "post-colonialist" narrative.

In the promotion of the fortunes of the homeland, its sacred character is often conjured up. It is doubtful whether all diaspora leaders actually believe in that sacredness, but in all cases it is stressed for mobilization purposes. The impetus for a territorially focused politicization came primarily from the diaspora – an illustration of the diffusion effect of ideologies dominant in the host countries; but there has been disagreement about the precise location and boundaries of the original homeland. Still, there is agreement about the location of the "holy places."

Whereas in the homeland, the territorial factor has become paramount once independent statehood was achieved or regained, in the diaspora, the existence or restoration of the homeland has continued to be associated with religion. This has been true in particular of the politically mobilized elements of the diaspora.

The territorial views of the diaspora have often been more religiously inspired, less realistic and more "maximalist" than that of their coethnics, including the builders and leaders of the "ethnonation," in the homeland itself. Exaggerated territorial claims are often based on the past presence in the area in question. For the Jews, the kingdom of Solomon represents the greatest geographical extent of national power; and although this was invoked in the past by Zionist revisionists,[21] this is not claimed even by the so-called "Greater Israel" advocates. Historical Armenia at its height extended into what is now Turkey, Azerbaijan, Georgia and Iran (and under Tigranes the Great [c.70 BC] even into Syria); the territory inhabited by the Sikhs once extended into West Pakistan, Kashmir and the Indian province of Haryana (Axel 2001: 101–2).

Changing relationships

The disconnection of the homeland from the diaspora implies a selective distancing of the latter from the former, signaling a growing divergence of interests. Members of a diaspora community may feel superior to the homeland because they may have greater economic and professional opportunities than are available in it. Some diaspora Jews argue that Judaism is freer and more pluralistic in the (North American and Western European) hostlands than in Israel. Others, in particular anti-Zionist Jews who are critical of that country, argue that it is less cultured and/or that it is more hostile to religious practice than are the diaspora communities (Cohen 1997). Neither this argument, nor the analogous assertion made by some that Canada is "more Punjabi than the Punjab" (G. Singh 2003) is to be taken seriously; but an ethnic community may have more freedom to mobilize in the diaspora than in the homeland, especially if there is greater political freedom in the former than in the latter. This is attested by Armenian political parties in Europe and the Middle East.[22] During the Cold War, the Catholicosate in the diaspora, the religio-administrative center based in Antelias, Lebanon, was much freer to voice its opposition to Communism than the compromised Church of the Armenian Soviet Republic; and it played an important role in presenting the Armenian cause in international circles. The promotion of Jewish settlement in Palestine and the establishment of a Jewish state were primarily the task of organizations in the diaspora. Some observers have argued that the claim for an independent Khalistan has in recent years been promoted more insistently in the diaspora than in Punjab itself.[23]

The influence of diaspora religion on state-building is not necessarily the same in all instances. In the Jewish case, for example, the evidence is ambiguous. On the one hand, Judaism, as ethnified and secularized, has contributed to a concrete homeland consciousness. But Judaism as a de-ethnified religion with universalistic pretensions has been relatively detached from Zionism. Finally, ultra-Orthodox Judaism, whether in its "fundamentalist" or ethnic guise, has been opposed to a physical return to the homeland and, a fortiori, to state-building, arguing that such a position preempts the eschatological task of the messiah.

The above indicates that the territorial aspect of diaspora is not without problems. More specifically, there is a discordance of views between the diaspora and the homeland regarding religion and territory, which is related to the distinction between *people* (community) and *nation* (a more political concept), the former applying more comfortably to the diaspora, and the latter generally associated with statehood. To illustrate: there are three "narratives" of the Sikh community: as a nation, in terms of ancestry, memories, culture, homeland and solidarity (Smith 1999: 13); as a diaspora; and as followers of a world religion (Tatla 1999: 11). The Sikh idea of a "community of the pure" is comparable to the Jewish notion of "a nation of priests and a holy people." The Sikh *panth* (community of believers) is transpolitical, whereas the *qaum* (nation) may be transreligious (Axel 2001: 4–5). This is analogous to the Hebrew distinction between *'edah* (religious community), *'am* (the [Jewish] people collectively); and *le'um* (nation), the latter having a more clearly political connotation; and the Armenian *azg* (nation) vs *zhobovourt* (people).[24] This is apart from ordinary Israeli "citizenship" (*ezrahut*), which is extended not only to Jews, but to Christians, Muslims and Druze as well and is based on *jus soli* or naturalization.

Religion extends beyond ethnicity and does not always substitute for it, nor vice versa. Many, if not most, Jews in the diaspora are secular and define themselves increasingly in an ethnic fashion. There are non-Sikh Punjabis in the homeland, but it is a moot question whether there are non-religious Sikhs in the diaspora in the same sense that there are "dejudaized" Jews.

The relationship between ethnicity and religion is even more complicated in the case of Armenians. Around 90 percent of the Armenians in the diaspora are nominally members of the Apostolic Church; but within that church there are two Catholicosates – that of All Armenians in Etchmiadzin, Armenia and that of Cilicia, centered in Antelias, Lebanon. Until the breakup of the Soviet Union, the latter was frequently able to play a more prominent political role than the latter. Until Armenians got a state of their own, the Apostolic Church was a "surrogate state," and the focus of their collective self-image. Church attendance of Armenians today is higher in the diaspora than in Armenia itself, but it has slackened – and is often limited to holiday celebrations and rites of passage. As Charles Aznavour, a prominent Frenchman of Armenian origin, put it, "our religion is Armenianship."[25] The Armenian Republic provides a vicarious secular identity, so that religion is less needed by the diaspora. Indeed, interest in the homeland territory has been eclipsing the church as a glue of collective diaspora identity. And as in the case of diaspora Jews, who have mobilized for economic and diplomatic support for Israel, so in the case of the Armenian diaspora, where organizational life has focused on the homeland (G. Minassian 2002).

In the diaspora, religious practices have undergone changes, often under the influence of practices of society and of dominant religions in host countries – among Jews, the growth of Reform, a German and subsequently American adaptation of Judaism, resulting in a sort of Protestantism without the cross; and among Armenians, sermons in the hostland language, and, though fiercely contested, increasingly in prayers. Among Sikhs in diaspora gurdwaras (especially in Canada and the United States), there has been a selective adaptation to Christian practice. Religion remains the principal identity marker of the Sikhs; one scholar, however, when referring to the Sikh diaspora, speaks of "interethnic solidarity" and the support by overseas Sikhs of their *coethnics* – rather than their *coreligionists* – in the Punjab (Tatla 1999: 76–8).

The watering down of religious observance in the diaspora – whether as a consequence of secularization or the replacement of one's ethnic religion by another – inevitably speeds up the de-ethnicization process and the weakening of ties with the diaspora. "For most Armenians, conversion to another Christianity is the beginning of assimilation."[26] Similarly, the primacy of the ethnic marker in the United States and France will in the long run be insufficient to preserve Jewish identity. Communities in the homeland, however, can more easily afford this watering down, because the "thickness" of their cultures, whose original matrix is religious, is such as to preserve the Apostolic, Jewish and Sikh identities respectively in Armenia, Israel and the Punjab. In the case of the Sikhs, ethnocultural identity can probably be preserved much longer, in part because the wearing of the turban as an ethnosymbol makes the feeling of "otherness" particularly pronounced. The ethnic identity of diaspora Jews is likely to linger because of widespread anti-Semitism, once theologically inspired and disseminated by the political Right, but now largely ideological, and increasingly associated with the political Left.

In the face of secularization, ethnically defined identity, expressed in a "hyphenated status," is increasingly taking the place of religion among Jews and Armenians. But such identity is flimsy because it is insufficiently informed by cultural content, such as language or knowledge of ethnonational history. Religion-based identity, however, has its own problems. In the case of the Armenians in the American diaspora, for example, the Apostolic Church is not very dynamic; its leadership has not been able to connect well with parishioners; there is no theology of exile; and the church has been marked by a lack of textual reinterpretation, an avoidance of a clear position on social issues, and an increasing use of English in liturgy. An ethnically flavored approach to religion is periodically replenished by immigrants, but their sources are drying up. Nevertheless, in the face of the growing secularization of both diaspora and homeland and the fact that each of these is pulling in opposite directions, religion remains the only effective connecting link. In the words of Tölölyan, "the Church remains the domain in which all other non-religious Armenian conflicts finally find expression" (Tölölyan 1988). This, however, does not mean the theological aspects of the religion but rather the use of religious symbols, that is, a selective orthopraxy rather than orthodoxy.

Much of the ambivalent relationship between religion and ethnicity that obtains in the diaspora is replicated in the homeland, due to the "mixed" and pluralistic character of its population. Although the majority religion has a dominant status in the homeland, its position is weaker than it might be in view of internal divisions. In Israel, these divisions are reflected not only in the existence of different religious streams, but also by the existence of separate chief rabbis for Ashkenazi and Sephardi Jews. In Armenia, the Apostolic Church, and specifically that of Echmiadzin, enjoys special legitimacy, but many members of the hierarchy were politically socialized under the Communist regime; moreover, there are also secular nationalist Armenians, the consequence of forced religious or ideological conversions aimed at weakening *national* identity.

Even among Sikhs, a secularizing "ethnification" has taken place. True, in the diaspora, clean-shaven Sikhs are in the minority, and Sikh life still strongly revolves around religion. The Punjab, too, continues to be strongly marked by Sikh religion and culture, but that region also contains many Hindu and Muslim inhabitants. That explains why there is a growing tendency among Sikh politicians and intellectuals to speak of a territorially based Punjabi identity that includes all residents of the area, that is defined by language, and in which non-religious minorities share equally in the destiny of the province (and, it is hoped, a future independent state). This was the view especially of the Akalis, who tended to define Punjabi identity in *national* rather than religious terms; but even they paid lip service to the Sikh religion for purposes of political mobilization (Tatla 1999: 22–7).

This heterogeneity explains the development of homeland cultures going beyond the Apostolic, Jewish and Sikh religions respectively. The exigencies of state-building and modernization have been such as to make it more necessary than before to focus on the task of creating and mobilizing common collective identities in increasingly "civic" and secular nations.

For the diaspora, modernization has produced a different set of challenges. The common argument that the more modern a hostland, the greater the pressure for ethnic groups to give up their identities, has a certain intuitive validity. But this argument must be reexamined. Diaspora ethnoreligious communities are just as likely to survive in modern hostlands as in traditional ones, if not more so, because they constitute one of the few remaining escapes from functionally oriented societies and one of the few substitutes for the extended family or *Gemeinschaft*.

The ethnoreligious orientation in the homeland, however, becomes much less important. Once statehood is achieved, other commonalities assume primacy, such as patriotism, political values, and the rights and duties of citizenship. The responsibility of maintaining political unity results in a process that diasporas can avoid more easily: economic growth, modernization, keeping domestic peace, defending state borders and acquiring international legitimacy. In this process, the territorial dimension becomes dominant, and national identity becomes increasingly secular and transreligious. Members of the political community are Israelis more than Jews,[27] and Armenians are more than members of the Apostolic Church.[28]

In the diaspora, too, the secularization trend is such that religion alone is not enough to keep alive the ethnonational consciousness of minority communities. Nor is language, due to the fact that the languages of the diaspora hostlands have crowded out the homeland languages. There is a question about one ethnosymbol that has played an important role in the homeland and the diaspora, namely, historical memory. Both Israel and Armenia have institutionalized the commemoration of the genocides of their respective peoples – in the form of remembrance days, eternal flames and documentary collections. At the same time, homeland governments are often too preoccupied with state-building to spend much time evoking unpleasant memories. In the interest of *realpolitik*, the Armenian government spends less time berating the Turks for their past misdeeds than it does dealing with more immediate challenges, such as relations with neighboring countries. Similarly, the Israeli government has been less uneasy cultivating good relations with Germany than have Jewish communities in the diaspora. In the diaspora, in contrast, the memory of the past, and especially of genocides, continues to fulfill an important role in the maintenance of collective identity. But there, too, historical memory tends to fade, especially in hostlands whose culture is basically ahistorical (as, for example, the United States).

Nevertheless, the two communities cannot easily separate from each other. As was pointed out above, there is a reciprocal need – of the homeland for financial and diplomatic support; and of the diaspora for infusions of culture and people. There is a symbiotic relationship between homeland and diaspora: during the nation-building process, homeland leaders feed on the diaspora religion; thereafter, the diaspora nourishes its identity on the secular achievements and needs of the homeland. Equally important, diaspora communities are held accountable by hostland and international opinion for the perceived misdeeds of the homeland. Thus diaspora Jews are stand-ins for Israelis, and anti-Israel attitudes are quickly translated into anti-Semitism.

The relationship between homeland, or ancestral, nations and diasporas will remain a matter of interest in the foreseeable future, because the latter are still growing as individuals continue to leave the homeland for economic, political and security reasons. Due to the growing permeability of international frontiers and improvements in global communication, it is now easier than ever for diasporas to be connected and identified with their homelands. This dual orientation has provoked a debate about "double loyalty," a phenomenon that, in turn, calls into question not only Gellner's notion of nationalism, according to which culture and nation are congruent and leave ethnoreligious communities no options between assimilation and exclusion (Gellner 1983), but also traditional notions of national sovereignty and citizenship. This debate is not confined to diasporas; it applies equally to the multiple loyalties of officials of multinational corporations. Unfortunately, while communication between diasporas and homelands has become easier in the technical sense, it has become more difficult in the cultural sense because the identity markers between the two communities are becoming increasingly differentiated.

Acknowledgments

I want to thank Walker Connor and Khachig Tölölyan for their useful comments on an earlier draft, presented at the conference on the Nationalism Debate organized by the Association for the Study of Ethnicity and Nationalism at the London School of Economics, April 23–24, 2004.

Notes

1 Compare this to the preference for the self-designation of "African-American" by American blacks, a hyphenated ethnicity analogous to "Italian-American" or "Irish-American."

2 It is a matter of debate whether Sikhs can set aside their appearance – whether the traditional turban can simply be dispensed with. Yet diaspora Sikhs are increasingly losing their distinctiveness, leaving only the most militant Sikhs behind.

3 The term "state-nation" is a translation of *Staatsvolk*, used by Marx, Hegel and other (mostly German) writers to refer to a collectivity that, unlike a mere *Volksgemeinschaft* (i.e. ethnic community) is sufficiently "evolved" to "reach their destination," i.e. to maintain a state (see Gellner 1983: 48).

4 During the Soviet and Nazi periods, exiled Russian and German intellectuals argued that they were better custodians of the authentic culture of their respective homelands than those who stayed behind. A similar argument can be made in the case of Tibetan exile culture today.

5 *Fort: Panth Khalsa – Information on the Sikh Nation*. Available online at www.panthkhalsa.org/panth/press_khalistan.html (accessed 20 June 2006).

6 These organizations were not entirely new; between 1925 and 1939 there already existed a philanthropic organization, the *Hayastani Oknoutioun Komité* (HOK), which had a branch in Armenia.

7 "Moses was not a man inspired by God in order to fulfill and reaffirm His covenant with Israel; he was really a national leader rising against colonial oppression. Muhammad may have been the seal of the prophets, but even more important, he was the founder of the Arab nation" (Kedourie 1993: 70). As Gellner (1983: 107) remarked, "Religion [was] used by Zionists for political ends. In the diaspora, the Jewish religion referred to Jerusalem; once back in Jerusalem, semi-secular Zionism for a time used the dated socialist populist clichés of nineteenth-century Europe."

8 Note that the Panthéon, the "temple" of the laic republic, is topped by a cross.

9 In Turkey, Iraq and Iran, the state has made the teaching of the Armenian language virtually impossible by imposing a state curriculum on Armenian parochial schools funded entirely by the community. But because these are essentially Muslim societies and inheritors of some version of the millet system and the *ahlu ul-kitab* ("people of the book") syndrome, they permit several hours of teaching of religion. During those precious hours a mélange of religion, history and, to a lesser extent, language is taught.

10 Even the Yiddish of the Bundists, who were socialist, anti-Zionist and anti-religious, was impregnated with Biblical expressions, and "secular" shtetl culture was permeated with allusions to the Holy Land.

11 Term employed by John Armstrong and cited by Smith (1986: 15 and *passim*).

12 See Will Herberg's notions concerning the "American religion" in his *Protestant, Catholic, Jew* (1960).

13 Reform Jews, in an attempt to "detribalize" Judaism, eliminated references to the ingathering of exiles and to Temple sacrifices, and even the general use of

Hebrew in prayers, but in the past generation many Reform congregations have returned to these and other "Zion-centered" practices.

14 Abrahamian and Sweeney (2001). See especially the chapters by Hamlet Petrosian, "The Temple," "The Sacred Mountain" and the "Khachkar or Cross-Star."

15 Note, however, that this practice is localized. "Van" people, and those from the region of Vasburakan or Vaskpuragan around it, have exceptionally strong local commitments and memories (Khachig Tölölyan, personal communication).

16 This is true of Yiddish, a secular diaspora language, as well. Based on Middle High German, it is written in the Hebrew alphabet and contains a significant number of Hebrew words, especially relating to religion, and many of its cultural and literary allusions are religious in origin (Safran 1992: 402–3).

17 Specifically, the breaking away from Byzantine doctrine of Christ's dual nature, as expressed at the Council of Chalcedon in 451.

18 "Two holocausts in the eighteenth century," "WaheGuru Ji Ka Khalsa" Available online at desix.5ucom (accessed 20 June 2006). For narratives of Sikh glory and displacement, see Axel 2001.

19 See also Tatla 1999: 196–200, who uses the term "holocaust" as metaphor for the "impact of the critical event" when he discusses the transformation of the attitudes of the Sikhs.

20 Personal communication from Khachig Tölölyan, March 2004.

21 A slogan of the Revisionist Zionists before the establishment of Israel was "The Jordan has two banks; this is ours, and that one, too."

22 Soviet Armenia had only the Communist party, while the diaspora had the ARF or Dashnaks, the bourgeois liberal ADL, and the socialist H'nchaks (see Nalbandian 1963; G. Minassian 2002; M. Hovanessian 2000: 90).

23 "Khalistan." Available online at www.fact-index.com/k/kh/khalistan.html (accessed 20 June 2006). In fact, the very idea of Khalistan was first put forth by Sikhs in the North American and British diasporas (Ahmed 1996: 277–8).

24 The concept of "Israel" itself has multiple connotations to both the homeland and the diaspora. It refers variously to the land, the state and to the Jewish people everywhere and their common destiny (See Sacks 1993, 8).

25 Paper read at the First Educational Seminar of AGBU Schools, May 1993. Available online at gardentowerhotel.com/MBWritings-SemEng93.DOC (accessed 20 June 2006).

26 Khachig Tölölyan, personal communication, March 2004.

27 Note, however, that Christian missionary activity is frowned upon even by secular Israeli Jews.

28 Since 1991 and the collapse of the Soviet Union, about 4–5 percent of Armenia's population has converted in response to financial and spiritual incentives brought in by Pentecostal and Adventist evangelizers and Jehovah's Witnesses.

References

Abrahamian, L. and Sweeney, N. (eds) (2001) *Armenian Folk Arts, Culture, and Identity*, Bloomington: Indiana University Press.

Ahmed, I. (1996) "Religious Nationalism and Sikhism," in D. Westerlund (ed.) *Questioning the Secular State*, London: Hurst.

Anderson, B. (1992) "Long-Distance Nationalism: World Capitalism and the Rise of Identity Politics," Working Paper 5.1, presented at conference on Nation, National Identity, Nationalism, Washington, DC, September 10–12.

Axel, B. (2001) *The Nation's Tortured Body: Violence, Representation, and the Formation of a Sikh Diaspora*, Durham and London: Duke University Press.

Beilin, Y. (2000) *His Brother's Keeper: Israel and Diaspora Jewry in the Twenty-First Century*, New York: Schocken.

Breuilly, J. (1996) "Approaches to Nationalism," in G.I. Balakrishnan (ed.) *Mapping the Nation*, London and New York: Verso.

Cohen, R. (1997) *Global Diasporas*, Seattle: University of Washington Press.

Crane, P.M. (1995) *Congressional Record*, June 7, E1184.

Gellner, E. (1983) *Nations and Nationalism*, Ithaca: Cornell University Press.

Gupta, D. (1996) *The Context of Ethnicity*, Delhi: Oxford University Press.

Hastings, A. (1997) *The Construction of Nationhood: Ethnicity, Religion, and Nationalism*, Cambridge: Cambridge University Press.

Herberg, W. (1960) *Protestant, Catholic, Jew: An Essay in American Religious Sociology*, Garden City: Anchor Books.

Hobsbawm, E.J. (1992) *Nations and Nationalism since 1780*, 2nd edn, Cambridge: Cambridge University Press.

Hovanessian, M. (2000) "La diaspora arménienne et l'idée nationale," in *Les Diasporas*, Paris: Cahiers d'études sur la Méditerranée orientale et le monde Turko-iranien, 30 (November–December): 83–109.

Kedourie, E. (1993) *Nationalism*, 4th edn, Oxford: Blackwell.

Marx, A.W. (2003) *Faith in Nation: Exclusionary Origins of Nationalism*, Oxford: Oxford University Press.

Minassian, G. (2002) *Guerre et terrorisme arméniens*, Paris: Presses Universitaires de France.

Minassian, T.T. (2002) "Erevan, Ville Promise," *Diasporas* 1 (2nd trimester): 71–81.

Nalbandian, L. (1963) *The Armenian Revolutionary Movement*, Berkeley and Los Angeles: University of California Press.

Sacks, J. (1993) *One People?*, London and Washington, DC: Littman Library of Jewish Civilization.

Safran, W. (1983) "France and Her Jews: From 'culte israélite' to 'lobby juif,'" *Tocqueville Review* 5:1 (spring/summer): 101–35.

—— (1992) "Language, Ideology, and State-Building," *International Political Science Review*, 13(4) (October): 397–414.

—— (2005) "Language and Nation-Building in Israel: Hebrew and Its Rivals," *Nations and Nationalism*, 11(1): 43–63.

Schwalgin, S. (2004) "Why Locality Matters: Diaspora Consciousness and Sendentariness in the Armenian Diaspora in Greece," in W. Kokot, K. Tölölyan and C. Alfonso (eds) *Diaspora, Identity, and Religion*, London and New York: Routledge.

Shani, G. (2002) "Beyond Khalistan? The Sikh Diaspora and the International Order," paper presented at the annual convention of the International Studies Association, New Orleans, 27 March.

Sicker, M. (1992) *Judaism, Nationalism, and the Land of Israel*, Boulder: Westview Press.

Singh, A. (2000) "Sovereign Cybernation of Sikh Diaspora," *Samar Magazine*, 12 (Fall–Winter): 42–5.

Singh, G. (2003) *The Global Indian: The Rise of Sikhs Abroad*, New Delhi: Rupa.

Smith, A.D. (1986) *The Ethnic Origins of Nations*, Oxford: Blackwell.

—— (1998) *Nationalism and Modernism*, London and New York: Routledge.

—— (1999) *Myths and Memories of the Nation*, Oxford: Oxford University Press.

—— (2001) "Nations and History," in M. Guibernau (ed.) *Understanding National-ism*, Malden: Blackwell.

Tatla, D.S. (1999) *The Sikh Diaspora: The Search for Statehood*, London: UCL Press.

Tölölyan, K. (1988) "The Role of the Armenian Apostolic Church in the Diaspora," *Armenian Review*, 41(1): 55–68.

—— (2005) "The Armenian Diaspora," *Encyclopedia of Diasporas*, New York and London: Kluwer Academic/Plenum: 35–46.

Viviano, F. (2004) "Armenia Reborn," *National Geographic*, March: 32–49.

Walinsky, L.J. (ed.) (1981) World Jewish Congress, Economic and Social Commis-sion, *Issues Facing World Jewry*, Washington, DC: Hershel Shanks.

Walker, B. (1998) "Social Movements as Nationalisms," in J. Couture, K. Nielsen and M. Seymour (eds) *Rethinking Nationalism*, Calgary: University of Calgary Press.

4   When is the nation no longer?

Edward A. Tiryakian

In the 1960s "the nation" began to come into its own academically, as a concept and a reality differentiated from "nation-state." The latter as an historical formation in different forms (federal republic, constitutional monarchy, etc.) became widely actualized in the nineteenth century – so much so that by the mid-twentieth century it had established itself globally, in "old" nation-states of Europe as well as in post-colonial entities in Africa and Asia. Historians, of course, had made it one of their favorite domains to provide narratives of the nation-state, and "nationalism," as more often than not nefarious activities of the nation-state toward its neighbors (and to "others" internally, perceived as not deserving full citizenship), received its fair share of attention (Hobsbawm 1990).

The 1960s provided a new climate and allowed for new perspectives to enter into the public sphere, perspectives on the whole critical of established societal structures and institutionalized patterns of authority which for a new iconoclastic generation became viewed as "oppressive." Among major structures of the new *ancien régime* was the nation-state. One new vista of this period was that "nation" and "state" are not essentially coterminous but are different entities, which in some circumstances may come together, as happened in Western countries in the course of modernity. "Nation," it has become increasingly clear,[1] refers to a certain sociological grouping; "state" to a political embodiment with bureaucratic structures and legitimated access to resources recognized (or challenged) by other such entities. As part of the new social movements of the 1960s and later decorating the "socioscape" were those within France, Great Britain, Spain and Canada in particular, movements seeking varying degrees of autonomy from the central state – not on behalf of an interest group (class, religious, gender or otherwise) but on behalf of a *nation*. The claims and aims of these groups, having a territorial anchorage within the boundaries of the nation-state,[2] generated a new wave of *nationalism* in terms of political and cultural activities directed against the monopoly of the state apparatus. In the European context, nationalism had been associated with state action against other states, and the experience of German, Italian and Soviet state actions against others (as well, of course, as state action internally) had considerably darkened the image of nationalism. But the general change in the social climate of the 1960s arguably allowed new, wider and perhaps more balanced perspectives on nation, state and nationalism. Moreover, nationalism had outside of Europe – in Asia, the Middle East, and Africa – gained *intellectual* respect and international standing as a mobilizing force against the colonial and imperial manifestations of the nation-state.[3]

Equally great legitimation for nationalism – and increasing interest in the nation as an irreducible phenomenon of modernity needing to be problematized as a source of agency – came in the late 1980s and 1990s in the wake of the Soviet reforms of *glasnost* and *perestroika* which allowed power shifts from the centralized apparatus of the Supreme Soviet to the peripheries. The power shift in the occidental part of the Soviet empire was to an important extent a function of nationalist mobilization in Hungary, Czechoslovakia, Poland and the Baltic States.[4] In these instances, the historical and cultural bases (e.g. the display of traditional flags) of the nation reappeared on the scene, after they had seemingly been shelved or dissolved in the larger postwar USSR entity. Tito's Yugoslav legacy, a delicately balanced federation of Communist parties given legitimacy by its separation from the postwar Soviet bloc, also imploded in the 1990s, with autonomous movements in Slovenia, Croatia, Bosnia and Macedonia rejecting Serbian hegemony. The relatively tranquil secession of Slovenia and that of Macedonia was seen as a benevolent form of nationalism against an oppressive state; the horrendous civil war that pitted Serbia, Croatia and Bosnia-Hercegovina in a tragic and classic triangular struggle gave nationalism a much darker image than it had enjoyed in the 1970s and 1980s. But it also helped to accentuate the contemporary significance of nationalism and its ability at ethnic mobilization, that is, of drawing attention to the *modernity* of nationalism.

In this chapter I strive to develop a more analytical, conceptual stance to open up new terrain for interrogation and research. In line with this, I would like to suggest that, while crosscutting a vast empirical literature, there is in fact a finite set of four interrelated questions sharply posing some basic queries. Three have been asked previously and have been extremely heuristic in generating interdisciplinary research. After briefly posing these, I will propose a fourth, which is anticipated in the title of this chapter. This will be accompanied by some suggested historical examples that might be appropriate for comparative analysis.

Defining the nation

The first foundational question is the one posed by the historian Renan in 1882: "What is a nation?" (Renan 1996). Although the historical context for framing the question was specific to strains in the emergent French Third Republic,[5] Renan's discussion has proven to be durable, with widespread applications. Critical to his formulation is that nationhood has a variety of *objective* necessary conditions – territory, culture, resources.

However, in themselves they do not suffice. There are also what might today be called *intersubjective* conditions: collective historical consciousness (what is remembered and, he pointed out, equally important, what is forgotten about the past), and the desire to do things together. As he summarized in a trenchant dictum of collective voluntarism: *the nation is a daily plebiscite*. The nation, following Renan, is thus a certain territorially grounded collectivity that requires ongoing purpose and validation in both great and small projects. The validation can occur in ritual activities (for example, flag-raising and -lowering, pledge of allegiance, observance of national holy days, the singing of national anthems, and the like) or in a variety of new ventures which enhance pride in national consciousness (for example, the setting up of the Tour de France in 1903, national participation in the modern Olympics), and of course, in national demonstrations against imperial/foreign hegemony (as witnessed in the Baltic states and elsewhere in Eastern Europe in October/November 1989). The nation is thus promoted from being an appendage of the state to being, as a collective being, an historical subject as much as, say, "class" is an historical subject for orthodox Marxism.

There is an obvious link between nation as a collective historical agent and another widely used sociological concept, that of "community," long ago recognized by Nisbet as a core idea of the sociological tradition (1966). Benedict Anderson's seminal *Imagined Communities* (1991) juxtaposes nation and community to make sense of the ubiquitous nation-ness as a cardinal feature of modernity – the result of transformations, material and psychological, by which from the eighteenth century to the twentieth colonial states and empires became national states. The emphasis Anderson gives to "community" adds greatly to an earlier Eurocentric and Romantic attachment to community by stressing its link to nation as "an imagined political community – and imagined as both inherently limited and sovereign" (Anderson 1991: 6), an active creation of consciousness by indigenous entrepreneurs. What is particularly distinctive is his endeavor to account for the development of national consciousness in communities outside the European heartland of nationalism, such as the Americas and Southeast Asia. In his innovative interpretation, it is "pilgrim creole functionaries and provincial creole printmen [who] played the decisive historic role" (1991: 65).

If nations are "imagined," that is, active constructions of collective consciousness, they are not "imagined" in any old way. Part of the appeal of Anderson's work is his illustration through a wealth of cases of various forms of imagining the nation, all of which require providing narratives linking the past to the present so as to link the nation today, its actors and its projects, to the past. Lastly, there is the question that Renan had clearly understood as necessary for the making of the modern nation, namely, what shall be remembered and what shall be forgotten? A nation is an historical and therefore dynamic entity: its consciousness – as promulgated in history textbooks, memorials, rituals and other aspects of collective memory – entails remembering who have been its significant actors (heroes and detractors) and forgetting its insignificant ones.

Talcott Parsons's work, which preceded Anderson's, provides us with sociological analytical tools by treating nation as a *societal community* (Parsons 1966, 1971). Parsons looked at societies as complex social systems which undergo, in dynamic processes of interaction, structural changes of differentiation that in turn, unless they fragment and dissipate, call for mechanisms of integration. Social institutions in different sectors of society provide continuity. At the core of a modern society, Parsons theorized, is the nation or societal community. Its significance in the total societal system is that nation is the "bearer" – or the anchor – of a normative order, a set of "value commitments" which "grounds the identity and solidarity of the community" (1966: 17).

If Anderson extended the notion of nation in space (as well as in time) with the theme of "imagined communities," Parsons extended it by invoking appropriate norms of modernity tacitly regarding the question of "whose nation" has rights and obligations defined by membership in the collectivity. That is, in the process of modernization, there is on the whole an enlargement of the modern institution of citizenship, an enlargement of those living in a territory who are said to share fully with others citizenship in the nation. Restrictions based on status, gender, race and other "ascriptive" criteria tend to become increasingly residual, allowing for a greater pluralism in the composition of those said to be members of the "nation."

Yet, obviously, this process of greater inclusion – which Parsons likened to the economic condition of "inflation" – has suffered setbacks at various occasions due to severe social strains regarding competing definitions of the situation as to what are the value commitments of the nation and who are core members. Parsons acknowledged counter-modern "deflationary" processes seeking restrictions of membership size in the nation, and he had in his own American setting the instance of McCarthyism seeking to remove alleged Communists from the public sphere. Looking backward to a previous period of the breakdown of modernization, Nazi Germany sought to remove cultural "aliens" from the roll of German citizens and Stalinist Russia engaged in purges against "rootless cosmopolitans." The problematic of "who belongs to nation" and just what are the core values of the nation and who can interpret these values (e.g. in the educational system basic to the socialization into core institutions) is not something of yesterday. In the past two decades the challenges of multiculturalism and (illegal) immigration have profoundly shaken the social and political landscape, in the United States with a burgeoning Latin American population and in Europe with its growing Islamic population. Parsons's vision of the American nation is not of a static entity, but one with a set of core values accessible to successive generations who can fine-tune the implementations and adaptations of these values to further modernization. And in the late 1960s and early 1970s, his basic perspective on the stability of the societal community prevailed against those on the far right or far left who questioned the adequacy of those commitments. However, September 11 and the first half of the present decade have put in jeopardy anew the viability of national core values and the societal integration of American society already manifested regarding multiculturalism and diversity for diversity's sake, undermining unity (Schlesinger 1998).

Questions of identity

The second question, so closely related to the first that they often become intertwined, is nevertheless worth asking: "What is national identity?" Anthony Smith has provided a general coverage of national identity issues (1991) and there is no dearth of more specific empirical approaches linking national identity to facets of nationalism, nation and national movements (e.g. Cameron 1999; Kriesi *et al.* 1999; Schöpflin 2000). What is important to note at the onset is that, just as "nation" is a dynamic concept, so is "national identity" subject to change, albeit it is often taken to be fixed, rooted in deep-seated structures of selfhood.[6]

The theme of identity is a general psychological one, namely how (by what symbolic means) does the subject represent or perceive himself/herself in the world *and* how does this perception reflect how other subjects perceive him/her? If this question of "Who am I?" is of importance to the basic human condition, it has increased salience with structural changes in the social environment of modernity. Asking "What is national identity?" has become both more acute and problematic as well as more extensive, I would argue, as a reflection of various changes in different parts of the world, including political, economic, cultural and demographic changes operating in different ways.

At one level, the separatists' questioning of the legitimacy and validity of the nation-state and the national culture that it generated in the integration of the societal community in the nineteenth and twentieth centuries in the West, has rendered problematic the meaning of collective identity for Canada, Spain and Belgium, for example. But so has the emergence of really new entities at the nation-state level, such as the Former Yugoslav Republic of Macedonia (Danforth 1995; Poulton 2000) seeking to develop a national identity different from adjacent countries like Greece and Bulgaria, but also seeking to accommodate a significant ethnic minority (Albanians). And some old entities newly liberated from the alien yoke of Communism also contain significant ethnic minorities, previously ruling elites, now finding themselves political minorities in the diapsora, where the "host" populations seek signs of political loyalty to the nation, for example, learning the indigenous language. Such is the case of the Russophone minority in the Baltic, notably in Estonia and Latvia (Kartlins 1994; Dreifelds 1996; Laitin 1998).

Europe itself provides much terrain, symbolic and material, for the study of collective identity. The construction of the European Union is a bold effort at the peaceful integration of a multitude of nation-states into a transnational reality which is still under construction, or perhaps, one might say "under invention" (Delanty 1995). While economic integration as a means of keeping the peace was an initial – and very successful – stimulus in the formation of the European Economic Community, the development of a common European identity requires greater effort, as witness the recent debates and negative referendum votes in France and the Netherlands regarding a European Constitution. Many of the primary symbols of national identity of European countries are versions of the Christian cross and mediaeval heraldry while others are embedded in Enlightenment secularism. The two have managed – uneasily at times, for example, during the polemic over the inclusion/exclusion of reference to "God" and Christianity in the preamble of the Constitution – to subordinate their tensions into a broader societal community. European Union officials have been very attentive to developing the cultural basis of a European identity, in effect a transnational identity that would satisfy a modern "E Pluribus Unum," as shown imaginatively in the coins and banknotes of the European Monetary Union (Shore 2000; Herrmann *et al.* 2004).

The European Union has been a successful collective endeavor in building a new Europe, successful in having a common currency accepted (which is one of the material bases of a national identity) and in preventing wars between member states. It may also be providing the institutional and cultural basis of new collective identities, providing actors with a sense of belonging both to an established nation and to a larger European identity. Here I will cite what is still a very rudimentary piece of evidence. A study of German students in both Eastern and Western German universities indicated that in terms of collective symbols that might provide pride of belonging, "Ossis" and "Wessis" alike rejected traditional symbols of nationhood but some positive symbols both found acceptable were what might be interpreted as a new identity: *being-German-in-Europe* (Ezell *et al.* 2003). It will be important to replicate this study both in Germany, which might discover if this is an emergent trend in a younger generation, a basis for a positive collective identity to replace the bane of an ongoing *negative national identity* (Tiryakian 2005),[7] and also elsewhere in Europe.

The European project has both a structural and a cultural challenge regarding its collective identity. Structurally, there is the question of how much can be absorbed in a short period of time within existing structures and institutions. In the Parsonian framework, problems of adaptation, goal attainment and integration can strain complex social systems, generating centrifugal tendencies away from the societal community. Attempts at federation where the units have different cultural and historical trajectories, and different economic and demographic characteristics, are more likely to result in failure than in success. The integration of Eastern Europe into the European Union is a mammoth task of economic, political and cultural integration. A greater challenge still is the question of the entry of Muslim Turkey into a Europe which had historically defined an integral part of its identity as the defense of its Greco-Roman-Christian civilization and its democratic secular ideals in the Enlightenment, from the non-European and mainly Ottoman "East" (Delanty 1995).

Even without the accession of Turkey into the European Union, the demographic trend of an increasing first- and second-generation Islamic population in various countries poses multiple questions of identity. For the immigrants and their descendants, being accepted as Frenchmen, Germans, Italians, etc., is at one level akin to the experience of immigrants who came to the United States in the great immigration wave of 1880–1912. Incorporation into the American societal community was a strain for both the "hosts" – primarily Protestant, English-speaking Americans – and the culturally distinct Catholic, Orthodox and Jewish "newcomers."

Integration of Muslim immigrants into Europe (and America) today is complicated even further by the global situation of anti-terrorism directed in response to what is perceived as radical Islam's war or jihad against the West. If the most concrete theatre of the war is Iraq and America's declared war against Al-Qaeda, the war's outreach touches Europe and its Islamic minorities. The question of their loyalty to the European nation-state or to an Islam outside Europe is one that profoundly marks the problem of identity, not only for the Islamic community but also for that of the larger societal community as a test of just how wide are its symbolic boundaries.

Europe is not the only region where questions of national identity are pressing. As this is being written, the question of Iraq's national identity – as well as that of virtually all countries in the Middle East – is of world importance. The American goal, via direct military intervention, is to remold the identity of traditional Islamic/Arabic states into "modern democracies" which hold free elections and engage in free economic markets. At least that is the *ex post facto* justification for its war in Iraq, and possibly for future interventions. At the time of writing, it is impossible to gauge how effective this attempt at changing societies and their established folk ways and mores, including their patterns of ethnic and gender social stratification will be in either the short or long term. It may be that if one transnational identity emerges from the continued American presence, it will be a pan-Arabic and pan-Islamic anti-American identity providing a modicum of unification that Nasser and the Ba'athists never could.

It is in retrospect clear that what Klapp highlighted years ago in his insightful study *Collective Search for Identity* (1969) remains a salient feature of the contemporary world. However, the question of identity has to be treated not merely in terms of the problems of individuals in mass society but equally in terms of the ambiguity of collective, national identity

Nations as process

The third heuristic question served as the theme of the 2004 meeting of the Association for the Study of Ethnicity and Nationalism, namely "When is the nation?"

Appropriately, the meeting was *de facto* a collective Festschrift to honor Anthony D. Smith who has labored mightily at the London School of Economics to make "nation" a critical field of multidisciplinary inquiry. An exemplar of this inquiry is Smith's own seminal work tracing the modernity of nations backward to their distant ethnic origins and reciprocally forward in history (Smith 1987: 2003).

History is crucial to the nation in many ways. A claim to the authenticity of a nation, its territory and members, is that it is attached to and validated by encounters with the historical process which is integral to the human condition. In nationalist narratives, the nation has been forged and tried in historical encounters with others. Primordialist narratives often place the nation's origins at the dawn of history; it is the nation which occupies sacred space (and itself sacralizes space), becoming a divine gift whose human inhabitants are "covenanters" or "trustees" in perpetuity. Historical origins merge with mythic beginnings in the designation of an "elect" or "chosen people" – whether these be the Jewish people, the Japanese, the Gauls or the Pilgrims and their descendants. To be sure, an alternative narrative – decidedly more secularist in tone – is that "nation" and (following Smith 1987) its progenitor "ethnie" have not been "always" but have undergone broad stages of historical development (the broadest being "ethnie," "nation," "nation-state").

This version of the historical narrative follows a simplified structural-functional evolutionary schema along the lines of Parsons's analysis. Namely, from the societal system of "ethnie" a development stage to "nation" involves structural *differentiation* of the national community into separate religious, political and economic institutions, which are interrelated by cultural and territorial ties. It is faced on occasions with crises that strain existing structural arrangements and call for collective attention to questions of societal *integration*. Core values, principles and collective symbols of belonging provide much of the ballast of national solidarity; these may have to undergo ordeals and sacrifices in order to survive. The historical narrative may well become one of evolutionary triumph after various trials and tribulations.[8] To extend the analogy, existing nations are like species of flora and fauna that have successfully adapted via evolution.

There is one aspect of "When is the nation?" which has received little attention in the vast literature pitting "primordialists" against "constructionists." It is that many, most and perhaps eventually all, nations are not fashioned once and for all, but that historical situations may challenge and promote a nation to be recast, even "reinvented." Rather than remaining static, nations are subject to new beginnings, institutionally, culturally and normatively.

As an illustration, asking "When is the German nation?" can provide different directives: one might look for the origins of German nationhood in the social institutions and cultural myths of Gothic tribes. Or, skipping many centuries, one can look for the emergence of a new Germany born with hegemonic Imperial Germany after its triumph over France in 1870. Yet one can say that the liberal aspects of the German nation only (and briefly) emerged as Weimar in the 1920s, while Hitler's equally brief Germany (1933–45) sought to establish a new "kingdom" (*Reich*) for the nation with an enlarged societal community based on ascriptive ties of pan-Germans as racial descendants of mythic Aryans. In terms of our ideals of modernity, a German nation only came into being in the post-1945 setting with the establishment of a federal republic and with a new set of institutional norms favoring equal treatment for all and a curtailment of centralized powers that could degenerate into authoritarianism. And even so, the partition of Germany into a bourgeois West and a socialist East made it problematic whether Germany was a nation separated by two states or two distinct nation-states that would go in divergent trajectories. So instead of the Anschluss of 1938 which gave consternation to others, the surprising German unification of 1990 was viewed with near universal joy as the birth of a new and democratic Germany. I would suggest that other illustrations might readily be found to demonstrate the point that *a nation may have multiple beginnings in the historical process, not all of which may be happy.*

The failure of nations

Opening the historicity of nations by asking their origins and development leads, at least theoretically, to posing one last general question, "When is the nation no longer?" Given a perspective which takes nation (or the societal community) as a dynamic entity, at least the theoretical possibility of its coming to an end should be entertained. Under what conditions may this happen and/or what historical instances may be shown to drive home the point as the significance of the question for a comprehensive examination of nationhood? The topic is not only of theoretical import but is also, in various guises, becoming one of timely interest. Prognoses predict the decline/disappearance of the nation-state in the face of globalization, or the decline of the hegemon and its empire due to global overstretch, or internally, because of multiculturalism and alien immigrants sapping away the common beliefs and core values of a beleaguered majority which is demographically not reproducing itself.[9]

To recall an earlier point: a nation is not its political apparatus, although this identification occurs frequently. A state may disappear as a result of conquest or perhaps even in conditions of anarchy, but this does not necessarily mean the nation behind the fallen state is equally no longer. The historical record shows many instances of what is sometimes referred to as "submerged nations" – cultural collectives maintaining all the essentials of Renan's "nation," a sovereign state. Such nations retain distinct orderings of institutions as well as separate traditions. "Submerged nations" remain subordinated to the polity of the dominant state, and their historical traditions may be submerged in the official history of the state, but they remain nations nevertheless at least *insofar as a critical segment of their population still view themselves as members of that nation's societal community.* Further, it is also possible that, with the process of modernization, what had been an autonomous but fragmented *ethnie* becomes a nation, different from the encompassing nation-state. Examples of such "submerged nations" that have not lost or even reasserted their national identity with modernity would be Wales, Scotland, Catalonia, Quebec and the American Indian Nations.[10]

Are there historical cases, however, where one might argue that the nation *qua* societal community became "no longer?" The following cases might be considered briefly (subject to much more careful scrutiny): from antiquity the Roman Republic, from the twentieth century the Republic of South Africa, and Yugoslavia. Doing this might stimulate discussion about other and perhaps better-documented instances.

The Roman Republic[11]

A case may be made for a Roman nation, or a "proto-nation," to have developed during the course of the Republic, dating the latter's beginning in 509/510 BC with the end of the monarchy and ending with Octavian Caesar assuming all powers and symbols of authority, first as Augustus ("venerable" or "revered") in 27 BC and then as *pontifex maximus* in 13 BC. If one can speak of a "peak" period of nationhood, it might be somewhere in the second century BC (say after Scipio's victory over Hannibal at Zama in 202 BC).

Rome from the onset stood out among other Latins as having exemplary military abilities, which enabled Romans to expand beyond their original locale on the Tiber River, establish colonies, drive out the Etruscans and the Gauls and, after definitively defeating their major rival, Carthage, in three Punic Wars, become the hegemon of not only Italy but of the Western Mediterranean.

The Roman (proto-)nation flourished by military conquest in developing the extremely efficient military machine of Roman legions, a machine whose efficiency was complemented by the outstanding engineering of an infrastructure of roads and aqueducts, such as the great Appian Way, begun by the censor Appius Claudius in 312 BC. The infrastructure that made Rome the first great metropolis (recall the saying "all roads lead to Rome") was complemented politically, at least initially, by the institutions of the *res publica*, such as the elections of offices that provided power-sharing between plebeians and patricians. Political empowerment in the nascent societal community of the Roman nation was anchored in Roman *citizenship*, which was extended in varying degrees to non-Romans, often as a reward for fighting for Rome in its wars; even freed slaves could become citizens and vote for offices, albeit not for themselves as officeholder. The cultural anchor of Republican Rome's identity, besides language and customs that had evolved from prehistorical times, Etruscan and Hellenic influences was Roman state religion, as Durkheim's teacher, Fustel de Coulanges, convincingly demonstrated (1980).

Rome by the middle of the second century BC might be said to have had all the accouterments of a nation: it had a mythic origin as a people with the foundation of Rome by Romulus and Remus; it had territory; it had a variety of political, economic and cultural institutions which provided it with unmatched administrative ability, and it had had a plethora of collective projects of military expansion beyond its original borders. The military underpinning of the Republic provided for the proliferation of colonies that could be settled by legionnaire veterans. Military booty and land acquisition by generals and their troops brought great wealth to Rome, particularly to the aristocracy or patricians.

When and how did the Roman nation end? Of course, there is a vast literature devoted to the fall of the Roman Empire, but that is not the question posed here. Part of the answer is already formally provided in seeing the Roman nation ending with the start of the empire. A second part of the answer is that the Roman nation, while advancing the notion of citizenship to a greater extent than Greek city-states had done with their *polis*, nevertheless operated restrictions with exclusion of women, slaves and foreigners.[12] Still, the boundaries of the Roman societal community, especially in the last 200 years of the Republic, were more porous than previous or subsequent city-states, at least in terms of allowing new entries into citizenship. With territorial and military expansion, the legionnaires began to be increasingly recruited from non-Roman mercenaries rather than from citizens, and their loyalty turned to their generals, away from loyalty to the state (Weber 1976: 319).[13] As the strains between factions and social classes increased, with growing economic disparity between haves and have-nots, the solidarity of the Roman nation gave way to civil wars and social disorders, which set up the stage for the military takeover of Julius Caesar (in 48 BC). One might say that the inchoate Roman nation dissolved in the long stretch of the Roman Empire. For example, the cult of the deified emperor stood in contrast to the Republican veneration of the collective representation of the nation, the Roman *genius publicus*. Moreover, the societal community of the *res publica* lost its normative cohesion as the virtues and moral sobriety extolled by, say Cato and Cicero, became diluted and washed away with a substitution of "bread and circuses." Commitment to the societal community of Rome, a commitment shown by the seriousness of electoral assemblies, on the one hand, and the extended military service to protect and extend the boundaries of the nascent Roman empire, gave way to partisanship, factionalism and the pauperization of the countryside. The nation became dissolved in the empire, the latter a multinational state resting uneasily on the vagaries of who might be emperor, without the checks and balances of power enjoyed by the Republic.

Augustus and his successor Tiberius instituted the practice of Romans taking an oath of loyalty to the emperor. The army of citizen-soldiers was transformed into a "professional army" and Augustus "ensured that it was now he and his family to whom all soldiers swore their oath of loyalty – not to their officers." As Boatwright *et al.* further note (2006: 265), with the continued erosion of citizen elections, "By the end of the second century, Roman citizenship was losing its allure."

South Africa

Today's Republic of South Africa represents extreme ends of the time spectrum of nationhood. At one end – the one immediately our own – South Africa is still in a nascent period of nationhood, barely ten years old if we date this with the popular acceptance in 1996 of a majority-rule constitution, enfranchising the total population in a bill of rights that bars discrimination in all forms. The new Republic, multiracial and multiethnic, has symbolized the inclusion of its societal community with a national flag unique among national flags in combining six colors representing the major tribal and national groupings of the country.[14] Like the Soviet reforms of the 1980s culminating in the unexpected breakup of a seemingly monolithic state apparatus, the new South African Republic emerged from international agitations and boycotts against its predecessor regime, but equally if not more importantly from domestic reforms put in motion in the 1980s, climaxing in President F.W. de Klerk turning power over to Nelson Mandela. Although the present formative period of the reinvented South Africa offers rich material for the theme "When is the nation?," it is the mirror-image question, "When is the nation no longer?" with which this essay is concerned. White-dominated South Africa did come to an end – miraculously, without the bloodshed many observers had predicted – but it is worthwhile to indicate the features of that nation.

The documentation for South Africa is extremely good and varied, and I shall provide only a condensed version of major aspects of nationhood of one segment of the population, the segment originating as a settlement of the Dutch East Indies Company in the seventeenth century and which in the course of several generations developed into the Afrikaner nation. This nation was politically at the helm of twentieth-century South Africa, but shared economic control with an English-speaking population that was to a large extent British.[15]

A salient aspect of the nationalism of South Africa was, like early American nationalism, the strong Old Testament-Calvinist orientation of a chosen people (Smith 2003: 141–4). An agrarian people on the move in the frontier setting of the Cape, at the beginning of the nineteenth century this group sought to distance itself from a newly imposed British administration which replaced Dutch rule. The nation saw itself with a divine mission and a divine justification for slaveholding. After an exodus (the "trek"), which for them repeated the exile and escape from Egypt, the original Dutch-speaking population evolved a language (*Afrikaans*) and the agrarian base of their economy was reflected in the two republics they founded beyond British reach, the Orange Free State and the Republic of the Transvaal becoming known as the *Boer* (*Boer* = farmer) republics. Equally important in the transformation from colonist to settler, the Boers were to modernize their name and start to call themselves *Afrikaners* i.e. Africans.

The unification of Afrikaners in the latter part of the nineteenth century was unwittingly promoted by British imperialism, when global industrial expansion necessitated not only new markets but also new sources of gold to provide capital. The discovery of rich gold fields in the Orange Free State and the Transvaal attracted Cecil Rhodes and British imperialism, and led to the bitterly fought British–Boer War (1898–1901), which did eventually bring about the unification of South Africa. As an unanticipated consequence, South Africa in 1910 became the Union of South Africa, with Afrikaners at the political helm, but with the English-speaking population retaining economic control.

Afrikaner nationhood developed strong bonds of identity and strong institutions, anchored in the Dutch Reformed Church, in the legal system, in universities (like Stellenbosch) that paralleled the English universities, and perhaps above all in the construction and reconstruction of history, which viewed the Afrikaners as having a sacred mission to bring a unique civilization to the African continent. The political triumph of Daniel Malan and his Nationalist Party in 1948, overthrowing the more moderate government of Jan Smuts, paved the way shortly after for Hendrik Verwoerd as Prime Minister to pass legislation deemed to ensure permanent white (minority) domination in South Africa. The separation of blacks and others, a large majority of the population, from political power and institutions of modernity (such as universities),[16] became known as the odious regime of *apartheid*. The South African republic reinvented itself into a reactionary nationhood.

If Afrikaner nationhood was so well formed and entrenched in power in the early 1980s, what factors led to the demise of the nation – or at least of the state in which the nation was nestled? First, and especially after the fall of Rhodesia, South Africa's borders were more porous and more open to guerrilla warfare, making it more costly to provide military defense. Second, the urban African population rallied around a major black nationalist party, the African National Congress, which became increasingly militant and able to mobilize its followers in violent clashes with the authorities. Third, international economic sanctions and the international community viewing South Africa – and white South Africans of all stripes – as a pariah became increasingly disconcerting, for professionals, athletes and others barred *de facto* if not *de jure* from participation at international events. The maintenance of a tight societal community became too high a price in a world order having no place for *apartheid*. This, at least, is an initial approximation of factors that brought the Union of South Africa to an end.[17]

The immense challenge for the new South African nation is, to return to

Renan, to develop collective projects: promoting public health (the HIV/AIDS adult prevalence rate is one out of five); advancing the African-ization of the economy in leading sectors (presently about half of the popu-lation lives below the poverty line); and, while remembering past injustices (in the peace and reconciliation measures), keeping open the goals of the framing of the new societal community. In this respect the challenge to develop a collective identity transcending the previous boundaries of nation-hood is very similar to that facing other multiethnic and/or multiracial soci-eties that have had constraining societal communities *de facto* – such as Northern Ireland, if not the United States.

Yugoslavia

Yugoslavia – the country of the "South Slavs" – was "invented" at Versailles by the victorious war powers partly under Wilsonian ideals of self-determination for national groups, partly to dismantle the Austrian-Hungar-ian empire and act as an important buffer zone. Eventually, after World War II and the Communist leadership of Josip Broz Tito, who had shown his mettle against Nazi Germany, Yugoslavia gained the respect (and the needed investments) of the Western world by functioning as a buffer zone against Stalin's Soviet expansion westward. The first invention of Yugoslavia had led to a Serb-dominated multinational unitary monarchy, first as the Kingdom of Serbs, Croats and Slovenes, and then in 1929 to the name change to Yugoslavia, which during the 1930s was in effect a royal dictatorship.

Tito's invention of a "second Yugoslavia" was to allow decentralized provincial autonomy as socialist republics to Serbia, Croatia, Slovenia, Mace-donia and Bosnia-Hercegovina (with autonomous ethnic enclaves in several of these). The institutional arrangement was intended to nullify the Serbian hegemony that had manifested itself in the first, prewar Yugoslav nation, a hegemony facilitated by the demographic dominance of the Serbs and the resources drawn by Belgrade as the seat of government and development. Although formal equality in the Yugoslav federal system was ideologically stressed and, in certain rituals such as the rotation of the presidency (which was intended to be instituted after Tito's death), power was still very cen-tralized, with Tito firmly in control of the state apparatus.[18] The political integration of Yugoslavia rested, thus, on a federal system and on loyalty (and obedience) to the head of the Yugoslav Communist system, whose aura was augmented as a wartime resistance hero (Marshal Tito) and subsequently as President of the new national entity, Yugoslavia. The Yugoslav "miracle" of being a Communist state that could say "no" to Stalin and the Soviet orbit was also promoted by the extensive economic development in the 1950s and 1960s made possible by substantial Western foreign investment, by exporting a surplus labor force to Western countries engaged in postwar reconstruction, and by the promise of a new form of industrial production giving greater weight to workers' councils ("auto-gestion"). By the early

1980s, at the time of Tito's death, many observers saw Yugoslavia as a viable multiethnic nation-state.

Yet, as part of the tragic history of Central Europe, the nation did not hold. Fearful of the resumption of Serbian hegemony when a nationalist (Slobodan Milosević) assumed the rein of Serbian government and indicated irredentist aims, Croatia and Slovenia broke off after their demands for a new confederation were rejected. This resulted in an atrocious civil war between Serbia, Croatia and Bosnia-Hercegovina, illustrating vividly what the sociologist Georg Simmel had analyzed nearly a century before as the basic instability of a triad, with shifting allegiances of two against one. The demise of Tito's Yugoslavia in the violent fragmentation of the 1990s led briefly to a "third Yugoslavia" when Serbia and Montenegro adopted a new constitution in 1992 as the reconstituted Republic of Yugoslavia, a skeletal remain of the former nation-state. In fact, even this reprieve was shortlived after the attempt of Milosević to recapture the autonomous province of Kosovo – (an enclave in Serbia) from the ethnic Albanian domination that had been promoted by Tito – culminated in NATO intervening to protect the Albanians. Serbia, the staunch World War II ally of the Western powers, was badly defeated by these, and the consequence of yet another Balkan war was a European Union-brokered agreement that kept the federal union of Serbia and Montenegro, but now gave equal recognition to the junior partner as the name "Yugoslavia" ceased to exist in 2003.[19]

Yugoslavia represents a stark example of a nation that was and that is no longer. Why did it fail so fast after seeming so secure? Ultimately, in terms of the analysis underpinning this chapter, it failed because there was insufficient across-the-board commitment from the significant components for the Yugoslav societal community. The nation and its institutions were "invented" but Yugoslav nationhood as a collective identity was insufficiently realized. Nationhood remained for the majority of Serbs and Croats a project for the realization, respectively, of a greater Serbia and a greater Croatia. On the other hand, a higher percentage of Bosniac Muslims identified themselves as Yugoslavs; younger people tended to identify themselves as Yugoslav more than older people; urban dwellers more than rural dwellers; and ethnic minorities within a republic identified themselves more as Yugoslavs than did the dominant ethnic group. Still, as Hodson *et al.* (1994) have convincingly shown in their analysis of 1985 and 1989 survey data, ethnic identity trumped Yugoslav nationhood where and when it mattered. Further, it may be noted that, in a complementary analysis, these researchers found that the political arrangements of the "new Yugoslavia" designed at Versailles and again after World War II by Tito to increase tolerance for the "other" and reduce conflict had very mixed results. Thus, in Croatia and Bosnia, where indices of tolerance were at high levels relative to other regions, ethnic conflict during the civil war was much more intense and brutal. They concluded in a follow-up study that "Yugoslavian state policies of modernization and controlled nationalism may have led to greater tolerance, but they also set the stage for the mobilization of groups around nationality, especially within nationally diverse and highly autonomous republics" (Sekulić *et al.* 1994: 1555).

There is no easy lesson to be learned from the examples discussed above, save that asking the question "When is the nation no longer?" opens up some vital queries in terms of which we may assess the viability of our own nations today. The cases discussed show different narratives of nations in the historical process. Rome, which has served as an exemplar of a republic, ended as a nation in a period of civil war and instability that willingly turned over power and authority to the authoritarian rule of an emperor. It waited twenty centuries to regain national identity as a republic; perhaps the championship win in the 2006 Football World Cup has provided its descendants with a welcome sense of unity that earlier generations had found missing. The Afrikaner Republic of South Africa, that had come into being in the mid-nineteenth century with the Orange Free State and the Transvaal, had become in the twentieth century a pariah nation because of its offensive apartheid regime of racial discrimination. Unexpectedly, its last state president, F.W. de Klerk, had the foresight and vision to alter a path headed for bloodshed; he ended the apartheid republic by turning the power over to Nelson Mandela, a man of peace and reconciliation in 1993–4. It can be said that a new South African nation has come into being peacefully, hopefully a new historical model for nation-building with racial diversity. Lastly, Yugoslavia, despite developing into the semblance of a viable nation-state (more of a federation than a single republic) under Tito, lacked internal cohesion after his demise; the last remnant of the vision of a "South Slav" nation came to a close in May 2006, when tiny Montenegro voted by a slim margin to secede from Serbia, which had been the backbone if not hegemon of Yugoslavia.

Notes

1 Clear at least to academics and to activists in new national movements. There is still a "cultural lag" in the media to accept the differentiation which is integral to our perspective. Nation-states are still seen as homogeneous and through the prism of the state and its dominant "nation-group." Nielsson (1985: 30f) provides an empirical refutation of this "one state, one national group" idea. Examining 164 political units including 161 sovereign states he demonstrated the variability of presence of "nation-groups" within state structures: 45 had a single nation-group, 62 had a dominant nation-group accounting for between 60–95 percent of the state's population, 17 had a dominant nation-group with fragmented minorities, and the remaining fourth ($n = 41$) were either binational or multinational states.

2 In a few instances, notably that of the Basques, the group straddled state boundaries. However, the French Basque region has not overtly experienced the autonomous movement of the Spanish Basque region.

3 I underscore *intellectual respect* because Third World nationalism with such figures as Nasser in Egypt, Mosaddeq in Iran, Castro in Cuba, the Sandanistas in Nicaragua, Lumumba in the Congo have been looked upon more with askance by Western governments and media than with sympathetic understanding.

4 One may include the German Democratic Republic (DDR), which in
   1980s had begun seeking greater autonomy, but not secession, from tl
   orbit.

5 There were deep cleavages in the first decade of the republic betweer
   chists, bonapartists, and republicans, with various shadings of each; cleavages
   regarding the place of religion in the public sphere; and cleavages regarding
   what to do about the lost territories of Alsace and Lorraine that Germany had
   annexed after the disastrous war.

6 A static or immutable approach to national identity would tend to treat it as
   "national character" – traits or characteristics taken to inhere in the "nature" of
   the collectivity.

7 Negative national identities are principally generated by other collectivities'
   perception of predominantly undesirable features of a given nation. Germany is
   not the only one to have had a persistent negative national identity based on its
   militarism toward others and treatment of racial minorities: Spain, for example,
   had for a long time (from the sixteenth century through the Franco regime) the
   stigma of a "dark legend." How an externally given negative identity impacts
   the self-awareness and self-consciousness of a population, with behavioral consequences ranging from collective denial to collective seeking for atonement is a
   matter awaiting important comparative research.

8 A rapprochement could be made viewing the narrative of the nation as forged in
   the anvil of history and the Marxist perspective of history as the midwife of the
   revolutionary process from which emerges the revolutionary class.

9 The animus toward multiculturalism and the apprehension regarding being
   swamped by immigrants from cultures inimical to traditional democratic values
   of the (American) nation are shared by the liberal left (Schlesinger 1998) and the
   conservative right (Buchanan 2002).

10 Regarding the last named, Deloria and Lytle point to the consolidation in urban
   areas of multiple Indian tribal entities, with the general temper of the late
   1960s facilitating the process of unification. In particular the March on Washington of multiple caravans during election week in 1972 was instrumental in
   demonstrating that "Indians shared a tradition of independence and nationhood,
   which the years had not erased" (Deloria and Lytle 1984: 237). In a sense this
   marked a "new beginning" for a unified Indian nation, which however still lacks
   the political and economic clout of other groups. The construction of the Indian
   nation parallels the construction of its colossal collective representation, the
   Crazy Horse Monument in Black Hills, South Dakota, which at its completion
   will be the world's largest art monument.

11 My discussion of Rome draws among others from Boatwright *et al.* (2004),
   Cornell (1995), and Crawford (1993).

12 By the third century BC, all Roman citizens had equal voting rights, and eventually after the Social War (90–88 BC) full citizenship was granted to all of Italy
   south of the River Po. See "civitas" in *Encyclopedia Britannica* 2005. *Encyclopedia
   Britannica Online*, search.eb.com/eb/article-9082770 accessed 16 October 2005.

13 Max Weber provides a keen analysis of the burdens of wars on Roman peasants
   and how this led to increased needs for unfree forms of labour, on the one hand,
   and to the pauperization of the peasantry, on the other (Weber 1976: 319).

14 For a full discussion of the flag designed to represent all segments of the population, see *Encyclopedia Britannica Online* search.eb.com/eb/article-9093959.

15 In what follows I am drawing partly on accounts of nationhood found in Moodie
   (1975); Patterson (1957); van Jaarsveld (1961); and Walker (1959). Biographies
   of major nationalist figures are not lacking.

16 Census enumerations up to 1990 tended to be fairly accurate for the white
   population but, for varied reasons, underestimated black South Africans by a

rather large factor. In the official 1951 Census, out of a total population of nearly 13 million, Whites had about 22 percent; in the 1996 Census of the new government, including the population of "homelands" previously left out, out of a population of 40.5 million, the White population had declined to 13.6 percent, with two other minorities, Indian and Coloreds, accounting for about 11 percent worldfacts.us/South-Africa.htm.

17 At least that was done without the bloodshed necessary to bring an end to the (American) Southern Confederation which also had a very restricted societal community.

18 "Tito, Josip Broz," *Encyclopedia Britannica*. available online at search.eb.com/eb/article-7297 accessed 18 October 2005.

19 "Yugoslavia" *Encyclopedia Britannica*, available online at search.eb.com/eb/article-228363 accessed 18 October 2005. As a final note on Yugoslavia's failed identity, Professor Slobodan Cvejic of Belgrade University informed me that in a large survey conducted in 2003–4 in Serbia – the heartland of the Yugoslav nation-state whose major institutions from the monarchy to the state airline were in the hand of Serbian management – only 1.3 percent of the respondents declared themselves as Yugoslavs (personal email communication, 9 September 2005).

References

Anderson, B. [1991] (1983) *Imagined Communities: Reflections on the Origin and Spread of Nationalism*, rev. edn, London and New York: Verso.

Boatwright, M., Gargola, D.J. and Talbert, R.J.A. (2004) *The Romans from Village to Empire*, New York: Oxford University Press.

—— (2006) *A Brief History of the Romans*, New York and Oxford: Oxford University Press.

Buchanan, P. (2002) *The Death of the West: How Dying Populations and Immigrant Invasions Imperil Our Country and Civilization*, New York: Thomas Dunne Books.

Calhoun, C. (1993) "Nationalism and Ethnicity," *Annual Review of Sociology*, 19: 211–39.

Cameron, K. (ed.) (1999) *National Identity*, Exeter: Intellect.

Cornell, T.J. (1995) *The Beginnings of Rome: Italy and Rome from the Bronze Age to the Punic Wars (c.1000–264 BC)*, London and New York: Routledge.

Crawford, M. (1993) *The Roman Republic*, 2nd edn, Cambridge, MA: Harvard University Press.

Danforth, L. (1995) *The Macedonian Conflict: Ethnic Nationalism in a Transnational World* Princeton: Princeton University Press.

Delanty, G. (1995) *Inventing Europe: Idea, Identity, Reality*, New York: St. Martin's Press.

Deloria Jr, V. and Lytle, C. (1984) *The Nations Within: The Past and Future of American Indian Sovereignty*, New York: Pantheon.

Dreifelds, J. (1996) *Latvia in Transition*, Cambridge: Cambridge University Press.

Ezell, E.D., Seeleib-Kaiser, M. and Tiryakian, E.A. (2003) "National Identity Issues in the New German Elites: A Study of German University Students," *International Journal of Comparative Sociology*, 44(3): 280–308.

Fustel de Coulanges, N.D. (1980) [1883] *The Ancient City: A Study on the Religion, Laws and Institutions of Greece and Rome*, Baltimore: Johns Hopkins University Press.

Gellner, E. (1983) *Nations and Nationalism*, Ithaca: Cornell University Press.

Gerhardt, U. (2001) "Parsons's Analysis of the Societal Community," in J. Treviño (ed.) *Talcott Parsons Today*, Lanham: Rowman & Littlefield.

Herrmann, R.K., Risse, T. and Brewer, M.B. (eds) (2004) *Transnational Identities: Becoming European in the EU*, Lanham: Rowman & Littlefield.

Hobsbawm, E.J. (1990) *Nations and Nationalism since 1780: Programme, Myth, Reality*, Cambridge and New York: Cambridge University Press.

Hodson, R., Sekulić, D. and Massey, G. (1994) "National Tolerance in the Former Yugoslavia," *American Journal of Sociology*, 99(6): 1534–58.

Kartlins, R. (1994) *Ethnopolitics and Transition to Democracy: The Collapse of the USSR and Latvia*, Baltimore: Johns Hopkins University Press.

Klapp, O.E. (1969) *Collective Search for Identity*, New York: Holt, Rinehart & Winston.

Kriesi, H., Armingeon, K., Siegrist, H. and Wimmer, A. (eds) (1999) *Nation and National Identity: The European Experience in Perspective*, Zurich: Verlag Rügger.

Laitin, D.D. (1998) *Identity in Formation: The Russian-Speaking Populations in the Near Abroad*, Ithaca: Cornell University Press.

Leoussi, A.S. (ed.) (2001) *Encyclopedia of Nationalism*, New Brunswick: Transaction Publishers.

Moodie, T.D. (1975) *The Rise of Afrikanerdom: Power, Apartheid, and the Afrikaner Civil Religion*, Berkeley: University of California Press.

Motyl, A.J. (ed.) (2001) *Encyclopedia of Nationalism*, San Diego: Academic Press.

Nielsson, G.P. (1985) "States and 'Nation-Groups': A Global Taxonomy," in E. Tiryakian and R. Rogowski (eds) *New Nationalisms of the Developed West*, Boston and London: Allen & Unwin.

Nisbet, R. (1966) *The Sociological Tradition*, New York: Basic Books.

Olson, M. (1982) *The Rise and Decline of Nations: Economic Growth, Stagflation, and Social Rigidities*, New Haven: Yale University Press.

Parsons, T. (1966) *Societies: Evolutionary and Comparative Perspectives*, Englewood Cliffs: Prentice-Hall.

—— (1971) *The System of Modern Societies*, Englewood Cliffs: Prentice-Hall.

Patterson, S. (1957) *The Last Trek: A Study of the Boer People and the Afrikaner Nation*, London: Routledge & Kegan Paul.

Poulton, H. (2000) *Who Are the Macedonians?* 2nd edn, Bloomington and Indianapolis: University of Indiana Press.

Renan, E. (1996) [1882] *What Is a Nation? Qu'est-ce qu'une nation?*, Toronto: Tapir Press.

Schlesinger Jr, A.M. (1998) *The Disuniting of America: Reflections on a Multicultural Society*, 2nd edn, New York: W.W. Norton.

Schöpflin, G. (2000) *Nations, Identity, Power*, New York: New York University Press.

Scullard, H.H. (2003) [1935] *A History of the Roman World 753 to 146 BC*, 5th edn, London and New York: Routledge.

Sekulić, D., Massey G. and Hodson, R. (1994) "Who were the Yugoslavs? Failed Sources of a Common Identity in the Former Yugoslavia," *American Sociological Review*, 59 (February): 83–97.

Shore, C. (2000) *Building Europe: The Cultural Politics of European Integration*, London and New York: Routledge.

Smith, A.D. (1982) *Nationalism in the Twentieth Century*, New York: New York University Press.

—— (1987) *The Ethnic Origins of Nations*, Oxford: Basil Blackwell.

—— (1991) *National Identity*, Reno: University of Nevada Press.

—— (2003) *Chosen Peoples*, Oxford: Oxford University Press.

Tiryakian, E.A. (2005) "Modernizing German National Identity," in H. Aretz and C. Lahusen (eds) *Die Ordnung der Gesellschaft. Festschrift zum 60. Geburtstag von Richard Münch*, Frankfurt: Peter Lang.

van Jaarsveld, F.A. (1961) *The Awakening of Afrikaner Nationalism 1868–1881*, Cape Town: Human & Rousseau.

Walker, E.A. (1959) *A History of Southern Africa*, 3rd edn, London: Longmans.

Weber, M. (1976) [1896] *The Agrarian Sociology of Ancient Civilizations*, London: NLB.

Part II

Memory and the persistence of nations

5 The appeal of nationhood

National celebrations and commemorations

Gabriella Elgenius

For many modernist theorists of nationalism, symbols and ceremonies belong to the world of myths and legends and are of marginal importance. I wish to argue to the contrary: symbolism is, as far as nationhood is concerned, as important as economic and political factors. Social life is a repository of symbols and ceremonies, whether in the form of totems, golden ages, flags, heroes, icons, capitals, statues, war memorials, football teams, national festivities or ceremonies, which are symbolic markers of national groups. Symbols and ceremonials provide shortcuts to the community they represent; they are by nature self-referential, subjective and boundary-creating (Mosse 1990; Cohen 1995; Armstrong 1982). Symbols and ceremonies are also public; they are manifested or performed in a public space. Moreover, national symbols and ceremonies provide us with a powerful testimony about the persistence of nations and the appeal of nationhood.

This chapter will focus on 'national day' ceremonies, phenomena through which the persistence of nations can be ascertained. The national day is one of a number of collective rituals by which nations project and advertise themselves to members as well as non-members. Together with other symbols asserting identity (such as national flags and anthems), the national day is used to glorify the nation before or after statehood has been attained. The intrinsic link between collective identities and collective ceremonies is central in this context. The hypothesis is that collective identities are manifested in collective rituals, the latter being an important factor in the making of and the maintaining of nations and national identities. In other words, national ceremonies express deeper aspects and meanings of the nation, provide comfort and anchorage, and raise awareness of 'who we are' and 'where we are from'.

The European context

National holidays (national days) are a mix of national and state elements, which it is not easy or necessary to separate.[1] Yet the embrace between the nation and the state produced a novel and unique festivity in honour of the birth of the sociopolitical unit. In this capacity, national days are holders of state-institutionalized practices with references to the community, its mythology and symbolism. The formalization of the European national days is often the result of negotiations between the people and the elites, a process that may be interpreted as an attempt by the latter to establish continuity with a living past through repeated and formalized ritual/symbolic complexes aiming to enhance the collective experience.[2]

The majority of national days in Europe appeared during the 1800s and 1900s and became established in the 1900s. The oldest national days emerged long before the French Revolution, originally as religious holidays, which survived into the modern era and, with time, took the form of national holidays, notably in the cases of Ireland eleventh century), Hungary (twelfth) and Spain (fifteenth).[3] In many cases we find that a late adoption is illustrative of interruptions in sovereignty and independence. For such reasons, few nations have an uninterrupted history of celebrating their present national day: Ireland (eleventh century), France (1790), Greece (1838), Switzerland (1891), Finland (1917) and Britain (1919). We may also note that many former Central and Eastern European countries under the rule of the Soviet Union, followed the cycle of Communist celebrations, which in many cases included Liberation Day or Victory Day (liberation from and victory over Nazism or Fascism), Constitution Day (new constitutions) and Labour (Workers') Day.

Recently, the significance of national days has been obvious in the nationalization process of Central and Eastern Europe, which, on the one hand, illustrates problems and stages connected to selecting a representative national day as a national symbol, and, on the other, suggests in a more general way that the national day is a significant element of nationhood.

Ceremonial statistics: content, style, choreography and participation

The national celebrations in Europe are not identical but we may find some common characteristics that describe the more general features and practices. The contours of a pattern have been formed, honouring in particular important political events (sovereignty, independence, the Republic, liberation, unification, the signing of a constitution), golden ages and national personifications (monarchs, saints, poets, etc.). They are all celebrations of historic events related to the birth of the nation-state.

The character of the national days varies to a high degree in Europe and accordingly there are several significant variables to consider. Some European national days are popular events, others elite celebrations; some are peaceful, others of a military nature; some are recognized by law as public holidays. The celebrations range from speeches given in public by government officials, to the participation of whole nations in processions, parades, carnivals and street parties. In other words, in some countries the protagonist is the people, in others the elite. On the one hand, the state-led military celebration of Independence Day in Belgium can be compared to the popular civilian celebrations of Portugal Day or of Constitution Day in Norway. On the other hand, the popular and military celebrations of Liberation Day in Bulgaria stand against the state-led national days in honour of the constitution in Denmark and in Sweden and of German unification, without encompassing participation.[4]

'Rallying and national symbols' give a national day definite shape and focus. They are integrated into the national ceremony; national flags are displayed and national anthems are sung. The location of the event, the public squares and national monuments involved are also intimately connected with national symbolism. These symbols all constitute essential rallying points intended to highlight the nation in a varied manner and to promote national pride. Music forms an integral part of the national day, whether provided by military units, mass bands or individuals. The music chosen sets the tone of the ceremony, the pieces played are naturally of great significance for the emotions that will be evoked. Processions or parades (military or civil) and popular carnivals are central features of national celebrations and connected to music performances.

Moreover, a successful national day relies on some form of collective participation. The usual pattern suggests that ceremonies are generally either characterized by military manifestations or by civil ceremonies with civilian participation. Military celebrations have usually been carefully orchestrated: timing and precision in marches and parades are paramount and point to the fact that the military is the characterizing element of the official ceremony. Likewise, military involvement implies that the ceremonies are elite-led with strong state presence and assertion. However, this does not mean that national days commemorated with the military forces cannot be transformed into civilian festivities after the official ceremony, which is clearly the case in France and Britain. Given the origin of the national days of Spain, France, Greece, Bulgaria, Belgium, Finland, Estonia, Latvia, Britain and the Czech Republic, it is not surprising that the armed forces in these countries still play a role in the official celebrations. It is also noteworthy that the Spanish and Greek celebrations are both military and religious in nature as they coincide with traditional religious festivities: in Spain the Feast of the Virgin Mary (Patron Saint of Spain and of the Spanish army), and in Greece the Feast of Annunciation.

As a general rule, however, we find that the majority of national days are popular days in which people participate. The reasons for their popularity are suggested in the main assumptions of this chapter that the national day is an expression of nationhood and that its popularity illustrates that its prerequisite, 'the nation', is still popular.[5]

Finally, the style of the national day partly depends on whether it is a matter of celebration or commemoration and on what historic event is being acknowledged. In most countries, notably in Norway, Greece, Spain, Portugal, Ireland, Lithuania and the Netherlands, the national days are associated with joyful manifestations of nationhood. As a clear contrast, and as the main exception to this rule, we find a solemn commemoration of the war dead all over Britain on Remembrance Sunday.

Thus a 'successful' national day constitutes a holiday especially set aside for the people and intended as an annual reunion of the community, a celebration in honour of an historical/national event or personification, and a symbol of the nation.

Case studies[6]

In order to further explore the development and importance, as well as character, of national days, we turn to three case studies. The selected national days are the military national day of France (Bastille Day), the popular and peaceful celebration of Norwegian national identity (Constitution Day), and the commemoration in honour of the British war dead (Remembrance Sunday).[7] The national days of France, Norway and Britain have emerged in different historical circumstances and represent various ceremonial types, with regard to differences in character and ceremonial variety (elite, mass, military, civilian, etc.).[8] The cases that follow will be discussed as ceremonies of high politics.

Bastille Day

Bastille Day (14 July) is the national day of France, even though the country enjoys other national holidays.[9] The Bastille, state prison and symbol of the Old Regime and its arbitrary rule, was stormed on 14 July 1789, a day which in due course became the symbol of the Republic and of its values of liberty, brotherhood and equality. On the anniversary of this date in 1790, citizens and delegates arrived from all over France to proclaim their allegiance to the new Republic and to participate in the Fête de la Fédération. The cult around 14 July was the first true celebration of the French nation (in a modern sense) and the need to commemorate it arose from a desire to break with the past. As an official national holiday of the Republic, 14 July was first celebrated in 1880, in memory of the capture of the Bastille but also in honour of the Fête de la Fédération (14 July 1790). The latter was national as well as ecumenical in character, which helped to shift the attention away from the violent reality of 14 July 1789 and the Revolution in general. In this way the sceptics were reassured at little cost to the Republicans. On such a basis, it has been said that Bastille Day turned from being a *Dies Irae* to becoming the national holiday of France (Amalvi 1996; Nora 1996).

Victor Hugo coined the expression: 'To overthrow bastilles is to deliver humanity'. A similar sentiment implying that a new moral federation was being created was expressed in an address by a founding father of the Third Republic Léon Gambetta, when he said that the storming of the Bastille was the Day when 'we received our New Testament' (Amalvi, 1996: 122), a statement challenging the Catholic community and pointing to the nation as the new and secular provider of community. As noted by Amalvi:

> Various forms of public celebration (including dedications of statues, parades, torchlight processions, and commemorations of all sorts) allowed the Republic to challenge the almost exclusive control that the Church had enjoyed over public space since 1815; some of the shared sacred character of religious celebration was carried over into the secular public domain.
>
> (1996: 132)

The sacred character of the Arc de Triomphe was further enhanced when the Unknown Soldier was buried there in 1920, which also provided a focal point for the nation's sacrifices. The Tomb of the Unknown Soldier underneath the Arc fully managed to draw the masses into the public sphere, first in the potent remembrance ceremony and then on Bastille Day.

To the French, Bastille Day is represented by the solemn military parade along the Champs-Elysées from the Arc de Triomphe to the Place de la Concorde in the presence of the head of state. Furthermore, it is also a holiday on which each commune holds a local dance and offers a fireworks display. There can be no doubt about the aim of the military parade, which clearly demonstrates the strength of French defence and sovereignty. The atmosphere during the 1.5–2-hour ceremony on 14 July is warlike rather than peaceful. There is, naturally, a difference between the highly organized parade of the French state and the celebrations stemming from feelings of belonging to the nation. The French participate in celebrations all over the country (fireworks, street parties and other festivities) and have done so since the official (state) establishment of Bastille Day in 1880. The military parade and the associations of military victory have also been at the centre of the 14 July celebrations ever since then. The manner in which the military procession is performed reinforces the importance of the ceremony with its geometric perfection and self-discipline, thereby creating an image of the efficiency of the French military apparatus and ultimately of the dedication to France, qualities also paraded in front of foreign heads of state. By stressing the Republican elements of 14 July as a national holiday and its Republican roots, the aim is to increase a feeling of inclusion in the Republican nation. However, neither the French Revolution nor political differences hold a major stake in the collective memory any longer, and it may be rightfully claimed that the French national day has been drained of its original political and historical substance (Amalvi 1996).

Besides the ceremonies with special connection to the national day, the main symbols to identify are naturally the national flag and the national anthem, both integral parts of Bastille Day. Reproductions of the French Tricolour are ubiquitous and the national anthem – the Marseillaise –

is heard on numerous occasions. The Tricolour and the Marseillaise play a vital role in the presentation of the national colours on 14 July, a noteworthy point in the celebrations. The dramatic chorus of the Marseillaise is played with increased meaning and emotion as it follows this flag ceremony: 'To arms, oh citizens! Form up in serried ranks. March on, march on. May their impure blood flow in our fields!'

Bastille Day is a celebration of pomp and circumstance, in which the military strength of France is displayed – nationally as well as internationally. The view from Place de la Concorde is dramatic. The majestic version of the French Tricolour, hanging from the Arc, also attracts particular attention to the Unknown Soldier and creates a patriotic background for the march in the Champs-Elysées. The President and his honorary guests are positioned in such a way (in Place de la Concorde) that they are able to follow the whole military procession from end to end along with the millions of television viewers. The celebration on 14 July is the manifestation of a nation-state examining itself nationally and moreover manifesting its potential to deal with aggression.

While 'emergency services' participate – as if to illustrate France's capacity to cope also with natural and civil disasters – the primary link is between the military procession and the violent and warlike history of France. With respect to the internal conflict in the aftermath of the Revolution, the military procession manages to convey the message that France was able to deal with serious domestic conflicts. In fact, the boulevards were built in order to counteract any domestic Revolutionary forces. With the military nature of Bastille Day in mind, the message from the French state is both contradictory and clear: 'France is a peaceful nation. It does not have any expansionist ambitions and has no declared enemies. All its actions are designed for peacekeeping, but it does have interests to defend, responsibilities to shoulder, and a world role to play' (French Ministry of Defence 2002).

Constitution Day

Norway has a longstanding tradition of celebrating Constitution Day (Grunnlovsdagen), in honour of the Norwegian constitution established in Eidsvold on 17 May 1814. To mark this historic occasion, Norwegians wear national costumes and large-scale processions are organized in towns and villages throughout the country. The central celebration takes place in Oslo, where the procession is held on Karl Johann Gate (Karl Johann's Avenue) in the presence of the Royal Family.

Norway's history is closely linked with the neighbouring kingdoms of Sweden and Denmark. Formerly independent, Norway had been united to Sweden from 1319. From 1380 onwards Norway and Denmark became a single unified state. The Treaty of Kiel (14 January 1814), however, changed the structure. A popularly elected National Assembly was summoned to Eidsvold outside Christiania (Oslo) in April 1814 to provide Norway with a constitution of its own. This work was successfully brought to a conclusion on 17 May 1814. On the same day the Assembly, as a final decision, elected as King of Norway Christian Fredrik, Prince of Denmark, and since 1813 'Stattholder' of Norway (Mykland 1996). The King was given the name Haakon VII, linking the newly formed Norway with the old free Kingdom of Norway and the dynasty ruling Norway before 1350. This supposed continuity has been described as 'entirely fictional' (Erikson 2002).

The independence movement of 1814 came into being owing to a variety of aspirations as well as fears. Some groups wanted a reunion with Denmark while others were clearly anti-Danish or anti-Swedish. Whatever the objections, the various political groupings united and the result was a powerful nationalistic movement, wishing to restore Norway to its former glory. As concomitants we find strong national elements in many areas of Norwegian society in the years to come and an identity began to form closely connected to national culture, history and symbolism. Another significant dimension of this identity-forming process was its relation to the neighbouring and dominant kingdoms, as identity becomes important when a nation feels threatened. In Norway, continuity with the medieval Vikings was promoted in order to make a case for the uniqueness of Norway in relation to Sweden and Denmark (Eriksen 2002). The new national resurgence was manifested in the celebrations of 17 May.

Constitution Day was officially celebrated for the first time in 1827 in the capital of Christiania. The celebrations provoked uproar in Sweden and the Swedish King, Karl Johan, regarded them as a demonstration against the union. It was not until after his death in 1844 that the anniversary was celebrated to the full.

The celebration of the national day has undergone many changes that are expressions of political developments. For example, in the 1820s, the Norwegian political focus was directed towards the defence of the constitution, i.e. the foundation of Norway's independence. Those were the themes of the first 17 May celebrations where 'Guard the Constitution' was a frequent motto on banners. In the 1830s Karl Johan had become resigned to the fact that the constitution was too protected by the Norwegians for him to be able to alter it. This was immediately reflected in celebrations becoming much less defensive and guarded. In 1870, a significant new element was added to the festivities and the national procession: a children's parade. Today this parade is the most unique and distinctive part of the Norwegian national day.

In the 1870s–1890s the old ruling elites stood against the liberal urban citizens and the farmers. As the conflict between these groups developed, the Conservative and Liberal parties were formed. In this era, 17 May turned into a day of discord and non-unity as the two political groups fought their battles. At the dissolution of the union (1905) the situation changed and the population became more united than ever before. This was manifest in elaborate 17 May processions all over Norway. The 1920s and 1930s brought new conflicts to the fore, this time between the middle and working classes. The middle classes participated in the processions and protested against the internationalism of the working classes. The workers were encouraged by their leaders to keep the class struggle alive and to keep away from 'the bourgeois celebrations of 17 May' (Mykland 1996) and as a result they held alternative celebrations. As could be expected, the Nazi occupation (April 1940–May 1945) drew the population together even more as all expressions of Norwegian nationalism – like the 17 May celebrations – were banned. During the postwar years, free from anti-democratic Nazi domination, the focus turned towards democratic rights and fellowship on 17 May. The question of Norwegian membership in the European Community aroused hostile sentiments and divisions and manifested itself on 17 May 1972.

Throughout its history, the 17 May celebration has been held with the neighbouring countries in mind. In the union era of the nineteenth century it was felt that Sweden to some degree represented a threat to Norwegian independence. Similarly, the experiences of being a small and powerless nation under German occupation gave the celebrations of 17 May a deeper meaning in the postwar-Cold War years.

The Oslo parade in Karl Johann's Avenue is a colourful affair. The plethora of national flags displayed and waved by participants and spectators define the whole atmosphere of celebration and national pride. The avenue itself is decorated with large national flags on both sides, intensifying the solemn identity-reinforcing character of the celebrations. National music is also essential in the festivities, with both solemn pieces and stirring national songs included in all celebrations throughout Norway.[10] Another important national symbol is the national costume called the *bunad*.[11] It is interesting to note that the *bunad* (with its regional variations) was designed by nationalists early in the twentieth century and manufactured to represent the whole of Norway. Most of the costumes depicted as typical came from specific mountain valleys in southern Norway (Eriksen 2002). A red ribbon is also worn over the heart by the participants and spectators symbolizing the link between Norway and the individual, something that underlines the strong feelings of belonging. As a most important national symbol, members of the royal family represent the nation in different parts of the country. In keeping with tradition, the King and Queen – together with the Crown Prince and Crown Princess – greet the parade from the balcony of the royal castle in Oslo.

Constitution Day is best described as a sincere and joyful national celebration marked by flag-waving, national music, national dress, parades, speeches, church services and the laying of wreaths at war memorials. Members of the royal family play a central role as they greet the procession of Oslo's schoolchildren from the balcony of the royal palace. In his capacity as the head of state, the King of Norway symbolizes the nation.

Remembrance Sunday

The British situation is complex as Britain consists of three main national groups: the English, the Scottish and the Welsh, and therefore a national day does not exist in the official sense. While the English have had the privilege of defining the concept of 'Britishness' historically, the different perceptions of nationhood are illustrated in the legendary commemorations of St George in England, St Andrew in Scotland, and St David in Wales. In Scotland and Wales, these national days have been days of national (political or cultural) pride, celebrated with a carnival of national symbols, even though they are not 'public holidays'. Recently, there has also been a growing interest in reviving St George's Day (23 April) in England, but it generally passes by fairly quietly. The lack of an official national holiday for Britain as a whole is compensated by the extensive commemorations on Remembrance Sunday or Armistice Day, and most communities in Britain have a war memorial, erected after the First World War, around which commemorations take place. Besides the extensive remembrance ceremony in London, church services and ceremonies are held all over Britain at precisely 11 am on 11 November (or on the Sunday closest to 11 November) in order to mark the signing of the Armistice in 1918. The main representatives of the state are also highly involved as the main sponsors and chief participants in the formal commemoration ceremony. So in this way Britain is united in mourning the war dead. Based on this empirical evidence, Remembrance Sunday can be considered as the unofficial national day of Britain.

Church services and ceremonies on Remembrance Sunday started in 1919 and were replaced by the Cenotaph ceremony in 1921, still the centre of the commemoration today. The solemn ceremony at the Cenotaph proved so popular that no new national memorial or new ceremony was created after the Second World War. Instead the remembrance ceremony was extended to honour all British and Commonwealth servicemen/women who died in the two World Wars and in other armed conflicts.

The concept of the Cenotaph itself, raised in memory of the fallen, refers to an empty tomb and, thus, symbolically a tomb of all war dead. The actual resting place for the Unknown Soldier is in Westminster Abbey (Winter 1995; Inglis 1993). The construction of a temporary 'Cenotaph' was proposed on 19 July 1919, in response to the need for a saluting point in Whitehall during the Victory March, and the foundation was laid for what was to become the Cenotaph ceremony.[12] More specifically, after learning that the French were going to include a 'saluting point' at the celebrations of 14 July, where French troops were to salute a great catafalque under the Arc de Triomphe, it was decided that the planned 'Victory March' through London needed a similar focal point (Mosse 1990). Britain had no Arc de Triomphe, so a design by Sir Edwin Lutyens,[13] was constructed as a Cenotaph and a non-denominational shrine of the nation in order to redirect the notion of the (French) Catholic catafalque.

The Victory March in London in July 1919, in which 15,000 troops and officers participated, boosted the Cenotaph's popularity; photographs of General Haig and Admiral Beatty saluting their dead comrades by the monument were reproduced in the British press. Lutyens's monument was so 'powerfully evocative of the mood of collective bereavement that later that year, it was transformed by popular demand into a permanent, indeed *the* permanent British war memorial, fixed to the place in Whitehall' (Winter 1995: 104).

The Cenotaph transformed the victory parade from a moment of high politics into a manifestation where millions could contemplate the reality of death in war. At the same time the monument was intended to reinforce national and patriotic feelings. A direct connection between the Cenotaph and the tomb was made by the King, who unveiled the Cenotaph and then walked behind the gun carriage, which bore the coffin of the Unknown Soldier into the Abbey. When Armistice Day was celebrated in November 1919 (with the placing of a wreath at the Cenotaph), it also included a two-minute silence – which was to develop into a tradition – commencing after Big Ben strikes 11 am. In the interwar period almost all activity was interrupted for two minutes to observe the 'Great Silence'. In places where there was no official ceremony, people gathered in the streets to form an impromptu congregation (Homberger 1976; King 1998; Mosse 1990).

In 1920 the permanent Cenotaph was constructed and the ceremony was combined with the (re)burial of the Unknown Soldier in Westminster Abbey. Huge crowds followed the procession through the streets of London to the Abbey. The inscription on the tomb reads: 'A British Warrior who fell in the Great War 1914–1918 for King and Country'. The term 'warrior' was chosen partly for its associations with a heroic age and heroic sacrifices (Inglis 1993). Starting in 1928, the BBC's broadcast brought the Remembrance Sunday ceremony to people throughout Britain.

There were commemorations of different kinds all over Britain, and memorials for the fallen were built in most British communities after the First World War in order to console the bereaved, for the government had as early as 1915 decided that the dead were not to be transported back to Britain. This 'caused a rupture in long-established patterns of grieving' (Moriarty 1991: 63), and the British needed war memorials as their million war dead lay in foreign graves and the majority of families had been touched by death in one way or the other.

The ceremony taking place at the Cenotaph in London[14] consists of the following important elements: (a) rallying of units round the Cenotaph before the ceremony starts; (b) procession of official representatives; (c) the two minutes' silence, the Last Post and the Reveille; (d) placing of wreaths of poppies at the Cenotaph by officials of the State; (e) service led by the Bishop of London; (f) depositing of wreaths by the participants of the parade. Appropriate music is performed during different stages of the ceremony.

The Cenotaph ceremony differs from Bastille Day as well as Constitution Day by being a commemorative and solemn event rather than a celebratory occasion. The Union Jack and the national anthem figure as prominent symbols in the ceremony, though here in particular in relation to the Unknown Soldier. The three flags hanging from the Cenotaph are there specifically to identify the fallen: St George's Cross refers to those dead for England, the Union Jack to those fallen for Britain in general, and the Commonwealth flag, displaying the Union Jack in the canton (corner), to soldiers of the Commonwealth nations. In the British case, the most potent symbol of the nation is the Unknown Soldier. Reverence for those fallen for their country, connected to religious and patriotic feelings constitutes a general background for the cult of the Unknown Soldier at the end of the First World War. The way in which he was chosen, the pomp with which he was brought back to Britain (and handled there), the care with which his final resting place was chosen testify to the symbolic significance and potency of the cult dedicated to the Unknown Soldier as a symbol of all fallen soldiers. In other words, the cult of the fallen constitutes a potent complex of symbols and myths:

> The return and burial of the Unknown Soldier was accompanied by a riot of symbolism. . . . The Unknown Soldier was transported over the channel by the French destroyer *Verdun*, so that this battle was included by name in the ritual. The coffin itself was made of British oak from a tree at the Royal palace at Hampton Court (a palace with many historical associations). Together with a trench helmet and a khaki belt, a Crusader's sword was placed in the coffin. The Unknown Soldier was brought to the Arc de Triomphe and the Cenotaph, situated in the middle of Whitehall, a broad avenue, was unveiled.
>
> (Mosse 1990: 94–5)

Remembrance Sunday is best described in terms of a national funeral and a day for national unity. The symbolism and behaviour of the participants, the silence, and the wreaths, have strong parallels to a Christian funeral, although the military presence highlights the sacrifice made by those who fought to defend the nation and its virtues. Although consisting of several nations, Britain may be argued, in terms of its symbolic and ceremonial expression (especially in the commemorations of Remembrance Sunday), to possess a national 'quality'.

Conclusions and comparisons

The national day is one image by which nations project and advertise themselves to 'insiders' as well as to 'outsiders'. Its *aim* is to reinforce and sustain the beliefs of a group and renew group identity. All aspects cannot be dealt with here, but the main meaning and function of these celebrations needs to be highlighted. Generally speaking, national ceremonies create awareness and may as a result reinforce and sustain the values of the community. National days can be powerful tools that bind past, present and future generations together. National virtues and values are derived from the past, and the 'moral' direction of the future is upheld by future generations celebrating the same ceremonies, and in effect, the same virtues and values.

National ceremonies may, in other words, provide anchorage in an unstable world and 'do not differ from regular religious ceremonies, either in their object, the results which they produce, or the processes employed to attain these results' (Durkheim 1976: 427). In a secular context, we can observe contemporary national communities – in form similar to the religious communities of the past – for which self-representation is as crucial as religious symbolism and ceremonials had been earlier. Nationalism in Europe hereby continues in a symbolic manner the Christian view of the world, where hopes and fears are controlled and acted out within ceremonial and liturgical forms (Mosse 1975).

Applying this line of argument to Revolutionary France, we can identify the encompassing transformation nationalism brought about. With nationalism came a new iconography and new rituals commemorating the nation, e.g. festivals marked by mass participation. 'A new political religion was being formed in which the people, now deified, worshipped themselves' (Hutchinson 1994: 39). It was essential to construct a new age and in this context rituals and symbols help to reinforce and maintain the new social structure. The nature of the Bastille Day celebration is still very much divided between the official and military state celebrations, manifested in the military parade, as compared to the festive celebrations of and by the nation all over France. The military nature of 14 July can only be understood by taking the conflict-ridden French past into account (nationally and internationally). The day was once celebrated in honour of the Republic formed through a bloody revolution during which the King was guillotined, whereas today national memory is presented in such a way that the past is forgotten and the official ceremonies can be performed even in the presence of royalty as guests of honour. Bastille Day is thus a good example, not only of national amnesia, but also of national formation and maintenance.

The surge toward creating a Norwegian culture and the rise of Norwegian nationalism in the nineteenth and twentieth centuries must be seen within the context of how important they are in creating and maintaining national identity. In the struggle for independence against the dominance of Denmark and Sweden, Constitution Day (17 May) provided Norway with a channel through which to express its uniqueness and distinctiveness after the establishment of the constitution, and was essential to the identity formation process. The anniversary has been at the core of renewal and maintenance of Norwegianness, and is a truly unique celebration owing to the high degree of participation. The celebration of 17 May is also unique as it has the character of a children's day and is a truly joyful commemoration of the birth of the nation.

The focus on the Unknown Soldier occupied several of the participating nations after the war. The British commemoration of the war dead began when a new 'democratic' kind of national consciousness came into being after the First World War in the age of mass politics (Mosse 1990). Remembrance Sunday has been commemorated ever since. It constitutes a national funeral and a day of unity for Britain where the nations of the British state mourn together, which is quite extraordinary in a time of devolution and ethnonational revival. The symbolism of the event (general conduct, the silence, the Last Post and Reveille, the wreaths) has strong parallels to the Christian funeral. This is clearly manifested throughout the solemn ceremony at the Cenotaph in Whitehall.

In modern societies, moral integration may take place through national ceremonies and the use of national symbols. In France it was with the new Republic and the ideals of 1789 that the nation was founded. In Norway the struggles against oppression from foreign domination were expressed via the fight to gain recognition for the Norwegian flag and the right to celebrate Constitution Day. The cult of the war dead in, for example, Britain after the First World War, further clarified the fact that conflicts and wars constitute a way in which nations achieve their virtues, in particular through the many sacrifices by the citizens/nationals for their country. National symbols and ceremonies are central to the long-term survival of nations.

Closely related to the forming of national virtues is the process through which the nation sanctifies itself. The national day is in many ways treated as a 'sacred' activity, and the symbols such as the flag attain the status of sacred objects. As central components of national worship they have, in other words, been raised above everyday life. Moreover, protests that would involve, for example, burning the Tricolour on Bastille Day or shouting during the two minutes' silence on Remembrance Sunday would be perceived as acts of desecration. The persistence of symbols and ceremonies over time also suggests that the nation is regarded as a sacred category, set apart from mundane activity. The respect shown national symbols and ceremonies can hereby be seen as an indication of the strength of national identity.

To sum up, the national day and other national ceremonies make people aware of who they are, in relation to 'us' and to 'others', through the celebration or commemoration of distinctiveness, and through symbols and micro-practices used on the day. The national days in Europe are repeated annual complexes of symbolism and constitute in many cases an anchor in an ever-changing world. It has been argued that national ceremonies serve as convenient means of analyzing the creation and maintenance of national identities. They facilitate social life by creating and reinforcing social values and can, on such a basis, constitute uniting elements. Although ceremonies make people aware of who they are, they do not necessarily create cohesion.[15] Ceremonies are certainly imbued with meanings, and can for this reason be contested and negotiated. This analysis appears to confirm Durkheim's proposition, duly amended, that national life is made possible only by a vast collective symbolism. The latter, in turn, provides us with empirical evidence of the persistence of nations and of the appeal of nationhood.

Notes

1 As a rule, national and state elements of the national day are conflated. The 'nation', in this coexistence, can be considered the bearer of identity and the ultimate justification for the state, whereas the 'state', which has the role of constraining that identity, constitutes the goal for most nations. In short, the 'nation' refers to a social group and a sense of shared cultural and/or political experiences and to its overall adherence to a complex of symbols that constitute the boundaries between 'us' and 'them'. 'Nationhood', in turn, is seen as the expression of cultural, political and symbolic elements of the nation. However, although nationhood rests on various degrees of a feeling of shared cultural and political experiences, it always includes an adherence to a complex of symbols and myths specifically relating to the 'nation' as a community. (See Elgenius 2005a: 23–4.)

2 Some European nations celebrate several days in honour of the nation, but one usually features as the paramount national day. The 'nation-state' does not exist as a homogeneous cultural or political unit, but usually as an aspiration of one dominant culture, and the focus here is on a significant national event, in which the national memory, connected to *the* dominant culture is being promoted with officially recognized national day celebrations/commemorations.

3 For an elaboration of the typology of 'old' (–1789), 'modern' (1789–1913) and 'new' (1914–to date) national symbols (national flags) and ceremonies (days), and the consequences of this pattern with regard to nation-building in Europe, see Elgenius 2005a.

4 Some national days are between these categories – 'mixed' celebrations which are relatively popular but honoured primarily by the state. The national days of Austria and Belgium are examples fitting this mixed model.

5 There are naturally nations in Europe whose national days are primarily celebrated by the state. However, it is worth noting that the majority of these nations have other national holidays in which participation is evident (see Elgenius 2005a).

6 The following case studies are based on firsthand observations, expert interviews and recordings such as televised broadcasts of 14 July celebrations and the parade along the Champs-Elysées in Paris, 14 July, 2001–2; of 17 May and the parade in Karl Johann's Gate in Oslo, 17 May 2002; and of Remembrance Sunday and the ceremony at the Cenotaph, Whitehall in London, 11 November 2001.

7 These countries have long traditions of national celebrations and popular participation is evident. Other cases, such as the recently established national day in honour of the unification of West and East Germany (Unification Day), may be characterized by a lack of display of national symbols and by elite participation. For a discussion on Germany see (Elgenius 2005b).

8 Four important elements in the systematic study of national days are:

   1 the event being celebrated/commemorated and its sociohistorical context;
   2 the location of the event and any national monuments that play an important role in the ceremony;

3 event participants; and
4 the symbolic expressions of nationhood: national flags and the singing of
   national anthems.

These essential elements produce the basic 'ceremonial statistics' for the national
day. Only a limited account of the selected cases can be provided in this chapter.
9 It should be noted that the international reference to Bastille Day is not recognized in France, where the national day is described by its date: '14 July'.
10 A few national songs in particular deserve to be mentioned: 'We are a nation
   too' (by Gretry/Wergeland), 'The Land We Inherited' (by G. Lorentzen), but
   above all the Norwegian national anthem 'Yes, We Love This Land' (by B.
   Bjørnson).
11 The *hunad* is a double-shuttle woven woollen shirt/dress with a jacket and a scarf
   for women. For men it consists of an embroidered and colourful three-piece suit.
12 The original march was followed by peace celebrations, entertainment and fireworks in central London parks (see Homberger 1976; King 1998).
13 Lutyens designed the two most important British war memorials – the Cenotaph and the Memorial to the Missing at Thiepval on the Somme (see Winter
   1995).
14 The description of Remembrance Sunday is based on the BBC TV broadcast of
   the ceremony at the Cenotaph, Whitehall 10 November 2002 (Lord Chancellor's Department 2003).
15 Durkheim maintained that societies become united through rituals that bring
   about feelings of exaltation and enthusiasm, which are carried over into daily
   life. It is in this way that consensus, or conformity, about social taboos and
   values comes into existence. National ceremonies, however, are intended to
   include larger and at the same time highly divided groups, in terms of class,
   religion, ethnicity, region and gender, compared to the rituals of the smaller
   societies studied by Durkheim.

References

Amalvi, C. (1996) 'Bastille Day: From *Dies Irae* to Holiday', in P. Nora (ed.) *Realms
   of Memory: The Construction of the French Past*, vol. 3, New York: Columbia Univer-
   sity Press: 117–62.
Armstrong, J. (1982) *Nations before Nationalism*, Chapel Hill: University of North
   Carolina Press.
Cohen, A. (1995) *The Symbolic Construction of Community*, London: Routledge.
Durkheim, E. (1915; 2nd edn 1976) *The Elementary Forms of the Religious Life*,
   London: George Allen and Unwin.
Elgenius, G. (2005a) *Expressions of Nationhood: National Symbols and Ceremonies in
   Contemporary Europe*, unpublished Ph.D. thesis, London School of Economics and
   Political Science.
—— (2005b) 'National Days and Nation-building: A Contemporary Survey', in
   Eriksonas, and Müller, *Statehood beyond Ethnicity*, Oxford: Peter Lang Academic
   Publishers.
Eriksen, T.H. (2nd edn 2002) *Ethnicity and Nationalism: Anthropological Perspectives*,
   London: Pluto Press.
French Ministry of Defence [Ministère de la Défense de France] (2002) 'Armées
   D'Aujourd'hui (Délégation à l'information et à la communication de la Défense)
   272', Julliet-Août 2002. Available online at www.defense.gouv.fr (accessed 11
   January 2006).

Homberger, E. (1976) 'The Story of the Cenotaph', *The Times Literary Supplement*, 12 November: 1429–30.

Hutchinson, J. (1994) *Modern Nationalism*, London: Fontana Press.

Inglis, K. (1993) 'Entombing Unknown Soldiers: From London and Paris to Baghdad', *History and Memory*, 5: 7–31.

King, A. (1998) *Memorials of the Great War in Britain: The Symbolism of Politics of Remembrance*, Oxford: Berg.

Lord Chancellor's Department (2003) 'Remembrance Sunday', Constitutional Policy Division, Available online at www.lcd.gov.uk/constitution/cenotaph/remsun.htm (accessed 11 January 2006).

Moriarty, C. (1991) 'Christian Iconography and First World War Memorials', *Imperial War Museum Review*, 6: 63–75.

Mosse, G. (1975) *The Nationalization of the Masses: Political Symbolism and Mass Movements in Germany from the Napoleonic Wars through the Third Reich*, New York: Howard Fertig.

—— (1990) *Fallen Soldiers: Reshaping the Memory of the World Wars*, Oxford: Oxford University Press.

Mykland, K. (1996) 'The 17th of May: A Historical Date and a Day of National Celebrations', Oslo: Ministry of Foreign Affairs of Norway.

Nora, P. (ed.) (1996) *Realms of Memory: The Construction of the French Past*, Vol. 1 *Division and Conflict*, New York: Columbia University Press.

Spillman, L. (1997) *Nation and Commemoration: Creating National Identities in the United States and Australia*, Cambridge: Cambridge University Press.

Winter, J. (1995) *Sites of Memory, Sites of Mourning: The Great War in European Cultural History*, Cambridge: Cambridge University Press.

Recordings

BBC 1. TV broadcast of Remembrance Sunday and the ceremony at the Cenotaph, Whitehall in London, 11 November 2001–3.

FRANCE 2. TV broadcast of 14 July and the parade at the Champs-Elysées in Paris, 14 July 2001–2.

NRK 1. TV broadcast of 17 May and the parade at Karl Johann's Gate in Oslo, 17 May 2002.

NRK 1. TV broadcast of highlights of 17 May, 17 May 2002.

ZDF1. TV broadcast of the Ecumenical Mass in Mainz Cathedral on Unification Day, 3 October 2001.

ZDF1. TV broadcast, *Festakt Tag der Deutschen Einheit*, 3 October 2001.

6 The persistence of the Turkish nation in the mausoleum of Mustafa Kemal Atatürk

Christopher S. Wilson

Introduction

The Republic of Turkey, founded in 1923 after a war of independence, created a history for its people that completely and consciously bypassed its Ottoman predecessor. An *ethnie* called "the Turks," existent in the multicultural Ottoman Empire only as a general name used by Europeans, was imagined and given a story linking it with the nomads of Central Asia, the former Hittite and Phrygian civilizations of Anatolia, and even indirectly with the ancient Sumerian and Assyrian civilizations of Mesopotamia. In the early years of the Turkish Republic, linguistic, anthropological, archaeological and historical studies were all conducted in order to formulate and sustain such claims.

Mustafa Kemal Atatürk, the revolutionary responsible for the Turkish Republic, was the driving force behind this state-sponsored construction of "the Turks" – even his surname is a fabrication that roughly translates as "Ancestor/Father of the Turks." It is no surprise then that the structure built to house the body of Atatürk after his death, his mausoleum called Anıtkabir, also works to perpetuate such storytelling.

Anıtkabir, however, is more than just the final resting place of Atatürk's body – it is a public monument and stage-set for the nation, and a representation of the hopes and ideals of the Republic of Turkey. Sculptures, reliefs, floor paving and even ceiling patterns are combined in a narrative spatial experience that illustrates, explains and reinforces the imagined history of the Turks, their struggle for independence, and the founding of the Republic of Turkey after the fall of the Ottoman Empire.

In this way, Anıtkabir is a collective monument that embodies the whole of the Turkish nation, not just a single man. It is a three-dimensional explanation and reinforcement of the Turkish nation. Additionally, Anıtkabir is used to represent both the Turkish nation and the people of Turkey during major national celebrations and on other more personal occasions. While Atatürk's mausoleum was originally designed and built to elaborate a Turkish identity, it is the monument's continued maintenance and usage in memorial rituals and commemorative ceremonies that demonstrate the persistence of this identity (or rather, the persistent need for such an elaboration).

Inventing a history and a language

Gazi Mustafa Kemal Paşa, known as Mustafa Kemal Atatürk after 1934, leader of the 1919–23 Turkish War of Independence and first President of the Republic of Turkey, clearly indicated his disdain for the former Ottoman Empire when he said in a 1923 speech that: "[The n]ew Turkey has no relationship to the old one. The Ottoman government has disappeared into history. A new Turkey has now been born" (Schick and Tonak 1987: 10; Öz 1982: 36). Atatürk and the other leaders of early Republican Turkey frequently described their Ottoman predecessor as old, outdated, inefficient, wasteful and disorganized. In contrast, their new democracy was to be modern, up-to-date, efficient, resourceful and well organized. This attitude of contempt for the new state's immediate predecessor shaped the ideology and hence policies of the young Republic of Turkey, including the construction of its representative architecture.

Ethnicity in the Ottoman Empire was not established exclusively according to territoriality or language, but defined more by religion: Ottoman Muslims, Jews and Christians identified first with those of the same religion before regional or language affiliations, although all were equally the subjects of the Ottoman Sultan. Conversely, the newly created Republic of Turkey sought to establish ethnicity not along religious lines but along the lines of language and history. The new Turkey was to be solely composed of Turks and Turks only – hence the population exchange between the Republic of Turkey and the Hellenic Republic of Greece that occurred in the early 1920s, in which ethnic Turks in Greece and ethnic Greeks in Turkey traded places.[1] Along similar lines, the appellation "Turk" would gradually be appropriated or changed from meaning "Muslim Ottoman" to meaning "a citizen of Turkey." That is, a new *ethnie* – the Turk – was created at the same time as the new nation of Turkey was also being created.

This new *ethnie*, however, needed a history – it needed a beginning or an origin myth. Given Atatürk's dislike for his Ottoman predecessors, it is no surprise that such a history was sought and eventually found in the time period before the Ottoman Empire. Eight years after the proclamation of the Republic of Turkey, two Turkish government institutions were founded that substantially contributed to the storytelling about "the Turks:" The Turkish Historical Society (*Türk Tarih Kurumu*) and Turkish Language Society (*Türk Dil Kurumu*). Over the following decade, each institution proposed theories about the Turks that, although eventually partially discredited,[2] shaped the discourse on these subjects well into the twentieth century.

The aim of the Turkish Historical Society, created under the patronage of Atatürk, was (and continues to be) "to study the history of Turkey and the Turks."[3] It began in 1930 as the "Committee for the Study of Turkish History," a subgroup of the Turkish Hearth Association, which in turn was an institution founded during the last decade of the Ottoman Empire to promote "Turkishness."[4] After changing its name and becoming independent of The Turkish Hearth, the Turkish Historical Society proposed the "Turkish History Thesis" at the First [Turkish] History Conference in Ankara in 1932.

This thesis, which attempted to counter the European opinion that the Turks were an inferior race, searched for a pre-Ottoman origin and proposed that current-day Turks descended from a branch of the nomadic Oğuz Turks, who migrated from Central Asia to India, China, Mesopotamia, Anatolia and even into Europe by crossing the Ural mountains, thereby populating almost the entire known world at that time.[5] This territorial approach to constructing a nation's origins has been described by Smith (1999: 63) as "the myth of location and migration" or "where we came from and how we got there." In this way, the Republic of Turkey conveniently theorized that contemporary Turks were the descendants of the ancient Anatolian Hittite civilization (among others), reinforcing Turkish claims to the territory that it prescribed for itself.

The first step toward language reform in the new Republic of Turkey was the ambitious 1928/9 replacement of Arabic script with Latin characters, several of which were specially adapted/adopted for Modern Turkish.[6] This not only allowed for a higher level of literacy in the general population (on the assumption that Latin characters were easier to understand than Arabic ones), but also permitted the vowel harmony of Modern Turkish to be represented more efficiently (since Ottoman Arabic script apparently did not have an agreed-upon system for indicating vowels).

The next and equally ambitious step toward language reform was the creation of the Turkish Language Society, which was founded in 1932 to help "purify" the Turkish language by inventing and suggesting Turkish equivalents for "foreign" words; that is, Ottoman words usually derived from Arabic and Persian.[7] In cases where a suitable Turkish replacement could not be found, the Turkish Language Society, encouraged by Atatürk, resolved the problem by means of the historically inaccurate but politically convenient "Sun Language Theory," initially made public at the First [Turkish] Language Conference in Istanbul in 1932. Simply put, this theory claimed that Turkish was a primal language from which all other languages emerged. Similarities between Sumerian and the other prehistoric languages of Mesopotamia, as well as contemporary Estonian, Finnish, Hungarian and Japanese, were given as examples to back up such claims.

The result of the "Turkish History Thesis" and the "Sun Language Theory" was the creation of Anatolia as a natural location for the Republic of Turkey and a conception of a Turkish race as its natural population. These theories implicitly upheld Anatolia as a kind of cradle of civilization that existed long before the Ottoman Empire – the place of origin for Turk ancestors who spoke a primal Turk language. The impact of these theories on a cultural level was a huge amount of state-sponsored archaeological, art historical, philological and scientific work that sought to physically exemplify the theories and prove them correct in material form.

The early Republic of Turkey actively supported and funded archaeological excavations, called "National Excavations," the establishment of "ancient civilization" museums, and the printing of publications in support of this pre-Islamic or pre-Ottoman origin myth. Archaeological finds consisting of sculptures, wall reliefs, architectural ruins and everyday artifacts from the Hittite, Urart, Phrygian and Lydian civilizations were collected, catalogued and exhibited in the new museums and published in the early Republic's propaganda literature.[8] Many motifs from these investigations such as deer, lions, doubled-headed eagles and Hittite sun emblems found their way onto the Turkish architecture and sculpture of the 1930s.

Such a reliance and dependence on archaeology should not be overlooked. As Smith (1999: 174–80) suggests, the nationalist is a sort of archaeologist: rediscovering, reinterpreting and regenerating the historic deposit of an ethnic past to find myths and memories for an *ethnie* on which nationalist identities can be constructed.

Parallel to this literal digging into the past was an increased interest in the nomadic traditions of the pre-Ottoman Turks, which represented a kind of ancestral lifestyle, before the Ottomans settled down. As a result, traditional nomadic crafts, particularly carpet-weaving, with its rich variety of visual motifs, and the design of traditional nomadic tents, were studied, documented and published widely in academic and popular journals. Such folk traditions were readily accepted and promoted by the Republican elite as symbols of a Turkish (or pre-Ottoman) identity.

With this background information about the Republic of Turkey's construction of a pre-Ottoman history of an *ethnie* called "the Turks," it is now possible to proceed to a discussion about the design and built form of the mausoleum for Mustafa Kemal Atatürk (Figure 6.1), which acts to reinforce a national (collective) identity for the citizens of the Republic of Turkey.

A mausoleum for Atatürk

Although Atatürk died in late 1938, it was not until 1953 that a permanent structure, called Anıtkabir (literally, "memorial tomb"), was opened to act as his mausoleum. An international competition for the design of Anıtkabir in 1942 received 49 entries from which three Turkish, three Italian, one German and one Swiss entry were shortlisted.[9] From among these, the design of the Turkish team of Emin Onat and Orhan Arda was chosen as the winner.

Ironically for a monument that tries to represent the Turkish nation, the winning design for the competition was a monumentalized and abstracted classical (Greek) temple containing small references to Anatolian decorative motifs. The winning architects did not deny this reading. In fact, it was highlighted. In an explanation of their design, Onat and Arda continued the story (or "history") of Turkey and the Turkish people that began with the Turkish Historical Society's "Turkish History Thesis":

Figure 6.1 Anıtkabir, the mausoleum of Mustafa Kemal Atatürk, Ankara, as seen on the back of the new Turkish five lira banknote (source: reproduced with permission of the Republic of Turkey Central Bank, in accordance with law no. 25383, pages 86–9, *Republic of Turkey Official Gazette*, February 24, 2004).

Our past, like that of all Mediterranean civilizations, goes back thousands of years. It starts with Sumerians and Hittites and merges with the life of many civilizations from Central Asia to the depths of Europe, thus forming one of the main roots of the classical heritage. Atatürk, rescuing us from the Middle Ages,[10] widened our horizons and showed us that our real history resides not in the Middle Ages but in the common sources of the classical world. In a monument for the leader of our revolution and our savior from the Middle Ages, we wanted to reflect this new consciousness. Hence, we decided to construct our design philosophy along the rational lines of a seven-thousand-year-old classical civilization rather than associating it with the tomb of a sultan or a saint.

(Bozdoğan 2001: 289)[11]

The design took 11 years to build, during which some changes were made, the most significant of which was that the vaulted ceiling of the main building was eliminated. Instead, a flat ceiling and roof were constructed assuring that the mausoleum more closely resembled a classical temple.

Anıtkabir sits at the top of a hill that used to be called Rasattepe.[12] In the 1940s and 1950s, before the rapid expansion of Ankara, this hill could be seen from most places in the city. This acropolis-like siting within Ankara also heightens the classical temple analogy. The location was also chosen for its symbolic value, as argued in Parliament by Minister of Parliament Süreyya Örgeevren:

Rasattepe has another characteristic that will deeply impress everyone. The shape of the present and future Ankara ranging from Dikmen to Etlik reminds [one] of the shape of a crescent while Rasattepe is like a star in the center. Ankara is the body of the crescent. If Atatürk's Mausoleum [were] placed on this hill, we would embed Atatürk in the center of the crescent of our flag. Thus the capital of Turkey would embrace Atatürk. Atatürk [would] be symbolically unified with our flag.

(Taylak 1998?: 22)[13]

In short, starting from the city-scale, the monument embodies an identity through the presentation of ethnosymbols, be they classical temples or flags.

Coincidentally, Rasattepe was also an ancient Phrygian tumulus and was consequentially excavated before the construction of Atatürk's mausoleum. The site yielded many archaeological finds, most of which went to the Museum of Anatolian Civilizations in Ankara. In this way, not only did Rasattepe provide the physical material to reinforce a mythical history of the Turks, but it also provided the metaphorical material: Atatürk, father of the Turks, would find his final resting place on top of the Phrygians, metaphorically and literally using this ancient civilization as a foundation.

Anıtkabir consists not only of the temple-like main building, but also a huge public plaza in front of the mausoleum, pavilions that surround the plaza, and a ceremonial approach. Visitors are first confronted by an imposing staircase with 26 risers which are intended to evoke the memory of August 26, 1922, the date on which Atatürk's forces could legitimately say that they had won control over the country during the Turkish War of Independence.

On either side at the top of the staircase are groups of sculptures: to the left, "Turkish Men" and to the right, "Turkish Women" (shown in Figure 6.2). The men include a soldier, a villager and a student – symbolizing defense, productivity and education. The two women in front are holding a wreath of wheat, a symbol of fertility, while the woman at the back is silently crying – symbolizing the nation's grief over the death of Atatürk. It is no exaggeration to say that these highly stylized sculptures physically represent the actual *ethnie* of "the Turk," the population of the Republic of Turkey, with the men strangely resembling Atatürk.[14]

Also on either side of this staircase are two stone pavilions, or "towers," that introduce the exterior architectural decoration scheme for the rest of the monument, which consists of Seljuk details like *mukarnas* ("saw-tooth" cornices), relief arches, water spouts, rosettes and bird houses. These pre-Ottoman architectural details, as already explained by the architects, were chosen to represent the "roots" of Turkish architecture. Additionally, the roof and the bronze arrowhead at the top of each "tower" (ten in total) represent a traditional Turkic nomadic tent (*yurt*),[15] still found today in parts of rural Turkey and Central Asia, the first of many examples of the appropriation of folk traditions found at Anıtkabir.

Figure 6.2 "Turkish Men" (left) and "Turkish Women" (right) at the entrance to the Street of Lions (source: sculptor: Hüseyin Özkan; photograph: Christopher S. Wilson).

Furthermore, each tower at Anıtkabir represents a theme related to the Turkish War of Independence.[16] Inscribed on the inside walls of each tower are quotes by Atatürk corresponding to the particular theme of each tower, such as "This nation has not, cannot and will not live without independence. Independence or death" (1919) in the Independence Tower or "Nations who cannot find their national identity are prey to other nations" (1923) in the National Pact Tower.

After the male and female sculptures, a ceremonial approach follows, known as the Street of Lions because it is lined on both sides by 24 stone lions (six pairs on either side). These lions are blatantly reminiscent of the Hittite lions found in archaeological digs sponsored by the early Republic of Turkey (Figure 6.3), a reference explicitly working to remind visitors of the pre-Ottoman origins of the Turks. This ceremonial approach ends physically at a huge public plaza, but visually beyond at the Turkish Grand National Assembly, or Parliament Building, and behind that, Çankaya Hill, the residence of the President of Turkey. In this way, the narrative of the ceremonial approach starts in the past (Hittite lions) but concludes in the present or even future (the Parliament and Presidential Palace).

Once into the huge public plaza, the main temple-like building of the

Figure 6.3 Left, lion sculptures from the neo-Hittite settlement of Carchemish/ Jerablos (source: Leonard wooley (1921) Plate B26a "Carchemish: Report on the Excavations at Jerablus on Behalf of the British Museum – Part II: The Town Defences," courtesy of the British Library). Right, a lion from the ceremonial approach to Anıtkabir (source: sculptor: Hüseyin Özkan; photograph: Christopher S. Wilson).

complex is on the left and more small pavilions frame the plaza on the right. The axis of this public plaza and the main building, known as the Hall of Honor, connects to the Old Citadel or Ankara Castle, which represents pre-Republican (read: Ottoman) Ankara, before it was declared the capital city of Turkey. Here again, the visitor is reminded of the past. However, this time, it is a past that is behind Atatürk – we cannot see it. Atatürk (or rather, the building housing his body) is literally blocking our view of this past because the Ankara Citadel is associated with the Ottoman Empire and is therefore not worthy of our attention, unlike the Hittite and Seljuk past that is.

The pavilions surrounding the public plaza contain a museum, opened in 1960, displaying Atatürk's personal artifacts like his identity card, clothing, medals, weapons and other memorabilia (including a wax model of Atatürk sitting at his desk with his stuffed dog at his feet). This museum leads to a new (Turkish) War of Independence Museum under the Hall of Honor. In the 18 vaults surrounding this museum are a series of "panoramic" exhibits, also themed according to the War of Independence and the revolutions that followed.[17] This experience ends in the Library of Atatürk, containing the 3,123 books in Modern and Ottoman Turkish, French, English, Greek and Latin owned by Atatürk, some of which are open to pages containing his notes in the margins.

The pavilions surrounding the public plaza are connected to each other with arcaded walkways that make extensive usage of Turkish carpet (*kilim*) decorative motifs on their ceilings (Figure 6.4). The public plaza in front of the Hall of Honor also has 373 abstracted carpet motifs on its floor, done with cobblestone paving (Figure 6.4). Just like the nomadic tent folk traditions that were appropriated for the towers of Anıtkabir, the Turkish carpet has also been seized upon to provide a visual identity for the Turks.

Figure 6.4 Turkish carpet ceiling decoration (top) and floor paving (bottom) at Anıtkabir (source: photograph by Christopher S. Wilson).

Approaching the Hall of Honor from the public plaza, there are two low-relief sculptures flanking either side. On the left is "The Battle of the Commander-in-Chief" (Figure 6.5); on the right, "The Battle of Sakarya." Both reliefs refer to the events of July–September 1921, during the Turkish War of Independence, when Atatürk was officially named Commander-in-Chief of the Turkish forces and a decisive battle occurred at the Sakarya River that brought both military and political victory for the young Republic.[18] Similar to the Street of Lions, these reliefs resemble archaeological Hittite finds in their composition and stylization. However, the subject matter of these reliefs is more recent than the lions and they function to fuse the recent past (War of Independence) with the present (public square), just before ascending the stairs to pay one's respects to Atatürk.

Before actually proceeding into the Hall of Honor itself, one is confronted in several instances with the words of Atatürk. First, in the middle of the stairs is a low wall with "Sovereignty Unconditionally Belongs to the Nation" inscribed onto it.[19] On the outside wall of the main building (the Hall of Honor), two of Atatürk's most famous speeches are emblazoned: on the left, Atatürk's 1927 "Address to the Youth," his call for vigilance against traitors to the Republic; and on the right, Atatürk's grand congratulatory 1933 "Speech on the Occasion of the 10th Anniversary" (Figure 6.6). Although visitors are just about to enter the personal burial place of

Figure 6.5 Detail of "The Battle of the Commander in Chief" by scupltor Zühtü Müritoğlo. Atatürk stretches one arm and says, "Armies, your first target is the Mediterranean, march!" (source: photograph by Christopher S. Wilson).

Figure 6.6 The Hellenic temple-like Hall of Honor, with two of Atatürk's famous speeches shining in gold behind the columns (source: photograph by Christopher S. Wilson).

Atatürk, they are still being reminded of the nation of Turkey (and not the Ottoman Empire) by means of these inscriptions.

Inside the Hall of Honor, the Turkish carpet motifs multiply in number and complexity. The roof beams of the ceiling are not even exempt from such treatment, with intricate patterns composed of gold mosaic tiles. At the far end of the Hall, framed by a single oversized window, is Atatürk's huge marble sarcophagus, a single block of red marble from Osmaniye (near Adana) weighing 40 tons, a symbol of the grave and body of Atatürk. The revolutionary's corpse is actually interred in a Seljuk-decorated, octagon-shaped chamber below the sarcophagus. This tomb is generally not open to the public, but has recently been made accessible via closed circuit television.

Although this point of the site is the most personal part of the experience, the sarcophagus, the end goal of a visit to Anıtkabir, completes the national narration: from the male and female sculptures to the pavilions/towers to the Street of Lions to the battle reliefs to the inscriptions of famous Atatürk sayings, the entire experience is meant to remind the visitor of the history (and future?) of the Turkish nation. Additionally, with the use of the pre-Ottoman architectural details, modern copies of archaeological finds and abstracted tent and carpet motifs, the monument presents a history of the Turks that existed long before the Ottoman Empire, thereby lessening the Ottomans' importance. In this way, Anıtkabir is a symbol of a constructed *ethnie* and history whose function is not simply commemoration but also education.

Persistence through maintenance

Architectural theorist Adrian Forty (2001: 4–8) has questioned the assumption that material objects can take the place of those memories formed in the mind, citing three phenomena to support his argument: the ephemeral monuments of some non-Western societies that function to "get rid of what they no longer need or wish to remember;" Sigmund Freud's theory of mental processes, which sees forgetting as repression (willful, but unconscious, forgetting) that decays differently than physical objects; and the difficulty of representing the Holocaust in physical form without diminishing its horror.[20]

Forty may be correct – material objects cannot simply replace mental memories – but what he does not recognize is the maintenance required to keep physical artifacts from decaying. It is this very maintenance that is significant in the construction of collective identity, memory and nationalism. The fact that physical objects, like architecture, need to be constantly maintained (or, literally, propped up) to achieve their purpose, means that there is always something or somebody behind that maintenance with a reason for doing it. This type of maintenance is more ideological than physical, although it sometimes manifests itself as physical changes, and can be categorized into two types: commemoration/ritualization and addition/subtraction.

Once Anıtkabir was constructed and opened in 1953, it immediately became the location of ritual commemorations and/or remembrance ceremonies associated not only with Atatürk, but also with the Turkish nation. Anthropologist Clifford Geertz (1973: 448) has called rituals the "stories people tell themselves about themselves." Similarly, John Skorupski (1976: 84) has commented: "ceremony says 'look, this is how things should be, this is the proper, ideal pattern of social life.'" At Anıtkabir, the stories told by the acting out of commemorations and ceremonies seem to reinforce the ideology of "how things should be" already advocated by the architecture, which then, in a circular fashion, leads to more commemorations and ceremonies.

The most significant ceremony conducted at Anıtkabir occurs on the anniversary date of Atatürk's death, 10 November. On this day at 9.05 am, a one-minute silence, a familiar device of remembrance ceremonies, takes place throughout Turkey. This commemoration is something that anyone in Turkey (national or not) is obliged to live through, even during heavy morning rush-hour traffic when all vehicles stop in their place; it is a major element in the collective memory of the Republic of Turkey. Although this minute of silence is simultaneously celebrated everywhere in the land, it is officially commemorated at Anıtkabir, despite the fact that the actual location of Atatürk's death was a bedroom in Dolmabahçe Palace in Istanbul.

After this one minute of silence, a wreath of flowers is typically laid in front of Atatürk's sarcophagus (the one accessible to the public) and the current Prime Minister and President write official statements in the

Anıtkabir visitors' book. This laying of a wreath and writing in the book not only occurs on the anniversary of Atatürk's death, but also at the opening of the Turkish Parliament every year and at any other time when it is deemed appropriate. When domestic associations and foreign dignitaries pay visits to Atatürk's mausoleum, they also act out this ritual, drawing both the national and international community into the collective memory and identity construction of Turkey.[21]

Wreath-laying and statement-writing also take place during periods of national crisis, especially national identity crisis. The most famous example of this occurred after the 1980 military coup when the Turkish armed forces took control of the country because a civil war had almost broken out between the political left and right in Turkey. General Kenan Evren, one of the outspoken leaders of the coup, immediately paid a visit to Anıtkabir, laid a wreath and explained the coup leaders' intentions in the visitors' book, addressing the text to Atatürk as if he were still alive:

> Our Great Leader: the Turkish Military Forces, as guardians of the republic that you founded, always faithful to your principles, had to halt those who were pushing the Turkish State a little closer toward darkness and helplessness, and were forced to take over the administration of the nation in order to renew democracy and your principles. We remember you once again with gratitude and a sense of obligation, and bow before you in respect.
>
> (Anıtkabir Association 2001: 439)[22]

Since Atatürk and the Republic of Turkey are frequently combined in the collective conscience of Turkish nationals, especially at Anıtkabir, the idea of Atatürk's immortality is equivalent to the continued survival (or persistence) of the Turkish nation.

Anıtkabir plays an equally important role in the rituals and commemorations surrounding the Turkish national day, October 29: the date of the declaration of the Republic of Turkey in 1923. Annually on this day, Anıtkabir's wide ceremonial approach (the Street of Lions), the large public plaza and the Hall of Honor are thronged with visitors, all paying their respects to both Atatürk and the nation of Turkey by visiting the monument. The significance of Anıtkabir and this date was not lost on those terrorists associated with the Islamicist Metin Kaplan, who have been accused of plotting to bomb the monument during the 75th anniversary of the Republic in 1998.[23] By attacking and possibly destroying the monument, the terrorists were attempting to eradicate (or at least nullify) the symbol of what they opposed. By attacking it on October 29 the symbolic nature of their act was greatly magnified.

Commemorative activity also takes place in a less formal manner that is not sponsored by the state itself. For example, political protestors often seek permission to end their rallies at the monument, both so that they can take their grievances directly to Atatürk himself and so that they can raise their concerns to national prominence. Grievances can be as petty as the proposal of insufficient pay increases for civil servants or as significant as recent opposition to military intervention in Iraq. In this way, Atatürk's mausoleum, more so than the Turkish Parliament itself, acts as a symbol of the nation. Likewise, schoolchildren, both in Ankara and from around the country, frequently make pilgrimage-like trips to Anıtkabir to pay their respects both to Atatürk and the nation, especially on April 23, the children's holiday in Turkey.[24] All of these ritual forms assure that Anıtkabir remains a place that simultaneously represents the past (a dead leader and an official history), the present (current crises and grievances) and the future (children).

Anthropologist Michael E. Meeker (1997: 163) has compared the wreath-laying assemblies in the public plaza at Anıtkabir to the so-called "Council of Victory" assemblies at the Topkapı Palace during the Ottoman Empire, where "thousands of the highest military and administrative officials assembled in [Topkapı's] middle court to manifest their personhood before the eyes and ears of the sultan ... for hours at a time." Meeker claims that the ranked formation at these Anıtkabir assemblies (from President to Prime Minister to military elite to Members of Parliament to provincial governors to the civil elite, as well as members of societies, political parties and associations) parallels that of the Ottoman Council of Victory and that in these ranked formations "[c]itizen and founder interact within a framework of constraints imposed by nationhood" (1997: 172). This is one of many parallels between the management of the Republic of Turkey and the Ottoman Empire, where the persistence or continuance of the Republic can actually be read as a persistence or continuance of practices started earlier and merely altered for new conditions.[25]

While Meeker's comparison is enlightening, more helpful still for understanding all of these commemorations and rituals is the argument developed by sociologist Paul Connerton who suggests that commemorations and rituals shape a collective or social memory not only by their persistent occurrence, but also by the performative bodily movements involved in carrying them out. He maintains that such bodily movements "act out" (in the psychoanalytic sense) a society's memory – its knowledge and images of its past. He refers to this specialized form of collective social memory as "habit-memory" and suggests that it includes those collective actions that are ruled by conventions and traditions. Connerton concludes:

> The habit-memory – more precisely, the social habit-memory – of the subject is not identical with that subject's cognitive memory or rules and codes; nor is it simply an additional or supplementary aspect; it is an essential ingredient in the successful and convincing performance of codes and rules.
>
> (Connerton 1989: 36)

To successfully participate in the rituals and commemorations at Anıtkabir is to perform from one's habit-memory. A visit to Anıtkabir is not an easy physical task. It means walking up a moderate incline for 600 meters through the Peace Park that surrounds it, ascending the 26 entrance stairs to the Street of Lions, walking on this "street" for 260 meters at a slow pace (due to the five-centimeter grass space between the paving slabs), ascending six more steps to the public plaza, crossing this expansive space (130 × 85 meters), ascending 42 more steps to the Hall of Honor and walking approximately another 35 meters to Atatürk's sarcophagus. All in all, from entry gate to sarcophagus, this journey takes at least 45 minutes on foot.[26]

According to archeologist Bruce Trigger, the monumentality of such long walks symbolizes the grandeur of the state and is designed to "impress people with the power of a ruler and the resources that he has at his disposal" (1990: 127). To lay a wreath at Atatürk's sarcophagus not only includes this extended journey, but also the bending down to place the wreath, always uncomfortably keeping one's back away from the sarcophagus as a sign of respect. To write in the memorial book may not be strenuous, but still involves perfunctory bodily movements by proceeding to the official writing spot at the official lectern and using the official pen.[27]

The second method of maintaining Anıtkabir concerns additions and subtractions to the monument since it was first designed and built. These additions and subtractions are significant because they are a direct reflection of the changing of circumstances over time, for which the process of maintenance constantly strives to compensate.

Beginning with the subtractions to Anıtkabir, the most radical change between the architects' competition-winning design and the actual built product was the elimination of the upper "attic" story over the Hall of Honor, which was a large mass covered in reliefs and projecting up from the columned base below that made it very similar to the first mausoleum in history, the tomb of Mausolus in Halicarnassus (located in present-day Bodrum, Turkey) built around 353 BCE. This attic story was not built, under consultation and with the approval of the architects, during the final phases of construction in 1950, in order to save both time and money. However, the removal of this attic story results in a plain and abstract columned main building that is even more like a Hellenic temple atop an acropolis, probably why the architects agreed to such a change (see note 11).

Also changed from the architects' original design was the number of torches flanking both sides of the Hall of Honor. Throughout Atatürk's laying-in-state, funeral and interment in a temporary tomb at the Ethnographic Museum, there were always six symbolic torches, three each side, representing the "six pillars of Kemalism": republicanism, secularism, nationalism, populism, statism and revolutionism. These "pillars" were the ideological manifesto of Atatürk's "People's Republican Party" and, since the early Republic of Turkey was a one-party state, these six concepts were also the ideological basis of the republic. Anıtkabir, as built, contains ten torches; five either side of the Hall of Honor. While it is difficult to pin-point exactly how and why the number changed from six to ten, this change in number can be counted as a subtraction and not an addition because the equating of Atatürk with his ideals, the six pillars of Kemalism, was lost (subtracted).

The next subtraction from Anıtkabir involves the public "Peace Park" around Atatürk's mausoleum, which is praised in the monument's promotional literature for its dedication to Atatürk's famous saying "Peace at home, peace in the world" and also for its wide variety of trees, flowers and vegetation from around Turkey and 24 other countries.[28] However, this park ceased to be public sometime in the 1960s or 1970s. No picnicking or bar-becuing is allowed in the park, both of which are favorite weekend pastimes of most Turks. Visitors are not allowed to even walk through it – they must stay on the prescribed paths when moving from the entrance gate to the monument proper. The change was made principally as a way to enhance security, but the end result is that the monument is maintained in a "time-less bubble" away from the hustle and bustle of the capital city that has grown up around it.

The last subtraction from Anıtkabir involves Cemal Gürsel, a former President of Turkey from 1960–6, and some martyrs of the 1960 military coup, all of whom were buried at the monument in the 1960s. These graves were all removed after 1985 when a "State Cemetery" in an Islamic-inspired style, openly acknowledged by the cemetery's architect (Anıtkabir is sometimes criticized for its non-Islamic look and feel), was constructed elsewhere in Ankara. Along with the 1981 law announcing that the State Cemetery will henceforth take all dead Turkish persons of national importance, it was also declared that Anıtkabir was not a graveyard but a national monument and gathering place:

> Only Atatürk's grave, and also his closest friend-in-arms and efforts Ismet Inönü's grave may be kept at Anıtkabir, which has been established as a gift to the Turkish people for the Great Savior. No one else may be buried on the property of Anıtkabir.
> (*Republic of Turkey Official Gazette*, November 10, 1981: 1)[29]

The declaration that Anıtkabir should not serve as a graveyard was made despite the fact that the mortal remains of Atatürk and Turkey's first Prime Minister (and Atatürk's best friend), Ismet Inönü, are buried there. Inönü died on December 25, 1973 and was quickly interred in a special tomb on the edge of the ceremonial plaza, directly opposite and on axis with the Hall of Honor. The interment of Inönü (and his non-removal to the State Cemetery after 1985) maintains the presentation of Anıtkabir as primarily a national monument, of importance to the whole nation and not to specific family members; and only secondarily as the location of the remains of Atatürk and Inönü.

The next additions to Anıtkabir were done in 1981, a celebration-packed year due to the 100th anniversary of Atatürk's birth. It was during these centennial celebrations that 68 small bronze pots of "Turkish" soil were placed around the subterranean grave of Atatürk, the one closed to the public that is directly below the sarcophagus in the Hall of Honor. The pots contained "Turkish" soil (in quotation marks) because at the time there were 67 provinces in Turkey – one pot came from each province. The 68th pot contained soil from the Turkish Republic of Northern Cyprus, the disputed territory occupied by the Turkish military and to this day not recognized by the majority of the world's nations as a legitimate state.

Since 1981, due to rapid development in Turkey, provinces have sometimes split as former small towns became larger cities and regional centers. As a result, there are currently 81 provinces in Turkey, and a brass pot for these new provinces seems to have been added each time. Lastly, like the "Turkish" soil from Northern Cyprus, three other "Turkish" soils have been added: from the garden of Atatürk's supposed birth-house in Thessaloniki, present-day Greece; from the area surrounding the Turkish monument in the UN Memorial Cemetery, Korea; and from the grave of the Selçuk commander Süleyman Shah (d. 1227), which is located in present-day Syria.[30]

All of these places are connected in some way with Atatürk and/or the Republic of Turkey: Atatürk's birthplace, a monument to fallen Turkish soldiers in the Korean conflict (1950–3), and the grave of the grandfather of the founder of the Ottoman Empire. Significantly, however, similar to the soil from Northern Cyprus, all of these supplementary pots contain soil from outside the current borders of Turkey – a very literal claiming of territory.

Another centennial addition to Anıtkabir was the inscription of more quotations onto the monument. Atatürk's final Republican Day address to the Turkish military on October 29, 1938 (in effect his last public speech since he died 12 days later) was inscribed at the lefthand entrance of the Hall of Honor; and İnönü's eulogy given at Atatürk's funeral on November 21, 1938 was inscribed at the righthand exit from the Hall of Honor. In between these two readings the visitor experiences Atatürk's sarcophagus inside the Hall of Honor. In this way, the placing of the inscriptions makes sense: 1) final words, 2) dead body, 3) funeral eulogy. What is significant, however, is that these inscriptions were not part of the original 1942 competition-winning entry, they were added almost 40 years later in 1981. In 1942 (and in 1953 when the monument opened), many people still had personal memories of the death of Atatürk. However, by 1981, several newer generations did not have such firsthand memories. It can be theorized that these new inscriptions were added to remind younger visitors that, although Anıtkabir is a national monument dedicated to the Republic of Turkey, its foundation stems from the death of Atatürk.

The most recent addition to Anıtkabir was made during the 2002 renovation of the original 1960 Atatürk museum. At this time, the museum was greatly expanded to become a "War of [Turkish] Independence Museum," which documents and explains post-World War I events, the creation of the Republic of Turkey and the political, economic and social revolutions that followed. Interestingly, the museum does not start with the beginning of the Turkish War of Independence, traditionally dated to Atatürk's landing at Sansum on May 19, 1919, but with the World War I battle of Gallipoli in 1915, when Atatürk first proved his military prowess to the outside world fighting in the service of the Ottoman Empire. In this way, the museum exhibits more blatantly equate the two concepts of "Atatürk" and "Turkish nation" than the architecture that surrounds the museum does.

The final significant transformation of Anıtkabir can be seen in the changing administration of the monument over the years. The 1941–2 architectural competition and the construction of the monument (minus the Hall of Honor's attic storey) from October 9, 1944 to its opening on November 10, 1953 were overseen by the Ministry of Public Works. The ministry continued to administer the monument until February 28, 1957, after which time it passed to the Ministry of National Education. The Ministry of National Education administer Anıtkabir until the 1974 establishment of the Turkish Ministry of Culture, which then took responsibility for the monument. The Ministry of Culture then managed the monument until the military coup of 1980, when the Ministry of the General Staff of Turkish Military Forces assumed control. This ministry still runs the monument, which means effectively that Anıtkabir is a military installation, albeit freely open to the public and to foreigners, which begins to explain much of the previous discussion about the changes to Anıtkabir: it is a national monument, but not one where citizens have the freedom to do as they please – they must act within the rules set out by the military administration, which ensure that all visits to Anıtkabir are only for the purpose of honoring Atatürk and the Republic of Turkey, and for no other reason.[31]

Conclusion

At the mausoleum of Mustafa Kemal Atatürk, officially called Anıtkabir, an authorized version of Turkish history is manifest in physical form. That is, official public (state) culture uses the architectural construction of Anıtkabir to set rules that govern both the nation-state and society. These rules are subsequently extended and maintained by means of the many and various visits to and commemorations at the monument that take place on both special and normal days and which are carried out by elites and the general public. Additions and subtractions to the construction also provide maintenance of sorts, as the symbolism of the monument is fine-tuned and its purpose(s) (re-)defined in concrete terms as circumstances change over time.

Can it be concluded that the Turkish nation persists because of the habit-memory that plays itself out at Anıtkabir – because of the bodily memory of "nation-ness" that is brought about by the commemorations and rituals that take place there? Or, is the persistence of the Turkish nation at Anıtkabir merely a reflection of the loyal military institution that runs the monument? Regardless of the answer to these questions, one thing is certain: Atatürk's mausoleum is the location of not only his physical remains but also his intellectual remains – it is an ever-changing (yet paradoxically ever-maintained) architectural representation of both Atatürk and the Turkish nation.

Notes

1 The exceptions to this population exchange were those ethnic Greeks who could establish their residency in Constantinople (Istanbul) prior to October 30, 1918 and those ethnic Turks who could establish their residency in Western Thrace prior to October 18, 1912, as agreed upon at Lausanne on January 30, 1923.

2 Most notably by Beşikçi (1977).

3 According to an informational brochure in English by the Turkish Historical Society, dated 2002. See also www.ttk.gov.tr/ingilizce/data/tarihce.html (last accessed June 21, 2006).

4 Turkish Hearth Association branches throughout Turkey later became known as "People's Houses" (*Halk Evleri*).

5 Although the Turkish History Thesis searched for a pre-Ottoman origin, it was in fact partly based on the Ottoman myth of beginnings as descendants of the Oğuz Turks, although not mentioning "a tribe of 400 tents." See Wittek (1958: 7–15) for more information about the Ottomans' own myths of origin. The Turkish History Thesis seems to have adapted the Ottoman myths by broadening the extent to which the Oğuz Turks migrated.

6 These specially adapted/adopted characters were:

   - Ç/ç (written as a "c" with a circumflex and pronounced like the English "ch");
   - Ğ/ğ (known in Turkish as a "soft g," this is a silent letter that prolongs the vowels that follow it);
   - İ/i (both a capital and lower-case letter "i" pronounced like the English "ee");
   - I/ı (both a capital and lower-case "i," but having no dot, pronounced like the English "uh");
   - Ö/ö (pronounced the same as the German);
   - Ş/ş (written as an "s" with a circumflex and pronounced like the English "sh"); and
   - Ü/ü (pronounced the same as the German).

7 For example, the Ottoman "*mektep*" (school) was replaced with "*okul*," derived from the Turkish verb "*okumak*" (to read). In English, the equivalent would be banning the French word "chauffeur" and replacing it with "driver."

8 Particularly as postcards or in *La Turquie Kemaliste*, a bimonthly magazine in French, English and German published by the Turkish General Directorate of Publications [*Basın Yayın Genel Müdürlüğü*].

9 Turkish short-listed entries: #24 Hamit K. Söylemezoğlu–Kemal A. Aru–Recai Akçay, #25 Emin Onat–Orhan Arda, and #29 Feridun Akozan–M. Ali Handan; Italian short-listed entries: #41 Giovanni Muzio, #44 Arnaldo Foschini, and #45 Guiseppe Vaccaro–Gino Franzi; German: #9 Prof. Johannes Kruger; Swiss: #42 Architect Ronald Rohn.

10 Implying the Ottoman era.

11 The original Turkish can be found in Onat and Arda (1955: 55–9).

12 Rasattepe literally means "Observation Hill," because of a meteorological station that existed on the site prior to building Anıtkabir. The name of the hill has been creatively changed to Anıttepe, or "Memorial Hill."

13 Translation by author. The original Turkish of this speech was also published in the Turkish newspaper *ULUS* on January 18, 1939.
14 Before Atatürk's body was moved to Anıtkabir on November 10, 1953, his temporary tomb was located in the Ethnographic Museum, Ankara – as if he was an exhibit himself.
15 According to the Turkish Ministry of Culture; see www.kultur.gov.tr/EN/BelgeGoster.aspx?17A16AE30572D313AC8287D72AD903BEB361049FDD41AE45 (last accessed June 21, 2006).
16 The "Independence" (*İstiklâl*) and "Freedom" (*Hürriyet*) Towers are at the beginning of the Street of Lions; "GI Joe" (*Mehmetçik*), "Victory" (*Zafer*), "Peace" (*Barış*), "23rd April" (*23 Nisan*), "National Pact" (*Misak-i Milli*), which established the borders of Turkey, "Revolution" (*İnkılâp*), "Republic" (*Cumhuriyet*) and "Defense of Rights" (*Müdafaa-i Hukuk*) Towers are around the public plaza.
17 The themes of these 18 vaults are as follows: Turkish Commanders in the War of Independence; Occupation of the Country; National Forces; The Congresses; Inauguration of the Turkish Grand National Assembly; National Struggles in Çukurova, Antep, Maraş Urfa and Trakia; First Victories at the Eastern and Western Fronts; Grand Victory–Mudanya Armistice–Lausanne Treaty; Political Revolutions; Reforms in Education, Language and History; Reforms in Law, Women's Rights and Family Names; Rearrangement of Social Life; Fine Arts, Press and Community Centers; National Security; Agriculture, Forestry, Industry and Commerce; Finance, Health, Sports and Tourism; Public Works and Transportation; Domestic and Foreign Political Events 1923–38.
18 It was after this victory that the French started to take Atatürk and his forces more seriously. The English would not do so until after the August 26, 1922 victory.
19 The Turkish is "*Hakimiyet Kayıtsız Şartsız Milletindir.*" There are many more sayings by Atatürk inscribed at Anıtkabir than the three discussed here. Most are on the inside walls of the towers, corresponding to the theme of each tower. For example, in the Tower of Independence: "We are a nation that wants life and independence, and we will pay with our life" (1921). Interestingly, the following quote can be found in the Tower of the National Pact: "Nations who cannot find their national identity are prey to other nations" (1923).
20 See also Young (1993) for a further explanation of the contradiction of Holocaust memorials.
21 By domestic associations I mean, for example, the Zonguldak Miners' Labor Union, which at one time also left a plaque that is located outside Atatürk's (real) subterranean tomb, or the Ankara Society of Women, who annually visit the mausoleum on its own commemorative date, World Women's Day (March 8). The ritual of laying wreaths and writing in the visitor book actually started at the Ethnographic Museum temporary tomb, but was institutionalized at Anıtkabir. The visitor books containing all entries are routinely compiled and publicly published. There currently exist 20 published volumes; see Anıtkabir Association (2001).
22 Translation by author. For more on the immortality of Atatürk, see Volkan and Itzkowitz (1984).
23 Metin Kaplan and his "Anatolian Federated Islamic State" planned to smash a small plane full of explosives into Anıtkabir during the October 29, 1998 ceremonies (strangely foreshadowing September 11, 2001), but were apprehended by Turkish police beforehand. As would be expected, the alternative date chosen in case of bad weather was November 10.
24 Delaney (1990: 517) likewise describes Anıtkabir as a place of pilgrimage, similar to the Ka'ba in Mecca, only secular.
25 Many authors have pointed out how the Republic of Turkey did not magically

spring from the ashes of the Ottoman Empire as perhaps Atatürk (in his famous "*Nutuk*" speech from October 15–20, 1927) and Kemalist historians present it. Instead, the "*Tanzimat*" reforms of the late nineteenth century and the early attempts at a constitutional monarchy of the twentieth century laid the groundwork for a nationalist view. See particularly Ahmad (1993), Berkes (1964), Heper *et al.* (1993), Kushner (1977), Poulton (1997) and Zürcher (1998).

26 Private vehicles are allowed to enter the grounds of Anıtkabir, which eliminates the first 600 meters uphill through the Peace Park, but the experience of the architectural promenade still begins at the 26 steps before the Street of Lions.

27 US President George W. Bush controversially used his own pen, rather than the official pen, during his visit in June 2004, setting off a string of commentary in Turkish newspapers.

28 The Turkish of Atatürk's famous saying is: "*Yurtta Sulh, Cihanda Sulh.*" The promotional literature of Anıtkabir states that the park contains around 50,000 decorative trees, flowers and shrubs in 104 varieties.

29 "*Türk milletinin, bir armağan olarak yalnız Büyük Kurtarıcı için tesis ettiği Anıtkabirde Atatürk'ün ve ayrıca en yakın silah ve mesai arkadaşı İsmet İnönü'nün kabirleri muhafaza edilir. Anıtkabir alanı içine başkaca hiçbir kimse defnedilemez.*" See also the Turkish Ministry of Justice webpage www.mevzuat.adalet.gov.tr/html/568.html (last accessed June 21, 2006).

30 The grave of Süleyman Shah on the banks of the Euphrates in Syria is guarded by Turkish soldiers who also have the right to fly the Turkish flag there, as agreed in the July 24, 1923 Lausanne Treaty.

31 Of the 19 official rules for visiting Anıtkabir posted at the entrance in Turkish and English, rule number 16 reads:

> While visiting the mausoleum, proper behavior must be adapted. Making a statement about political and social issues to the press, addressing to the crowd (sic) and handing out leaflets is prohibited. Shouting and screaming is forbidden. Respect must be shown within Atatürk's eternal rest grounds.

References

Ahmad, F. (1993) *The Making of Modern Turkey*, London: Routledge.

Anıtkabir Derneği [Anıtkabir Association] (2001) *Anıtkabir Özel Defteri (1953'ten Günümüze Anıtkabir'i Ziyaret Eden Yerli ve Yabancı Heyet Başkalarının Atatürk Hakkındaki Duygu ve Düşünceleri)* [*The Private Guestbook/Register of Anıtkabir (Feelings and Thoughts about Atatürk by Domestic and Foreign Committee Heads Who Have Visited Anıtkabir from 1953 to the Present)*], 20 vols, Ankara: Anıtkabir Derneği Yayınları [Anıtkabir Association Publications].

Atatürk, M.K. (1982) *Quotations from Mustafa Kemal Atatürk*, trans. Y. Öz, Ankara: [Turkish] Ministry of Foreign Affairs.

Berkes, N. (1964) *The Development of Secularism in Turkey*, London: Routledge.

Beşikçi, I. (1977) *"Türk-Tarih Tezi," "Güneş-Dil Teorisi" ve Kürt Sorunu* [*The "Turkish History Thesis," the "Sun-Language Theory" and the Kurdish Question*], Ankara: Komal Publishers.

Bozdoğan, S. (2001) *Modernism and Nation Building: Turkish Architectural Culture in the Early Republic*, Seattle: University of Washington Press.

Connerton, P. (1989) *How Society Remembers*, Cambridge: Cambridge University Press.

Delaney, C. (1990) "The Hajj: Sacred and Secular," *American Ethnologist*, 17(3): 513–30.

Forty, A. (2001) "Introduction," in A. Forty and S. Küchler (eds) *The Art of Forgetting*, Oxford: Berg Publishers.

Geertz, C. (1973) *The Interpretation of Cultures*, New York: Basic Books.

Heper, M., Öncü, A. and Kramer, H. (eds) (1993) *Turkey and the West: Changing Political and Cultural Identities*, London: I.B. Tauris.

Kushner, D. (1977) *The Rise of Turkish Nationalism, 1876–1908*, London: Cass Publishers.

Madran, E. (ed.) (1986) *Anıtkabir Rölöve Projesi [Anıtkabir Contour/Outline Project]*. Ankara: Middle East Technical University Architecture Faculty Press.

Meeker, M. (1997) "Once There Was, Once There Wasn't: National Monuments and Interpersonal Exchange," in S. Bozdoğan and R. Kasaba (eds) *Rethinking Modernity and National Identity in Turkey*, Seattle: University of Washington Press: 157–91.

Onat, E. and Arda, O. (1955) "Anıt-Kabir," *Arkitekt*, 280: 51–61 and 92–3.

Öz, Y. (trans.) (1982) *Quotations from Mustafa Kemal Atatürk*, from an original compilation in Turkish by Akıl Aksan, Ankara: Ministry of Foreign Affairs.

Özyürek, E. (2004) "Miniaturizing Atatürk: Privatization of State Imagery and Ideology in Turkey," *American Ethnologist*, 31(3): 374–91.

Poulton, H. (1997) *Top Hat, Grey Wolf and Crescent: Turkish Nationalism and the Turkish Republic*, London: Hurst & Company.

Republic of Turkey Official Gazette (1981), Law No. 2549, November 10, available online at www.mevzuat.adalet.gov.tr/html/568.html (last accessed June 21, 2006).

Schick, I.C. and Tonak, E.A. (eds) (1987) *Turkey in Transition: New Perspectives*, New York: Oxford University Press.

Skorupski, J. (1976) *Symbol and Theory: A Philosophical Study of Theories of Religion in Social Anthropology*, Cambridge: Cambridge University Press.

Smith, A.D. (1999) *Myths and Memories of the Nation*, Oxford: Oxford University Press.

Taylak, M. (ed.) (1998?) *Etnografya'dan Anıtkabir'e [From the Ethnographic Museum to Anıtkabir]*, Ankara: Şekerbank Kültür Yayınları [Şekerbank Cultural Publications], no. 7.

T.C. Genel Kurmay Başkanlığı [Ministry of the General Staff of Military Forces of the Turkish Republic] (1994) *Anıtkabir Tarihçesi [A Short History of Anıtkabir]*, Ankara: Genel Kurmay Baskanlığı.

Trigger, B.G. (1990) "Monumental Architecture: A Thermodynamic Explanation of Symbolic Behaviour," *World Archaeology*, 22(2): 119–32.

Republic of Turkey Official Gazette (2004) Law No. 25383, February 24.

Turkish Historical Society (2002) "Short History of the Society," [Brochure] available online at www.ttk.gov.tr/ingilizce/data/tarihce.html (accessed June 21, 2006).

Turkish Ministry of Culture (2006) "Anıtkabir (Atatürk Mausoleum)," available online at www.kultur.gov.tr/EN/BelgeGoster.aspx?17A16AE30572D313AC 8287D72AD903BEB361049FDD41AE45 (accessed June 21, 2006).

Volkan, V. and Itzkowitz, N. (1984) *The Immortal Atatürk: A Psychobiography*, Chicago: University of Chicago Press.

Wittek, P. (1958) *The Rise of the Ottoman Empire*, London: Royal Asiatic Society of Great Britain and Ireland.

Wooley, L. (1921) "Carchemish: Report on the Excavations at Jerablus on behalf of The British Museum – Part II: The Town Defences," London: The British Museum.

Young, J. (1993) *The Texture of Memory: Holocaust Memorials and Meaning*, New Haven: Yale University Press.

Zürcher, E. (1998) *Turkey: A Modern History*, London: I.B. Tauris.

7 Which 'nation' persists?

The competing notions of the Thai nation as reflected in public monuments

Andreas Sturm

Nationalist events, including parades and official festivals filled with pomp and ceremony, make it clear that nationalists consciously endeavour to project a unique and united nation. Bastille Day celebrations in France (see Elgenius in this volume), for example, project nothing less than the existence of a singular French nation which, beyond any political differences, is supported by all French citizens, regardless of social class; alternative interpretations of the nation are dismissed out of hand as the work of outsiders or, worse, traitors to the nation.

In this chapter, however, I will argue that the unified front presented by these national celebrations obscures the far more telling behind-the-scenes *process* of nations. Far from exemplars of consensus, nations are actually the result of ongoing contestation. Elite groups within at least some nations constantly engage in a vital and ongoing intellectual debate concerning how the nation should be presented. This constant reinterpretation and adaptation of the nation by elite groups ultimately produces distinguishably different nationalisms – a process of (re-)creation that perpetually revitalises the appeal of the nation to the majority of national citizens. This process of reinterpreting the nation is crucial for the persistence of the nation in the face of threats such as globalisation.

In an effort to illustrate this process, this chapter offers a careful study of the development of nation and nationalism in Thailand using an ethnosymbolist lens. The essay is divided into two parts. The first section focuses on three competing notions of Thai nation and nationalism: monarchical, political/statist and royal. The second section deals with monuments as reflections of these interpretations of the Thai nation. When combined, these two sections provide a vivid depiction of how elite debates help perpetuate the nation.

The competing notions of the Thai nation and nationalism

The current academic perception of Thai nation and nationalism is dominated by three main ideas. First, the Thai nation is a modern invention of royal elites and came into existence at the end of the nineteenth century with the help of nationalism. This nationalism was triggered by the aggressive behaviour of the colonial powers, especially the French gunboat policy in the so-called *Paknam* crisis of 1893. Categorised as 'royal nationalism', this nationalism, continues to the present (Thongchai 1998: ch. 8; Thongchai 2001: 57 and 62). Second, Thai elites constructed a nation in order to safeguard their claim to absolute power in the face of growing calls for democracy. Thai nationalism is therefore classified as an *official* nationalism (Anderson 2003: 99–101). Finally, the biggest challenge for the Thai nation and for Thai identity is globalisation and the development of cyberspace (Thongchai 1995: 37). Unfortunately, these three ideas suggest that, once created, Thai national identity remained static. Yet the reality is that Thai identity underwent frequent change and development – a fact that begs a new tactic for explaining Thai nationalism.

The ethno-symbolist approach offered by Anthony D. Smith provides a very useful starting point. According to Smith, nations (but not nationalism) did exist before the advent of modernity and are a result of a long process, not of a singular event; it is the 'nation' that precedes and determines 'nationalism' and not the other way round. For that reason, an analysis of nationalism should look into perceptions of the nation in different historical periods and the way in which members of a given nation develop their national sentiments. Nations have been able to persist through time because their component groups and individuals joined together to overcome dangers and to find a unique meaning and purpose through the development of national myths, symbols, and traditions. Further, the ethno-symbolist approach accepts that different interpretations of the nation can both coexist and compete with each other. John Hutchinson categorised these competing forces as political and cultural nationalisms whose rise and fall is part of an interactive cycle (1985: 426). Although all protagonists in the opposing camps lay claim to the 'same' nation, their views on descent, history, culture and tradition vary. Particularly interesting is the way in which myriad groups interpret the same set of symbols, myths and traditions at various times (Hutchinson 2001: 76–83).

If the ethno-symbolist model is applied to the Thai case, the following points become clear. First, although it is beyond the scope of this chapter to discuss the early development of Thai identity, elements of a pre-modern Thai nation can be found in the core area of central Thailand from the end of the sixteenth century onwards. If, as Smith suggests, the pre-modern nation was 'a named community possessing a historic territory, shared myths and memories, a common public culture and common laws and customs' (Smith 2002: 15), then the Thai nation was not invented by the Thai elite in the 1890s.

Next, because Thai nationalism was never static, it cannot be categorised as 'royal nationalism' throughout its history. Royal nationalism is usually defined by its use of the symbolic power of the monarchy to achieve national goals. Although coined by Tom Nairn to describe the United Kingdom, royal nationalism might also be applied to Japan in the second half of the nineteenth century. In both cases, nationalisms in the reign of Queen Victoria and in the time after the Meiji reforms were driven by the 'state' (Nairn 1988: 11).[1] Royal nationalism requires that the monarchy, the principal symbol of the nation, play a passive but cooperative role, strengthening the state (government and/or bureaucracy) by providing symbolic support, without yielding any real power. Over time, as the monarchy lost power, royal nationalism played a vital role in both democratisation and secularisation. In nineteenth-century Thailand, the same degree of transformation noted in Japan and Britain was present, but monarchy played a far more active role in developments. While the British state took control of the nation away from the monarchy, leaving Queen Victoria and her heirs to a largely symbolic role, Thai monarchs actively tried to create loyalty to the nation through the monarchy itself; it was the monarchy that used the state as a means to achieve this aim and not the converse. I see the Thai nation in the mid-nineteenth century as an essentially indigenous national group that I will term 'monarchical nation'. This nation developed its specific nationalism which could be termed 'monarchical nationalism'.[2] *Monarchical nationalism* is nationalism under the intellectual leadership of the monarch himself. It calls for a charismatic monarch who is able to bind the loyalty of the people to the nation that he personifies. The monarch is less the symbol of the nation than an embodiment of the nation. In monarchical nationalism the 'state' plays only a supportive role and a strong monarchy is required.

In another respect, Thai nationalism in the nineteenth century can hardly be categorised as 'official nationalism'. Anderson defined 'official nationalism' as 'a willed merger of nation and dynastic empire' developed 'by power groups threatened with exclusion from or marginalisation in popular imagined communities' (2003: 99 and 109). A merger would naturally require the existence of two distinctive elements but there was never such a distinction in the Thai case. The pre-modern Thai nation gradually developed from the sixteenth century and was always defined by the monarchy. During the nineteenth century Thai nationalism started to appear as an ideological movement within the royal elite. At that time, there was no 'popular imagined community' challenging the monarchy and therefore no need for a response. King Mongkut (r. 1851–68) used nationalism as a tool for intraelite struggle between himself and the nobility. Due to the lack of an anticolonial struggle that might have formed a unified nationalism, the intra-elite struggle inaugurated by Mongkut continued through the decades; Mongkut set the standard for his successors by promoting a nationalist ideology developed by the monarchs themselves.

To underline my argument concerning the different periods of the Thai nation and nationalism, I discuss public monuments that represented the specific nationalism of the ruling elite group of each period.

The three periods of the modern Thai nation and nationalism

The monarchical nation: Its nationalism, and its monuments (mid-nineteenth century–1932)

Undisturbed by direct colonisation, the pre-modern Thai nation developed into a unique entity compared with its neighbours in Southeast Asia. The Thai monarchical elite (royal family) *actively* sought to transform their kingdom into a modern nation by cultural renovation rather than revolution in order not to endanger the cultural essence of the existing society. This decision was not unusual because cultural processes in Southeast Asia generally followed the long-established principle of selective adaptation (Dahm 2001: 6). Traditional Thai kingship and Buddhism are both excellent examples of the integration of indigenous and foreign elements without the loss of a basic cultural identity. The Thai elite saw it as natural that the king was to be the embodiment of the modern nation, just as he was regarded to be at the centre of the universe in pre-modern times when the kingdom was seen as a terrestrial copy of the heavens.

Beginning in the mid-nineteenth century, Thai monarchs legitimated themselves in a new way. When Mongkut became king in 1851, the nobility's position was so powerful that it was they who chose candidates for the throne. Mongkut was selected because he had been a monk for decades and had neither a preexisting power base (such as the military) nor enough money to endanger the nobility. To break the dominance of the nobility, Mongkut decided to build up direct connections with the people, bypassing the control of 'people/manpower' by the nobles in the traditional organisation of society. Unlike former kings who had no contact with people outside their courts, Mongkut incorporated the masses into his monarchical nation by reviving the myth of the Kingdom of Sukhothai (founded in the thirteenth century) as the 'Golden Age' of Thainess and as a role model for modern kingship. He reintroduced its paternalistic kingship, where the monarch as 'father' has to look after his 'children'. To reach out to the common people, Mongkut organised traditional festivals and ceremonies that involved the public in grand spectacles. Mongkut's awareness of the importance of a public image distinguished him as the first Thai monarch to allow the people to look upon him openly. The king, therefore, was able to disseminate his idea of the monarchical nation long before the arrival of print-capitalism. The ideology of the monarchical nation and nationalism became more sophisticated over the decades and the power of the monarch increased tremendously during the reign of King Chulalongkorn (r. 1868–1910). With an implementation of a trans-ethnic idea of Thainess in monarchical nationalism, everybody, regardless of ethnic or religious background, could be Thai provided loyalty was given to the king.

In 1886, King Chulalongkorn erected the *anusawari prab ho*, a monument to commemorate the fallen soldiers of the campaign against the rebellious Ho Chinese who took control of several cities in the Mekong region between 1877 and 1886. Situated in the province of Nongkhai on the Mekong River, the monument was a traditional *chedi* (stupa) blended with Western design elements; it featured a pyramid in the centre and small transepts on all sides. Each of the four sides was decorated with a commemorative text in one of four languages – Thai, English, Chinese and Lao – that praised those who had died for their loyalty. The text promised that their 'name will be honoured forever' while also emphasising that they died 'with loyalty to the king, with braveness and without fear of death' (Krom Sinlapakon 1998: 125–9). Although this earliest nationalist monument did not portray the trans-ethnic idea fully formed, it is nevertheless significant that it was dedicated to the people.

Despite the populist dedication, the king was the focus of this narrative. The fallen soldiers became immortal first and foremost for their loyalty to the monarch and the nation. In addition, the use of four languages to present the commemorative texts speaks either to the monument's role as a border marker denoting the boundary between Thailand and French-controlled Laos or to its role as a symbol of the trans-ethnic nature of the monarchical nation. This polyglot monument intended to eulogise fallen heroes also invited readers of different ethnic backgrounds to become a subject/hero of the king as well. The monument was heavily influenced by European models and reflected a growing tendency to create monuments that 'invited' the people to join with the heart of the nation while using religious symbols to represent individuals rather than depending on a single hero, usually a general or other 'great man', as shorthand for the ordinary masses (Smith 2001: 580). This was a monument erected as a reaction to an external threat and was not a tool in the intra-elite power struggle.

The king's idea of a monarchical nation became clearer in 1887 when he organised an exhibition during a royal cremation ceremony in Bangkok. The exhibition, which could be interpreted as a kind of mobile monument, featured 92 paintings depicting events from Thai history. Every painting was accompanied by poems designed to explain whichever episode was depicted graphically. Chulalongkorn, writing many of the poems himself, basically introduced a 'national history' aimed at the masses that attended the funeral. The main theme of the exhibition was the defence of the nation by the heroic deeds of former kings, civil servants and common people. The king argued in these poems that the past *barami* ('perfection'/charisma) of a monarch was not enough by itself to prove his claim to the throne. The king must constantly acquire new *barami* by doing beneficial deeds for the people (Chulachomklaojuhua 1983: 21). To underline his point, Chulalongkorn ordered that leftover wood from the royal pyres be used to build the Siriraj Hospital (Chulachomklaojuhua 1983: 4–5). The hospital on the bank of Chaophraya River, named after the king's dead son, can be interpreted as a monument of the benevolent monarchy. It also became the blueprint for future monuments of the monarchical nation: a connection between the monarchy and their humanitarian deeds.

One of the most important monuments erected during the monarchical nation period is the equestrian statue of King Chulalongkorn (*phraborom-rachanusawari phrapiyamaharat*) in Bangkok. The statue, the first public depiction of a human being (except Buddha) in Thailand, was unveiled with a big ceremony in 1908.[3] Besides the current incumbent King Bhumibol, King Chulalongkorn was the most beloved Thai monarch ever. The feelings of the people towards their monarch were expressed by the donation of a large sum of money to build the monument and the surrounding plaza on the occasion of a celebration marking Chulalongkorn's status as the longest reigning monarch in Thai history. Crown Prince Vajiravudh dedicated the monument in the name of the people. During his speech, he connected the monument with the idea of the monarchical nation:

> [King Chulalongkorn's] reign is a record in the history of the Siamese nation that surpasses those by all previous sovereigns, from ancient Ayutthaya down to the present. The statue is a testimony for future generations of shared feelings which shall forever stand as a national monument of our heartfelt devotion to Your Royal Person.
>
> (cited in Peleggi 2003: 4)

Chulalongkorn placed his statue at the heart of a new square which was to be the centre of Bangkok and therefore symbolically the focal point of the kingdom/monarchical nation. The king, portrayed as an elegant and West-ernised horseman, was the embodiment of this nation. The statue became an object of veneration and its surrounding plaza was used for important state ceremonies as well as a place for relaxation: a role that the plaza began to play once more during the 1990s when rapid economic growth sent many Thais looking for emotional and spiritual comfort.

King Vajiravudh (r. 1910–25) followed most of the basic ideas of monar-chical nationalism and erected monuments that were beneficial to the popu-lation. A good example is the establishment of Chulalongkorn University. In 1910, Vajiravudh used the leftover money from the equestrian statue to introduce new departments such as medicine and engineering to the School for Royal Servants. In 1915 the name of the school was changed to Chula-longkorn University with the intention of making it a monument for King Chulalongkorn. In January 1915, at a ceremonial placement of the founda-tion stone for one of the new university buildings, Vajiravudh declared that, while Chulalongkorn had never achieved his goal of creating a university for the Siamese people:

> it is my duty as his son to make his wish come true. When it is finished it will be the royal monument to remember him. It is necessary to con-

struct this big and permanent royal monument as it will be the benefit for the Thai nation eternally.

(Chulalongkorn University 1997: 347–8)

While King Vajiravudh endeavoured to reflect his father's conception of the monarchical nation, his actions inadvertently lessened the appeal of monarchical nationalism by introducing elements of a competing brand of nationalism – political nationalism. Rather than focusing exclusively on the monarch as national totem, Vajiravudh emphasised the Thai race and civilisation. By giving utmost significance to the nation, an act symbolised by his slogan 'Nation-Religion-King', Vajiravudh weakened the position of the monarchy. The subtle rhetorical change opened the door to at least one oppositional group who used the new formulation to legitimise their demands for an abolition of the absolute monarchy, claiming that it was necessary to change the system of government out of love for the nation.

The political nation and its monuments (1932–50s)

In the 1920s, the absolute monarchy faced increasing political opposition within the civil and military bureaucracy. Initiated by Western-trained military and civil officials, a new vision of the nation emerged: a nation with a constitution as its centre and greatly influenced by Western ideas. A *coup d'état* brought the era of absolute monarchy to an end in 1932. The initial plan of the coup promoters was to build a national identity based on constitutionalism. Seen as 'quasi-holy relic', the constitution was declared the 'soul of the country' (*mingkhwam*) (Chai-anan 1989: 256). However, the events in Europe and East Asia in the 1930s and the apparent success of authoritarian regimes, supported the emergence of the 'statist' vision of the political nation initiated by Phibul Songkhram, who became Prime Minister in 1938, and his intellectual associate Luang Vichit Wadakarn. The nation was to be represented by a strong state, ruled by a 'leader' (*phunam*). To strengthen the state, Phibul wanted a total redesign of Thai culture. In his opinion, Thai identity did not originate from Buddhist culture but from the civil tradition deeply rooted in the cultural heritage of all Thais. Phibul did not hesitate to eliminate traditions and ceremonies, one example being the abolition of prostration and crawling in front of the royal family. Next, he introduced the state cultural laws known as *ratthaniyom* ('Cultural Mandates of the State'), the 12 Cultural Mandates in which the government prescribed how people must behave. There was no room for regional cultures or traditions of minorities in Phibul's new Thainess.

Phibul and his followers should be categorised as 'statist nationalists' due to their emphasis on the state. Similar to other systems of *statism*, the leaders of the Thai state in this period aimed 'to control ... economic and social affairs' (McLean 1996: 477; Breuilly 2001: 786). They did not understand the state as a purely rational entity, as in Schiller's famous comparison with a machine (Kedourie 2000: ch. 3), but rather fostered a more emotional view. Therefore, the term *statist nationalism* takes into consideration this altered form of *statism* and should be understood as a subcategory of political nationalism. According to Hutchinson, political nationalists are people who

> perceive the nation in rationalist terms as a homogenous collectivity of educated citizens. They wish for a state representative of the nation that will break with tradition and raise the people to the level of the advanced 'scientific' cultures. Although essentially modernist, they appeal to historic ethnic sentiments in an instrumental fashion in order to mobilize religious and rural support for their goal (1985: 426).

This nationalism was mirrored in monuments erected by the Thai government in the 1930s and 1940s.

In 1936, the first public monument of the political nation, the *Monument for the Protection of the Constitution* (*anusawari phitak ratthatammanun*) was unveiled. Its function was to commemorate the victory of government forces against royalist rebels in 1933. The monument is in the shape of a bullet with the constitution laid on top. Its decoration includes images of a farmer's family and the wheel of Dharma, symbolising the willingness of the state to defend the constitution, the Thai people, and Buddhism (Krom Sinlapakon 1998: 191–3).

The most famous landmarks from this period are the *Democracy Monument* (*anusawari prachatipatai*) and the *Victory Monument* (*anusawari chaisamoraphum*) in Bangkok. While the first was to celebrate the introduction of democracy in Thailand, the latter was constructed after the outbreak of armed skirmishes with French troops in 1940 on the border to Indochina and the subsequent retrieval of territories originally lost during the colonial period. Heroic realism dominates this monument, centred on a huge obelisk. Five lifesize bronze figures are at the base, displaying the activities of army, navy, air force, police and civilians. The purpose of the monument was to evoke nationalist feelings against an outside enemy and to represent the new role of Thai citizens in contrast to their former role as subjects. At the opening ceremony in 1942, Phibul asserted:

> This Victory Monument will eternally remind all Thais that this country successfully retrieved its honour by the hands of the Thai heroes of the five groups namely the army, the navy, the air force, the police and the civilians. This important monument, apart from being a memorial to the glory of the Thai heroes, it implants [the idea] in the next generation of Thais to have perseverance, patience and braveness and to be without fear of dying for retrieving the honour of the nation. It also implants the perfect love of the nation as well. Every time our fellow countrymen pass by this monument, they will remember all this goodness. The Victory Monument is the destination of the solidarity of all

the Thai people to integrate and to preserve the Thainess of Thailand forever.

(cited in Chatri 2005: 81)

Phibul's words make it clear that the Victory Monument is an excellent reflection of statist nationalism in the political nation.

Had it been constructed, the *Thai Monument* (*anusawari thai*) might have embodied the fullest representation of the political nation possible. The monument was designed as a huge stupa with a base length of 100 metres on each side. It was to be surrounded by buildings that were intended to house an economic museum to showcase products, a restaurant and ball-room, a hotel and a conference centre. Foreign guests were supposed to feel, in the words of project leader Luang Vichit, 'immediately how prosperous our country is' (cited in Chatri 2004: 383). This stupa was not supposed to have any religious function but was solely to create the feeling of national-ism. It was the combination of a building in the style of a stupa, represent-ing Thainess, and the modern amenities representing progress, that was revolutionary. Vichit enthused:

> When the Thai Monument is finished it will not only be the most important and lasting piece in Thailand but could be one of the 'wonders-of-the-world' in terms of culture and art. We can show the world the history of Thai architecture in a way no one or no king could ever do. If we can build this monument in our period this will be a great and lasting honour for us. King Chulalongkorn invested five million Baht to build the Anantasamakhom Throne Hall without benefit for the glory of the nation. This monument will be for the glory of the nation and of us.
>
> (cited in Chatri 2004: 383)

Budget cuts assured that all plans to build the monument were scrapped.

No matter how much Phibul attempted to create statist nationalism as seen through these monuments, he was not able to replace the monarchy with the state as the focus for loyalty to the nation. Underestimating the emotional appeal and sacred dimension of the monarch, Phibul failed to con-vince the masses about his idea of the nation. An incident in 1948 was a good indicator of the collapse of Phibul's statist nationalism. When an exhi-bition of statues of King Chulalongkorn and Phibul were presented in a government shop, it was heavily criticised by visitors because the statues were the same height and were placed on the same level. The criticism was so intense that the government had to publish an explanation in the news-papers stressing that the display was not intended to be a scale representa-tion of the 'real' figures depicted (Chatri 2005: 195).

The period of royal nationalism and its monuments (1950s–1970s)

After the Second World War, the leaders of the political nation found a new cause to help unite the Thai people: the American-led struggle against Communism. Communism was regarded as un-Thai and seen as a vehicle for a foreign takeover the country. The huge amount of US money pouring into Thailand enabled a new group inside the military and civil bureaucracy to build a power base on their own. Led by Field Marshall Sarit Thanarat, this faction ousted Phibul and took control of the state in 1957. Having a different vision of the nation from their predecessors, the new regime acknowledged that the Thai nation was best unified by the symbolism of the monarchy. Sarit was willing to support the young King Bhumibol (r. 1946–) in various activities as long as those activities were beneficial to Sarit's government while leaving Bhumibol with only a symbolic role.

In the anti-Communist atmosphere, the proponents of royal nationalism started to erect monuments featuring historical royal heroes who had reportedly fought against intruders at various points in the past. One of these champions was the warrior King Naresuan who restored the sovereignty of the Kingdom of Ayutthaya after it had been lost to the Burmese in the sixteenth century. His monument (*phraboromrachanusawari somdetphranaresuanmaharat*), unveiled in Suphanburi province in 1959, is located on the battlefield where the struggle between the Ayutthayan king and the crown prince of Burma reportedly occurred. Naresuan is depicted on a war elephant in an attacking pose with his weapon ready to strike. The statue faces the Burmese border in the west (Krom Sinlapakon 1998: 25–9). The monument aimed to inflame patriotism against an external enemy, using historical figures to remind Thais of their obligation to fight for the nation in the manner of their ancestors.

In the late 1960s, royal nationalism came under increased pressure from left-leaning intellectuals because of its close relationship with military dictatorship under Prime Minister Thanom Kittikachorn. A democratic period between 1973 and 1976 resulted in political turmoil and convinced various elite groups that only a firm stance against Communism would save the country from becoming another domino in the international Communist conspiracy. This time previously competing elite groups started to cooperate to ensure the survival of their respective visions of the Thai nation.

The growing cooperation of elites led to an expansion of commemorative activities to include ordinary people as well as historical figures. This change resulted in one of the most unusual monuments in Thailand: the *Monument of the Bangrachan Heroes* (*anusawari wirachonkhaibangrachan*), which was erected in Singburi province in 1976. Depicting a group of villagers with water buffalo and all kinds of homemade weapons attacking the Burmese while yelling full throated war-cries, this monument was to commemorate the heroic struggle of villagers during the Burmese invasion in 1767 (Krom

Sinlapakon 1998: 424–9). According to national myth, the villagers, although small in number, fought the foreign invaders to the last man. The aim of the monument was to re-create the spirit of the battle of Bangrachan and to motivate the Thai population to help the government fight against the Communist 'intruder'.

The *Monument for the Heroic Deeds of Civilians, Policemen and Soldiers* (*anusawari wirakamphonlaruen tamruat tahan*), a war memorial unveiled in the northern province of Nan in 1976, is another striking example in the struggle against foreign invaders. The installation is located in one of the most embattled areas between Communist and government forces and depicts one soldier, one policeman and one civilian erecting a flagpole with the Thai national flag on it (Krom Sinlapakon 1998: 419–23). The government aimed to show that the province was Thai territory and all Thais were working together to defend the land even if they had to sacrifice their lives. The monument was intended to emphasise that Communism was un-Thai.

Other monuments from this period frequently represented the brother of King Rama I, Prince Mahasurasinghanat, a famous general who was crucial to the defeat of the Burmese and the unification of the country during the reign of King Taksin (r. *c.*1767–82). The main statue was erected at Mahathat Temple, facing the royal plaza in Bangkok in 1979. The statue (*phrabowonrachanusawari somdetphra bowonraratchao mahasurasinghanat*) depicts the general standing with folded hands while offering his sword (Krom Sinlapakon 1998: 291–4). Viewers might interpret the general's stance as suggesting his desire to protect Buddhism or, in this context, the land of Buddhism, though the orientation of the statue in the direction of the royal plaza also indicates dedication to both monarchy and nation. Construction of the figure was executed on the initiative of Admiral Sa-ngad Chaloryu who led two *coup d'états* in 1976 and 1977 and the statue could be seen as a personal justification for his actions while also proving his loyalty to the king. This monument aimed to rekindle the spirit of the fighting ancestors, a spirit now so desperately needed in the fight against Communism.

The revival of monarchical nationalism as reflected in monuments (1980s–2000)

The breakdown of the military and bureaucratic dictatorship in the 1970s led to a philosophical shift among a new generation of military leaders. They ousted ultra-conservative colleagues and offered a fresh approach to solving the problem of insurgency inside the country. Prime Minister Prem Thinsunalonda (1980–8), a close associate of King Bhumibol, supported the growth of civil society by stressing a democratic and just state with the king as its centre. King Bhumibol's own vision of the nation as a moral society with a self-sufficient economy was exemplified by the execution of thousands of royal projects designed to improve the wellbeing and prosperity of the people. He also promoted a trans-ethnic approach to Thainess by visiting and supporting ethnic minorities such as hill tribes and the Muslim population in the far south. In his eyes, as long as a citizen was loyal to the king, he was loyal to the Thai nation as well. The economic crisis of 1997 gave his idea of the nation a significant boost when the king's leadership was called upon to provide emotional reassurance to the people. Following in the footsteps of the absolute monarchs, Bhumibol made an effort to promote his vision of the nation by endeavouring to embody the nation, not just symbolise it.

The activities of the king together with changing attitudes among a new generation of military and political elites led to a revival of the monarchical nation that was reflected in the design of new monuments. At first, the construction of monuments to historic heroes continued, but gradually designs grew milder and less aggressive. The memorial commemorating those who sacrificed their lives in the battlefields of Khao Kor in the northern province of Phetchabun (*anusawari phusiasalakhaoko*) is an excellent example of the new monumental style. The installation consists of a tall obelisk housing a small museum in its basement. Not only was the shape less aggressive, the inclusion of a museum celebrating all participants in the battle illustrated the Thai government's acknowledgment that Communists were Thais as well and were worthy of reintegration into Thai society. The monument reflected policy order 66/2523, issued in 1980 under Prime Minister Prem (Krom Sinlapakon 1998: 159–63). According to the directive, the state would target Communism using political and not military means; for example, an amnesty was granted to Communist fighters and supporters.

Officials adopted a similar approach in 1990 when developing a memorial to war dead in Tak province (*anusawari phusiasala*). The monument is designed in a traditional stupa form, with bas-reliefs depicting soldiers as protectors of religion, farmers, families, development and education. Once more, the government insisted on a neutral depiction of combatants from both sides because 'the conflict was between Thais who all loved the Thai nation but had different ideas of how to develop it. This monument should therefore not blame any side' (Krom Sinlapakon 1998: 153–7).

Yet the most significant change in monumental form since the 1990s was the revival of monuments depicting the monarch as a benevolent father who cares for the well-being of his children.

The King Rama VIII Bridge (*saphan phra ram 8*) over the Chaopraya River in Bangkok stands as one of the most outstanding examples of modern monarchical monuments. The bridge was opened under the watchful eye of the king himself on Chulalongkorn Day (23 October) in 2002 (Sayamrat 26. 9. 2001: 12). The whole idea behind the bridge and its design mirrored the shifting presentation of the nation toward the monarchical ideal.

In 1993, the king initiated the construction of a new bridge to tackle the city's notorious traffic problems. The king himself determined the placement of the structure and also insisted that it be named after his elder brother, King Ananda Mahidol or King Rama VIII (r. 1935–46). From the first blueprint, the project was to be a 'royal memorial' and a 'royal gift'. Ultimately, the project's 300-metre span proved an impressive technical feat while the design became a showcase for Thai art. The royal seal of King Ananda inspired the theme of the bridge. In the seal, Phra Bhodhisatva (a future Buddha) sits on a lotus blossom with his right foot on a smaller lotus blossom (symbolising 'land') and his left hand holding an unopened lotus flower, while a crystal palace in the background symbolises radiating light. The bridge design reflects this seal through the addition of a glass observation deck with metal frames in the shape of an ornamental closed lotus. The shape of the 165-metre high pylon is based on the crystal palace of Phra Bodhisatva, while the anchor span for the stay cables is decorated with a lotus blossom motif using four different materials to symbolise unity between the four regions of Thailand. Beyond this, the design includes traditional *bai sri* ceremonial trays at the foot of the bridge meant to illustrate deep reverence for the institution of monarchy.

Beyond the bridge itself, the King Ananda Bridge project also includes a park and museums, one to commemorate the king and one for regional arts and crafts (Manas 2002: 47–118). The bridge can be interpreted as a symbol of the king's ideal of Thai national identity, representing the monarchy and Thai culture in a modern world. On the occasion of the opening of the bridge, the Thai Post Office issued a special series of stamps featuring four 'royal' bridges. This ensured that the meaning of the bridge as a monarchical monument was disseminated all over the country ("Maihet stamp thai 2004: 21").

Parks represent very popular monuments to the monarchical nation. 'The Princess Mother Memorial Park' (*uthayan chaloemphrakiat somdechphrasri-nakarintharaboromratchonnani*), located on the other side of the Chaophraya River in Thonburi, is an excellent example.[4] It was built on King Bhumibol's initiative in 1993 to restore an old building in the area where his mother lived during her childhood. The park is in the middle of a densely populated area and aims to give the visitor a respite from the heat and noise of the surrounding city. Besides being a recreational zone, the park also functions as a place for carrying out rituals and activities (Munnithi Chaipathana 1996: 57). The space was opened to the public in 1996 and includes two exhibition halls. The first hall celebrates the life of the Princess Mother and shows the history of the local community, depicted by the official brochure as a 'multi-racial and multi-religious society living together in perfect harmony' (Princess Mother Memorial Park, no date: 6). The second hall focuses on the Princess Mother's activities and conduct. Further, a full-scale model of the Princess Mother's house, very simply furnished, gives the visitor the impression that she was a modest person living like an ordinary Thai. Two elements at the centre of this park, however, make it an important monument to monarchical nationalism. The first element is a great two-sided bas-relief. The first side portrays the development and welfare activities of the Princess Mother, including her 'flying-doctor' service to remote parts of the country, while the other side shows a traditional procession of northern people both celebrating and honouring the Princess Mother. The second element is a central plaza, regularly used for free concerts, overlooked by an octagonal pavilion with a lifesize statue of the Princess Mother. The statue shows the Princess Mother in a benevolent pose, looking at the people to whom she gave this relaxing and pleasant park; in return, almost every visitor pays respect to her statue. The park management organises activities designed to provide useful knowledge, including occupational training and cultural and traditional handicraft (Princess Mother Memorial Park, no date: 14). According to the Royal Chaipathana Foundation:

> This park should be considered a historical park, so that future genera-
> tions will be able to reminisce about the 'Princess Mother of the Thai
> people' who performed her activities for the benefit of the people. It will
> also be a symbol of His Majesty the King's most devoted kindness to
> provide a place where everyone can come and relax.
>
> (Munnithi Chaipathana 1996: 61)

Conclusion

Which 'nation' persists? Judging from the popularity of the monuments, the 'monarchical nation' is the most vivid representation of the Thai nation. Due to their beneficial function, many people use monarchical sites on a daily basis and so are constantly reminded of the deeds of the various monarchs. Monuments depicting 'royal nationalism' are sometimes used for ceremonies, though these events seem to celebrate a specific individual and do not appear to embody the original goal of the monument itself: the strengthening of Thai patriotism. Monuments of the political nation are the least popular. Some monuments, such as the Democracy Monument, were reinterpreted and are now understood in a totally different context. Other monuments of the political nation such as the Victory Monument are now seen as traffic obstacles. Rare ceremonies, such as on Veterans' Day, receive little attention from the media or the public.

The Thai case shows that a constant reinterpretation of the nation by various elite groups is strengthening the ability of the nation to resist challenges. The development of the Thai nation and its nationalisms indicates that the form of nationalism that appeals to common traditions, myths and symbols is most successful, while also pointing out that 'a nation is never an affair of a single generation, a nation is by its nature a transgenerational entity' (Shils 1995: 100). Because the Thai nation itself was formed over a long period of time, traditions, myths and symbols are the most powerful instruments for creating loyalty to the nation due to their emotional resonance. The Thai nation also persisted so effectively because there was no all-dominating theme such as the fight for independence which is found in most neighbouring countries. What could be understood as a hindrance toward successful mobilisation of the masses turned out to be a strength, closely fitted to a Thai emphasis on the value of flexibility and adaptation to changing circumstances. Challenges such as the current wave of globalisation are answered by a change in popular interpretation of the nation.

At its core, the persistence of the Thai nation seems to be secured for the near future. It remains to be seen, how future nationalisms will be reflected in public monuments.

Notes

1 For similar arguments see Arblaster (1989) and Hobsbawm (1983). For Japan see Breuilly (1993).
2 Monarchical nationalism in Thailand should be categorised as a type of 'cultural' nationalism. Hutchinson defined cultural nationalists as people 'who perceive the nation not as a state but as a distinctive historical community, which continuously evolving, embodies a higher synthesis of the "traditional" and the "modern"' (1985: 486).
3 The first statue of a monarch in Thailand was produced during the reign of King Mongkut; it was, however, not on public display. The first statue of a ruler on public display was, ironically, a foreign ruler: Queen Victoria. Her statue was placed in front of the British consulate in Chiang Mai. See the photograph taken by the German biologist Carl Hossens (1912: 299).
4 A similar project but on a much larger scale was finalised recently in the east of Bangkok: 'The Royal Park of King Rama IX' (*Suan Luang Ro 9*).

References

Anderson, B. (1991; revised edn 2003) *Imagined Communities: Reflections on the Origin and Spread of Nationalism*, London: Verso.
Arblaster, A. (1989) 'Taking Monarchy Seriously', *New Left Review*, 174: 97–110.
Breuilly, J. (1993) *Nationalism and the State*, 2nd edn, Manchester: Manchester University Press.
—— (2001) 'The State', in Alexander Motyl (ed.) *Encyclopaedia of Nationalism*, San Diego: Academic Press: 769–92.
Chai-anan, S. (1989) 'Political Institutionalization in Thailand: Continuity and Change', in R. Scalapino, S. Sato and J. Wanandi (eds) *Asian Political Institutionalization*, Berkeley: University of California Press: 241–60.
Chatri, P. (2004) *Kanmueang lae sangkhom nai sinlapa sathapattayakam sayam samai thai prayuk chatniyom* [Politics and Society in Arts and Architecture in the Periods of Modern Siam], Bangkok: Matichon.
—— (2005), *Khanaratsadon chalong ratthammanun: prawattisat kanmueang lang 2475 phan sathapattayakam 'amnat'* [The Kana Ratsadon Celebrating the Constitution: Political History after 1932 as Seen through the Architecture of 'Power'], Bangkok: Matichon.
Chulachomklaochaoy[j]uhua, P. (reprint 1983) *Klong pap phraratchaphongsawadan* [Poetry Depicting the Paintings from the Royal Chronicles], Bangkok: Amarin Printing.
Chulalongkorn University (1997), *Nangsue Mahawitthayalai* [University Annual Book], Bangkok: Chulalongkorn University.

Dahm, B. (2001) 'Cultural Traditions and the Struggle for Nationhood in Asia', paper Presented at the sixteenth IAHA-Conference at the University Malaysia Sabah, Kota Kinabalu, July 2001.

Hobsbawm, E. (1983; reprint 1996) 'Mass-Producing Traditions: Europe, 1870–1914', in E. Hobsbawm and T. Ranger (eds) *The Invention of Traditions*, Cambridge: Cambridge University Press: 263–307.

Hossens, C. (1912) *Durch König Tschulalongkorns Reich*, Stuttgart: Strecker & Schröder.

Hutchinson, J. (1985) *The Dynamics of Cultural Nationalism: The Gaelic Revival in Late Nineteenth and Early Twentieth Century Ireland*, unpublished thesis, London School of Economics.

—— (2001) 'Nations and Culture', in M. Guibernau and J. Hutchinson (eds) *Understanding Nationalism*, Cambridge: Polity Press: 74–96.

Kedourie, E. (2000) *Nationalism*, 4th edn, Oxford: Basil Blackwell.

Krom Sinlapakon (1998) *Anusawari nai prathet thai* [Monuments in Thailand], Bangkok: Department of Fine Arts.

McLean, I. (ed.) (1996) *The Concise Oxford Dictionary of Politics*, Oxford: Oxford University Press.

'Maihet stamp thai [Remarks on Thai Stamps]' (2004) *Warasan Trapraisaniyakon*, 12 July, 34: 21.

Manas Kowanich (2002) *Saphan phraram 8 – an nueng ma chak phraratchadamri* [Rama VIII Bridge under the Royal Initiatives], Bangkok: Bangkok Municipality Administration.

Munnithi Chaipathana (1996) 'The Park in Commemoration of Her Royal Highness the Princess Mother', *Munnithi Chaipathana*: 52–61.

Nairn, T. (1988) *The Enchanted Glass*, London: Century Hutchinson.

Peleggi, M. (2003) 'Siam/Looking Back – Thailand/Looking Forward: King Chulalongkorn in Thai Collective Memory', Paper presented at the Conference 'King Rama 5: Siam and Southeast Asia', Bangkok: Maha Chakri Sirindhorn Anthropology Centre.

Shils, E. (1995) 'Nation, Nationality, Nationalism, and Civil Society', *Nations and Nationalism*, 1(1): 93–118.

Smith, A. (2001) 'Will and Sacrifice: Images of National Identity', *Millennium: Journal of International Studies*, 30(3): 571–82.

—— (2002) 'When Is a Nation?', *Geopolitics*, 7(2): 5–32.

Winichakul, T. (1994, reprint 1998) *Siam Mapped – A History of the Geo-body of a Nation*, Honolulu: University of Hawaii Press.

—— (1995) 'Chat thai, mueang thai lae nithi iaosiwong [Thai Nation, Thailand and Nidhi Aeusrivongse]' in Nidhi Aeusrivongse, *Chat thai mueang thai baep rian lae anusawari wa duai watthanatham rat lae rupkan chitsamnuek*, Bangkok: Matichon Press.

8 The cross, the Madonna and the Jew

Persistent symbolic representations of the nation in Poland

Geneviève Zubrzycki

Every nation has its myth of foundation: its linked plots of growth and development, crisis and resistance, doom, victory and rebirth. These myths change over time, with the times, but always remain, their origins occluded; it is in that sense that nations are timeless. The most common and pervasive Polish myth is that of Poland's intrinsic Catholicity: *Polonia semper fidelis* (Poland always faithful), the bulwark of Christendom defending Europe against the infidel (however defined); the Christ of nations, martyred for the sins of the world and resurrected for the world's salvation; a nation whose identity is conserved and guarded by its defender, the Roman Catholic Church, and shielded by its Queen, the miraculous Black Madonna, Our Lady of Częstochowa; a nation that has given the world a pope and rid the Western world of Communism. If this representation is a caricature of the myth, it is, like all caricatures, distorted only by the picture being drawn with rather over-sharp angles.

This chapter analyzes Polish national identity and its association with Catholicism through a study of key symbols and core narratives: the cross and Poland as Christ of nations, the Black Madonna of Częstochowa, and the Jew as prime "Other." These symbolic representations were brought to bear in a recent crisis at Auschwitz, when in the summer and fall of 1998 self-defined "Poles-Catholics" erected hundreds of crosses just outside the former death camp. The "war of the crosses," as I call the event, materialized and crystallized, within a single site and series of events, social conflicts regarding the role of Catholicism in defining Polishness, the place of religion and the Church in the new polity, and the role of anti-Semitism in the construction and affirmation of Polish national identity. The controversy had two interlaced layers: the most evident is the ongoing Polish–Jewish conflict over the memory of Auschwitz, and the Christian–Judaic dispute about the presence of the cross at this site of the Shoah. The second layer concerned the meaning of the cross in post-Communist Poland and involved, more broadly, a debate among Poles about the appropriateness of the association between Polishness and Catholicism in an independent Poland. It is on this second layer of the controversial cross-planting action that I focus here.[1] I first analyze the use of the cross by ultra-nationalist "Poles-Catholics" at

Auschwitz and examine the meaning of the cross in the discourses of multiple communities in Poland. The war of the crosses serves as a window through which I analyze the persistence and transformation of national symbolizations and the reconfiguration of the nation–religion relation in post-Communist Poland.

The war of the crosses and religio-national scripts

The controversial cross-planting action was spurred by rumors regarding the possible removal of an eight-meter high cross, popularly known as the "papal cross," standing proudly just outside Auschwitz, in the backyard of what had been, from 1984 to 1993, a Carmelite convent (Figure 8.1).[2]

In June 1998, Kazimierz Świtoń, a former Solidarity activist, initiated a hunger strike that lasted 42 days, demanding a firm commitment from the Catholic Church that the papal cross would remain.[3] After failing to secure such a commitment, Świtoń appealed to his fellow Poles to plant 152 crosses on the grounds of the former convent, the so-called gravel pit, both to commemorate the deaths of 152 ethnic Poles executed at that specific site in 1941 and to "protect and defend the papal cross." This appeal proved successful: during the summer and fall of 1998, the gravel pit in Oświęcim[4] was transformed into the epicenter of the war of the crosses, as individuals, civic organizations and religious groups from every corner of Poland (and from as far away as Canada, the United States and Australia) answered Świtoń's call to create a "valley of crosses," encouraged by the popular and controversial radio station Radio Maryja.[5] During that summer, the site became the stage for prayer vigils, Masses, political demonstrations and general nationalist agitation. It was the destination of choice for pilgrims, journalists and tourists in search of a sacred cause, a good story or a free show, respectively. Religious images of the national Madonna (Our Lady of Częstochowa), as well as secular symbols like red and white Polish flags and coats-of-arms with the Polish white eagle wearing a crown,[6] commonly adorned the crosses and added to their symbolic weight and complexity. The papal cross itself was transformed into an improvised altar, with flowers, candles and small flags spread at its foot. The fence surrounding the area, where crowds of the curious gathered to observe the spectacle, was likewise covered with political banners and flowers. By the time the Polish army finally removed them in May 1999, there were a total of 322 crosses at the gravel pit (Figure 8.2). The papal cross, however, remained, and is still standing. There was thus no resolution of the initial conflict concerning the presence of that specific cross.

As we shall see, individual actors taking part in the war of the crosses were the authors of a tableau borrowing, in its narrative script and symbolic form, the core narrative of Polish Catholicism and Poles' martyrdom. That narrative was forcefully created in the nineteenth century by Romantic poets who equated the Partitions of Poland with its crucifixion.[7] Poland, in these

Figure 8.1 Papal cross at the gravel pit. The large brick building in the background is Auschwitz I's Block 15, the so-called Block of Death, where prisoners were tortured and executed at a nearby shooting wall. Next to the cross is a placard with the words "Defend the Cross," spoken by John Paul II during a homily in Zakopane in 1997 (source: photograph courtesy of the Auschwitz-Birkenau Museum).

Figure 8.2 Papal cross surrounded by smaller crosses planted in the summer of 1998 on the invitation of Kazimierz Świtoń (source: photograph courtesy of the Auschwitz-Birkenau Museum).

writings, was the Christ of nations: sacrificed for the sins of the world, it would be brought back to life to save humanity from absolutism. This representation of Poland's political situation rapidly left the confines of literature to be part of popular culture: religious holidays such as Easter, for example, became the occasion to commemorate Poland's "crucifixion" and pray for its resurrection.[8] The Virgin Mary was represented in prayers, songs and art as the crucified nation's protectress and comforter. The icon of the lady of Częstochowa, by far the most popular virgin of the lands of partitioned Poland, resonated with special intensity. Her scarred face and the miracles associated with her represented Poland's mutilation and gave hope for national independence. She had saved Poland from the Swedish invasion during the Deluge (1655–60); she could certainly defend the nation from the Muscovite and German tyrants. With Poland transformed into Christ of nations, the cross was metamorphosed into a core Polish symbol representing the plight of the nation and its imminent salvation *qua* independence.

This representation of the Polish fate became canonical, securely anchored in national self-understanding, and it resurfaced with special intensity under Communism. Catholicism and the Catholic Church were portrayed by the opposition as the basis of a moral community fighting an evil totalitarian regime imposed from outside and from above, and succeeded in providing a powerful narrative of the nation, one able to mobilize support against the party-state. The narrative evoked a glorious past and carried emotionally loaded analogies between present misery and the painful experience of the Partitions. It was built around Poland's historical suffering and the alleged role of the Church in the nation's survival, the notion of Poland as chosen people (*lud polski ludem Bożym* – "the Polish people is God's people") and of Poland as *Antemurale Christianitatis*, defending Europe against the infidel (Islam in the seventeenth century, atheist Soviets in the twentieth). The iconography of national identity and resistance to the oppressive foreign regime emphasized symbols traditionally associated with the nation, such as the miraculous Black Madonna of Częstochowa, as well as motifs taken from the Passion, such as the cross and the crown of thorns (Osa 1996; Rogozińska 2002: 28).[9] The cross especially was a significant symbol of collective fate which, together with other symbols, gestures and practices, provided a frame to organize resistance to the regime and created a language to express rebellion against it. Crosses were frequently carried during political manifestations, and it is with three giant crosses that the victims of the 1970 strikes were memorialized a decade later, a demand explicitly formulated by the Gdańsk shipyard strikers on August 14, 1980.[10]

Poles' "singular secular gospel," as literary critics Maria Janion and Maria Żmigrodzka (1978: 10) call this specific form of Romantic messianism, was especially mobilizing in the context of statelessness; when identities could not be constructed through legitimate national institutions, such as during the Partitions (1795–1918) and during Communism (1945–89). With an independent state recovered in 1989, would Poland be a nation with the cross, or without?

The crosses of Auschwitz as iconography of pain and Polishness

The great majority of the crosses brought to the gravel pit in Oświęcim bore a small commemorative plaque indicating the name and prisoner number of the victim in whose memory the cross was being erected, or a specific slogan, message, poem, biblical inscription or testimony: Defend the Cross; For God and Fatherland; Only Poland. Most of them were signed by their sponsors, whether private individuals or organizations: A. Biedak and F. Binkiewicz; Zdybniów Parish, Sandomierz; Patriotic Association "Wola-Bemowo" in Warsaw; Falanga (a fascist group); Society of Saint Pius X (a schismatic organization); Polish-American Committee in the Defense of the Cross. Some preferred to remain anonymous: Academic teacher from Warsaw; Son; Attorneys of the Capital.

While some crosses were delivered individually in a relatively anonymous, subdued manner, others were transported with maximal flourish and fanfare in processions accompanied by songs and prayers. Typically, a small ceremony would attend the planting, complete with speeches, personal testimonies, flowers, banners and flags. The subsequent blessing of crosses was accompanied by more developed ritual performance such as prayers, religious chants and the sprinkling of holy water as photographers and crowds of the curious observed from the distance of the street, standing behind the gravel pit's chain-link fence that bounded and distinguished "sacred space" from everyday space (Figure 8.3). Crosses were brought from Poland's four corners: Warsaw, Cracow, Łódź, Łomża, Katowice, Sandomierz and Wrocław, to name only a few places. At least three crosses were dedicated by members of Polish communities in the United States (Chicago), Canada (Toronto) and Australia, testifying to the transnational mobilization of the action.

The most common theme expressed on the crosses' inscriptions is the martyrdom of Poles and the implicit claim to Poles' right to the site, in an effort to counteract the recent revision of Auschwitz's history away from a focus on Polish martyrdom toward an emphasis on the Jewish Holocaust.[11] Recall that the cross-planting action was initiated by Świtoń, who invited Poles to commemorate the execution of ethnic Poles at the gravel pit in 1941, thereby sufficiently sacralizing (and Polonizing) the site such that the papal cross would remain. In this vein, one woman intended her cross as a testimony of the crimes against Poles, her cross's inscription reading: "As an inhabitant of [nearby village], I was a witness of those brutal murders of Hitlerites on Poles in the camp and at the Gravel pit. Let this birch Cross attest that I remember you. Anna Chrapczyńska." Another cross, offered by Świtoń's son, is dedicated to the memory of five priests "tortured to death on 26 August 1941 . . . martyrs for [their] Faith and for Poland," marking the site as a holy Catholic and national one. The cross here is associated with some of the most painful chapters of Polish history. By emphasizing suffering and martyrdom on these crosses' inscriptions, their authors implicitly compete with Jews for the "ownership" of Auschwitz.

Other crosses stressed the Catholic identity of Poles by fusing, sometimes in creative ways, Catholicism and Polishness. In addition to a multitude of crosses bearing inscriptions like, "To the Poles-Catholics murdered at the Gravel pit" and "Here died Polish patriots-Catholics," many were inspired by a poem commonly attributed to Adam Mickiewicz (1798–1855) Poland's national bard: "Only under this cross/Only under this sign/Poland is Poland/and a Pole is a Pole." The author of one inscription, in a significant inversion or Freudian slip, replaced the poem's last verse with the line ". . . and a *Catholic is a Pole*" (my emphasis), illustrating the complete conflation of national and religious categories. The cross, moreover, is often described as Poland's protector and main attribute, its totem. Without it, Poland would no longer be Poland, as the short poem suggests, or exist at all, as Świtoń argued: "This cross, it is for Poland to be or not to be" (*Rzeczpospolita*, July 20, 1998). Opposing the cross is therefore equal to treason, as expressed on this other cross: "He who fights the Cross, who sells Polish land and the Nation's property, is the enemy of and traitor to the Fatherland." A true Pole, according to this inscription's author, is a traditional

Figure 8.3 A Catholic priest blesses crosses planted at the gravel pit during the summer of 1998 despite the official condemnation of the action by the Episcopate of Poland in late August (source: photograph from the personal archives of Kazimierz Świtoń).

Catholic opposing the presence of foreign capital in Poland. Jews are the obvious enemy, and liberal secular elites their accomplices – if not actually Jews disguised as Poles, like wolves in sheep's clothing. This is a position freely expressed in the pages of the Right-wing Catholic daily *Nasz Dziennik*, associated with Radio Maryja. Its editors encourage the boycott of foreign products, oppose the selling of Polish land and industries, and specifically promote a traditional Catholicism in a section of the paper called "the Faith of Our Ancestors." In it, ethnic, religious and economic nationalism are fused into a conservative, traditional vision of Poland closing itself off to the West and the European Union because the designs of both are supranational, therefore antinational. Jews are represented as linked to both Communism and capitalism; either way, they deal with money, whereas "good Poles" cultivate the land, their national traditions and their Catholic faith.

Several other crosses bear Biblical quotations and conjoin religious anti-Semitism with Polish nationalism. Two merit special attention. The first is four meters' high, ornately decorated by metal panels attached to its sides, painted in green, and inscribed by hand in white (Figure 8.4). Beneath the main inscription is a coat of arms in red metal featuring an embossed white eagle that has a crown nailed onto its head, symbolizing Polish independence. The main inscription contains a passage from the Gospel according to Matthew that is frequently invoked to explain (and justify) the tragic fate of Jews:

> Then said Jesus to the crowds and to his disciples, "The scribes and the Pharisees sit on Moses' seat; so practice and observe whatever I tell you, but not what they do; for they preach, but do not practice. . . . Therefore I send you prophets and wise men and scribes, some of whom you will kill and crucify, and some of whom you will scourge in your synagogues and persecute from town to town, that upon you may come all the righteous blood shed on earth. . . . Truly, I say to you, all this will come upon this generation."
>
> (Matt. 23: 1–3, 34, 36. RSV)

While Jews are depicted as Christ-killers whose death at Auschwitz is therefore justified, Poles, in contrast, are rendered as truly sacrificial victims and heroes. In a messianic interpretation of their fate, Poles were not killed at Auschwitz as a punishment for any sin, but rather *to redeem sin* and save the world, as we can see from the inscription on another cross. More somber than the previous one, the sign is professionally engraved and, like the aforementioned one, its authorship remains anonymous (although the author's gender, profession and place of residence are revealed):

> And the whole earth followed the beast with wonder. Men worshiped the dragon, for he had given his authority to the beast, and they wor-

Figure 8.4 Cross featuring Biblical references (Matthew 23:1–3, 34, 36) (source: photograph by Geneviève Zubrzycki).

shiped the beast, saying, "Who is like the beast, and who can fight against it?" (Revelation 13.3–4. RSV).

In the name of the Lord Jesus Christ, the Holy Spirit and the Father, let no human dare to raise his unworthy hands on this Cross – symbol of the Catholic faith and of a free Poland, but also of the bloodiest Golgotha of Poland and of the heroism of Poles murdered at this gravel pit and in Oświęcim – since It stands on Polish Land, soaked with Polish blood.

– Offered by an Academic Teacher from Warsaw (capital letters in original text)

The inscription mixes a Biblical passage with a personal interpretation of the events and issues at stake in the war of the crosses. Since the first century, this passage from the book of Revelation has often been read as an end-times prophecy of an Antichrist/world power that represents the ultimate manifestation of evil. In the Polish context, the passage could be used to describe a multitude of enemies: colonizers and occupiers as well as traitors. It is not clear who "the beast" is, in the eyes of the academic teacher from Warsaw: Nazism? A Jewish world conspiracy against Poland? The personal inscription proffers other indications. First, the cross is here again the symbolic fusion, within one material sign, of Catholicism and Polishness. The cross is the symbol of Catholic faith *and* of Poland – not any Poland, however, but more specifically a *free* Poland. Removing the cross, by implication, would signify the loss of independence. The cross also stands for another symbol, "Oświęcim," invoked here as Poland's "bloodiest Golgotha," a religious metaphor borrowed from John Paul II's homily during his Mass at Birkenau in 1979. Just like Jesus, Poland was crucified to save the world from evil, a powerful contemporary extension of the Romantic, messianic myth of Poland as the Christ of nations. Thus the cross also represents the sacrificial, redemptive heroism of Poles. The last part of the inscription justifies the presence of the cross at the site and warns against its removal: the cross cannot be removed because it stands on "Polish Land" ("Land" spelled with a capital *L*, emphasizing its sacredness and sovereignty), and because that land is soaked with Polish blood (as opposed to Jewish ashes), which sanctifies its grounds. The injunction against the cross's removal, made in the name of the Holy Trinity, could be addressed either to Jews or to Poles who supported the relocation of the papal cross.

The cross in the crossfire: debating a polysemic symbol

These representations of Poland were made by a very specific group of Poles, who not only expressed anger and indignation at the possibility of the papal cross's removal, but condensed and materialized these sentiments into iconography that they then actually brought to the gravel pit, even in open disobedience of the Episcopate of Poland's request not to erect crosses at the site in late August. The actors' obdurate persistence in the ritualizations serves as solid evidence of the depth of their conviction and dedication to "the cause." But this dedication was far from general, and interpretations of the event and of the symbol itself were far less unanimous than the Defenders of the Cross attempted to convey.[12]

As this section shows, the cross is not only a multivocal or polysemic symbol (Turner 1967); it contains various sets of associations, various layers of meaning for various groups. The war of the crosses, as social drama or "crisis event," polarized and mobilized different segments of Polish society and, ultimately, is linked to central cleavages in society. It is related to a crisis in Polish–Jewish relations, but also, if not primarily, to one within Polish society and within even the Catholic Church. I now turn to the analysis of these discourses, and these multiple "publics" through the arguments made for or against the removal of the cross(es) from the proximity of Auschwitz.

Bracketing the theological arguments against the presence of the cross and other religious symbols at Auschwitz, for Jews the cross has traditionally been seen as a sign of menace, and stands as a symbol of indifference during the Holocaust, or even as a symbol of aggression and persecution (Krajewski 1997). In the words of Dawid Warszawski,[13] a Polish Jew:

> This cross in Auschwitz is in our eyes the sign of the persecutors, not of the victims. Its erection at the cemetery of Jewish victims by Christian Europe insults us. . . . In Auschwitz, the place of death not of one Jew, but of one million, there should be no crosses.
>
> (*Gazeta Wyborcza*, April 21, 1998)

A similar argument was made by a reader of the Jewish monthly *Midrasz* in a letter to its editors:

> In Jerusalem, one Jew died on the cross – Christ; in Auschwitz, more than one million Jews perished, and this with much greater suffering. In Oświęcim, Jews constituted almost 99 percent of victims. . . . This cross is the disgrace of Polish Catholicism.
>
> (Narmi Michejda, *Midrasz*, April 1998)

The argument is cast in religious categories (Jews vs Christians), and suffering is measured quantitatively and qualitatively. The cross, however, is not only a universal, Christian symbol: its presence at that site is more specifically associated with Polish Catholicism. The cross at the gravel pit thus signifies an attempt to "Christianize" Auschwitz and to "Polonize" its memory. According to Stanisław Krajewski, Jewish activist, public intellectual and co-chair of the Committee on the Christian–Jewish Dialogue, "The planting of crosses is the expression of Christian triumphalism" (*Midrasz*, April 1998). For many ethnic Poles, on the other hand, efforts to remove the cross are understood as attempts at "de-Polonizing" and further "Judaizing" "Oświęcim;" it is interpreted as the exclusive appropriation of the symbol by Jews and their refusal to allow Poles to commemorate their own victims.

Under Communism, the cross marked the group's boundaries: "us," the nation, against "them," the alien, atheistic Communist regime. This was especially true in the late 1970s and the early 1980s, when the secular Left took pride in the "Polish Pope," supported workers demonstrating with religious symbols in 1980 and more generally "embraced the Church" following the declaration of martial law in 1981. The cross was understood by those who opposed the regime, including atheists and Jews, as a sign of diversity against an imposed monolithic worldview. In 1983, for example, during the fortieth anniversary of the Warsaw Ghetto Uprising, Marek Edelman, the Uprising's last living leader, decided that Solidarity's independent commemoration of the event should be marked by the laying of a cross with flowers at the Ghetto's Heroes monument.

In post-Communist Poland, however, the cross in the public sphere – and especially at Auschwitz – now signifies for liberal intellectuals from the Left (and for some liberal Catholic circles), the imposition of a set of values and intolerance toward Others. It stands as the rejection of the principles of the *Rechtsstaat*, where particular allegiances are relegated to the private sphere. The symbol of the cross at Auschwitz for them stands for an ethno-Catholic vision of Poland which excludes not only Jews from its present and past, but also all of those who do not think of themselves or of Poland in those terms. For editors of far-Left, anticlerical publications such as the satirical weekly *Nie*, the cross also stands for fundamentalist tendencies in Poland since the fall of Communism and represents the "narrow-minded clericalism and bigotry" of the so-called "Catho-Right." In the words of Jerzy Urban, *Nie*'s owner and editor-in-chief, the "crossomania" is a "comedy in which the crusaders, like madmen escaped from mental institutions, play Cathonationalist gardeners ... planting crosses on gravel, like dogs and cats feeling the need to mark their territory" (*Nie*, 35, 1998).

In the discourse of conservative Catholic groups, attempts at removing the cross are still associated with the Communist past of forced atheization and religious repression. The presence of the cross in the public sphere here signifies, in a paradoxical twist, religious freedom and religious *pluralism* associated with Western culture and values, as expressed in this Catholic organization's declaration arguing against the removal of the papal cross from the gravel pit:

> Signs and symbols are the testimony of [the living's] faith and national identity, their dignity and freedom, their endurance and hope. For Christians, for the majority of Poles, the cross is such a sign. In our forefathers' history, the partitioner or the occupants more than once have fought against the presence of the sign of the holy cross on Polish land. Today, in a free and independent European country, in a state based on

the rule of law and democracy, the battle with the symbols of religious faith is contrary to the spirit of Europe and the expression of lack of respect for people of other faith or nationality...

(Civitas Christiana, in Katolicka Agencja Informacyjna *Biuletyn Prasowy*, March 24, 1998)

Generally speaking, the cross for Christians symbolizes suffering, love, and victory over evil. But it is also said to refer more specifically to Poland's Christian heritage, to resistance to occupation under the Partitions, during World War II, and under Communism. Consider, to wit, Józef Cardinal Glemp's words about the cross:

The Polish people [*lud*] have been put up on the cross. That is why they love this cross, a sign of love in suffering wherever it is: in the shipyards, in Warsaw or in Oświęcim. In Oświęcim the cross has been standing and will stand. [...] The Eiffel Tower did not and does not please everyone, but it is not a reason to remove it and take it down.

(*Tygodnik Powszechny*, June 6, 1998)

The sites enumerated by Cardinal Glemp are closely associated with the nation, with Polish martyrdom and resilience. All three are symbols of the moral victory of Poles under occupation: Oświęcim and Warsaw during World War II, and the Gdańsk shipyards under Communism. The Polish nation is identified here with Christ, in continuation with Polish Romantic messianism, so its history and destiny are intimately linked to the cross. Finally, the analogy Cardinal Glemp draws between the cross at Auschwitz and the Eiffel Tower in Paris shows the extent to which he downplayed and belittled the Jewish objection.

For traditionalists and the Catholic Right, the cross represents the endurance of the Polish nation through centuries, the resurrection of the Polish state and now the reaffirmation of Poland's mission in the new Europe as well. In a more narrow connection to "Oświęcim," it represents years of national domination and religious repression during the German occupation, but also under the Communist rule. The cross stands as a sign of resistance to occupants and oppressors and as a sign of victory over them; the symbol of national persistence. For many Poles, then, the cross at Auschwitz is above all a symbol of Polish sovereignty. This is especially so after pressure from some Jewish organizations to remove it and in the face of Jewish proposals for the extra-territoriality of the former death camp.[14] In the words of Świtoń: "The time has come to make a choice: the Cross or servitude. [...] If we do not defend this Cross – the time has come for the fifth partition of Poland" (in Marszalek 1998: unnumbered pages).[15] Some 130 parliamentarians, mostly from the Right-wing coalition Akcja Wyborcza "Solidarność" (AWS, Electoral Action "Solidarity"), signed a letter to the Prime Minister asking him to ensure the presence of the cross at the gravel pit, and emphasizing that the defense of the cross is the state's "legal and moral duty." The parliamentarians justified their position by, among other arguments, defining the cross as part of the "national heritage" and the site where it stands as the site of "Polish martyrdom:"

> The cross standing in the site sanctified by the mass martyrdom of Poles and of representatives of other nations, should last as a sign of suffering and sacrifice and at the same time as the sign of faith and hope for those who in great numbers gave their lives in this inhuman place. [. . .] The sovereign Polish Republic guards all those signs [of faith, and of religious and national identity] against all attacks.
>
> (Katolicka Agencja Informacyjna, *Biuletyn Prasowy*, no. 12, March 24, 1998)

"Oświęcim" here is represented as the symbol of martyrdom of "the Polish Nation and other nations," following the socialist narrative of World War II the Polish state propagated until the fall of Communism. As the site of Poles' martyrdom, the gravel pit is sacralized. Here again the cross is associated with national identity in addition to Christian faith. It is implied that it is the Republic's duty, now that it is sovereign, to defend the symbol against all attacks – whether from secular post-Communists, Jews or foreign powers.

The Christian symbol thus summons historical and contemporary echoes far removed from its religious semantics. In the Right's discourse, it is clearly related to what a free and "truly Polish" Poland should be. For Świtoń and his *ad hoc* group, the Defenders of the Cross, the cross symbolizes the Catholic "essence" of Polishness. Here is what Świtoń told me:

> The cross is the fundament of our identity – that's the cross. Poles have won under the cross, they went to death with the cross. If a Pole is not defending the cross, I think he's not a Pole; he's just an ordinary person. If a Pole allows the removal of crosses, he also stops being a Pole . . .
>
> (Interview, April 25, 2001)

Polishness here is equated to Catholicism, and the cross is the symbol of that fusion. Therefore, the removal of the cross not only signifies the stripping of one's Catholic identity, but also of one's national identity. Without the cross one is condemned to her pre-social state with no "self;" an "ordinary person," in the words of Świtoń. Polishness, we may also deduce from this view, is "extra-ordinary."

Even among Catholics the cross has various significations, linked with a variety of positions that could be heard during the war of the crosses. In fact, that event brought to light and to life serious differences and divisions within the institutional Church itself (Zubrzycki 2005). The hierarchy's position on the papal and the other crosses was far from unified, and clearly unfolded and shifted in accord with developing events. Bishops publicly expressed different opinions, and Cardinal Glemp's declarations were inconsistent, ranging from open approval to condemnation of the action. Nearly two months after the war of the crosses was declared by Świtoń, the Episcopate of Poland finally issued a much expected official declaration in which it condemned the action and decided that all but the papal cross would be removed from the gravel pit. The Church's hierarchy from then on attempted to restrict the semantic orbit of the cross and regain discursive and ritual control of the symbol. The Bishops convened to emphatically promote a "correct theology of the cross," because, as they put it, it became apparent that "a deeper reflection about the meaning of the cross [was] lacking" (Katolicka Agencja Informacyjna, *Biuletyn Prasowy*, August 25–26, 1998). According to Archbishop Henryk Muszyński, "the cross is a sign of love, forgiveness, and unity; and not exclusively the symbol of a rather narrow conception of identity that can then be freely exploited in the fight with others" (ibid.). As he saw it, it had been easy to mobilize Poles around the symbol "because of their emotional attachment to the cross, attacked and destroyed by two totalitarian regimes," which had therefore become "a beautiful patriotic-religious symbol, worshiped as such" (ibid.). Interviews with priests, scholars and other public figures on the meaning of the cross appeared in the press: While Świtoń claimed in Right-wing Catholic publications that the cross was the symbol of Polishness, Father Wacław Oszajca asserted that

> When one says that the cross is a sign of national identity, the meaning of the cross is denied – national identity is put above the cross. For Christians, it should be the opposite: national identity [and] the identity of every human being ... is understandable only through the cross and Christ.
>
> (*Wprost*, August 23, 1998)

The Church's rather late efforts at disseminating a "more orthodox" theology of the cross were in vain. The Episcopate's condemnation of the action remained unheard: crosses continued to appear at the gravel pit throughout the fall of 1998, and two Catholic priests even consecrated the crosses along with a small chapel built by Kazimierz Świtoń, supplying the Defenders of the Cross with fresh ammunition. The group now argued that not only could the papal cross not be removed, but that the other crosses could not be touched either. According to Świtoń and his followers, the Church had no monopoly over the symbol – a position Cardinal Glemp himself had articulated in an early declaration. What is more, they argued, "*We* are the Church." Świtoń explained to me what he meant by that:

> Our Church did not defend [the cross]. Because the Church is divided: there's the administration and there's the People of God. ... But the

Church, in fact, it is the People of God, just like Christ founded it, and not the administration, bureaucrats who are priests, Bishops or Cardinals.

(Interview, April 25, 2001)

In this explanation, Świtoń distinguishes between the institutional Church – the administration and its bureaucrats who did not come to the defense of the cross and Polishness – and the People of God, a "truer" Church, faithful to its mission of guarding the nation. Though the statement "We are the Church" is reminiscent of the democratic, post-Vatican II definition of the Church as a "community of believers," Świtoń's comment smacks of something closer to the Weberian distinction between Church and sect, between a routinized and institutionalized movement and a charismatic one whose objectives have not been bent by the needs of the institution (Weber 1978: 456). What defines Świtoń's "People of God," however, is their "true" Polishness. According to Świtoń, "a Pole who does not defend the cross stops being a Pole." Moreover, for him the hierarchy of the Catholic Church in Poland was no longer Catholic at all, since at one point the Bishops stopped defending the cross *as the symbol of Polishness*.[16] Just like only those who defend the cross are Poles, only those who defend the cross *qua* Polishness are Catholic. The statement "*We* are the Church," therefore, opposes the "no longer Catholic" Catholic Church (because not nationalist enough) to a truer Church, the People of God, defined here as "true Poles," i.e. those who defend the cross as a symbol of Polishness. "By defending the cross," Świtoń told me,

I was defending Polish identity. *Polish identity*. Because Poland without the cross would not be Poland. Mickiewicz already said it a hundred something years ago: "Only under this cross/Only under this sign/Poland is Poland/and a Pole is a Pole."

(Interview, April 2001)

These reflections might be the best contemporary articulations of the fusion of Catholicism and Polishness within a single category, that of "Polak-katolik."[17]

As these few quotes illustrate, for Świtoń, the Defenders of the Cross, and many other national-Catholic groups, Catholicism is so closely associated with the Polish nation that there is no perceived tension between the universalism of the religion and its nationalist interpretation. The supranational dimension of Catholicism is simply absent from the logic of this discourse, and although the Defenders of the Cross borrow freely from the rhetoric of Vatican II, their interpretation is far removed from the post-council teachings.

Persistent myths and symbols?

The analysis of the specific crosses' inscriptions and the diverse discourses about the symbol of the cross suggest important leads for our consideration: First, the war of the crosses highlights divisions within Polish society and the different ways in which various groups actually articulate, "on the ground" and in the public sphere, the relationship between national identity and religion. Though the controversial event is an extreme example of national-religious fusion, and may at first glance suggest that nationalism and religion are even more tightly linked in post-Communist Poland than they were before, the analysis of the public debates surrounding the war of the crosses actually revealed the opposite: namely, that the fusion of religious and ethnonational identifications is seriously questioned by several communities of discourse and that the equation between Polishness and Catholicism is eroding.

This erosion is prompted by a change in the structural relation between state, nation and Church (Zubrzycki 2006). In the traditional model that was operative, *grosso modo*, during the Communist period, the nation and the Church were united against a "foreign" state. National identity was consciously constructed through religion and supported by the Church in opposition to the state.[18] The religion-nation fusion that had emerged in the nineteenth century and was codified by the nationalist Endecja at the beginning of the twentieth, gained force and became more or less taken for granted. When in 1989 the state acquired legitimacy and became "truly Polish," however, it was no longer the "third element" against which nation and Church could be mobilized, but rather the prism through which identities could be viewed and consciously constructed. As a result, religion's ability to carry national identifications has declined and the provisional nature of what appeared to be a solid fusion began to show its seams. The war of the crosses therefore should be seen as an attempt to revitalize a version of national identity in decline. It is precisely at the moment when the fusion of religious and ethnonational categories is being loudly contested in public discourse and civic life that strident counter-efforts by minority voices are deployed in an attempt to ossify a vision of the nation that is slowly disintegrating. The symbol of the cross, in this context, actually operates as a site for the profound contestation – even fission – of the Polish–Catholic fusion. Rather than representing monolithic unity, it contains and brings to light conflict and fragmentation. Contrary to the myth of Poland's intrinsic Catholicity and of the monolithic authority of the Church in that country, tension, fissure, and lines of division run deep. And although the overwhelming majority of Polish citizens are ethnically Polish and (at least nominally) Catholic, what Polishness and Catholic identity "are" is polysemic and contested.

This is not to say, of course, that prior to the fall of Communism the ethno-Catholic vision of Polishness was unanimously accepted. As a coveted symbol constructed out of sub-symbols, events and narratives, the nation is always and everywhere a crossroads where diverse discourses intersect, with political and cultural actors fighting over the direction of advance. Like an active volcano, the nation is made of the sporadic eruptions of competing discourses and practices about what it purportedly is and should be. The nation in fact "happens" (Brubaker 1996) through these bursts of creativity, contestation and redefinition that do not appear *ex nihilo*, but rather are embedded in and caused by their social, historical, cultural and economic environments. It is a work-in-progress constituted through events like the war of the crosses, in which actors manipulated core Polish symbols, and the public debates about those events. A key point here is that, although persistent, these symbolic representations of the nation are far from unchallenged and unchanging.

Needless to say, the war of the crosses was not only a debate among Poles over the meaning of the nation, the nature and future of Polish Catholicism, and over what constitutes a legitimate national symbol. There is no question that anti-Semitism was at the core of the event. Although the debate rarely involved Poles and Jews in direct dialogue, Jews remained the implicit (and often explicit) external and internal "Other" in exchanges between Poles. Jews and Jewishness served as a trope to discuss Polishness and the role of Catholicism in defining and shaping the latter.

Revisiting religious nationalism: sacred secular symbols

Whereas dominant paradigms in the literature on nationalism maintain that nationalism replaced traditional religion and even is a modern religion itself through the sacralization of politics (Durkheim [1912] 1995; Hayes 1960; Llobera 1996; Tamir 1995; Marvin and Ingle 1999), this case suggests a much more complex and subtle relationship between nationalism and religion. Historically, the formation of Polish nationalism cannot be related to religious decline. Religious symbols and stories instead provided a vocabulary and grammar to speak of the nation and its mission after the last Partition of Poland (1795). Romantic messianism found a congenial niche for the expression of this emerging form of nationalism in Catholic rituals and everyday practices. Through a slow and complex process in the nineteenth and twentieth centuries, Polish national identity and Catholicism became fused.

This process is far from conforming to the functionalist model, however, according to which nationalism, after having superseded religion, replaces it, or even becomes a religion itself. The paradigmatic term for this model is "civil religion." Civil religion, following the Durkheimian trajectory, attempts to describe or interpret the social sacralization of a given group's symbols.[19] In the modern era, according to this view, state symbols like the flag are worshiped by citizens as religious totems, and national martyrs are revered as "saints." Nationalism becomes a religion. But this model of the relationship between nationalism and religion will not do either.

Liah Greenfeld (1996) suggested that the treatment of nationalism as a modern religion stems from the fact that nationalism is a form of consciousness that sacralizes the secular, hence the temptation to treat it as a religion, albeit a civil religion. Although this is useful, it does not go far enough. The Polish case points to a different and overlooked process. Because of Poland's peculiar political history, it was not political institutions and symbols that were sacralized and became the object of religious devotion (following the French revolutionary model), but religious symbols that were first secularized, and then *resacralized as national*. Biblical allegories, religious symbols, hymns and iconography as well as religious practices like processions, pilgrimages or simple participation in Sunday Mass were largely politicized as carriers of national identity during the period when the Polish state disappeared from the European map or was a Soviet peon. As such, religion served as an alternative space providing civil society with an area of relative freedom of action in defiance of an oppressive or totalitarian state. Catholic identity, symbols and practices were secularized through their politicization and eventual fusion with national identity. Their significance was heightened or loaded; they became neon hyper-markers, but of Polishness.

The Polish case therefore suggests a peculiar form of the secularization of religion and religious symbols, through their political instrumentalization, and then their *resacralization*, now as *national* symbols. The cross in Poland is therefore a *sacred secular* symbol. It is sacred not only because of its Christian semantics (or even in spite of them), but because it traditionally represents, since the nineteenth century, Poland. In the place of religion yielding to nationalism or nationalism becoming a religion, here *religion becomes nationalism*.[20] The national sacralization of religious symbols, however, is meaningful and garners consensual support only in specific politico-structural contexts, namely in periods of statelessness or when the state is not regarded as truly national, as under Communism. This study therefore points to the necessity of looking at the relationship between religion and nationalism as it is embedded within broad systemic processes related to state formation on the one hand, and as it is reflected in specific cultural dramas and practices on the other.

Acknowledgments

This chapter adapts material from Geneviève Zubrzycki's *The Crosses of Auschwitz: Nationalism and Religion in Post-Communist Poland*, © 2006 by The University of Chicago. All rights reserved.

Notes

1 For an exhaustive analysis of the war of the crosses that includes an examination of the Polish–Jewish conflict regarding the memory of Auschwitz and the presence of Christian symbols at the former death camp and its immediate vicinity,

see my book *The Crosses of Auschwitz: Nationalism and Religion in Post-Communist Poland*, Chicago: University of Chicago Press, 2006.

2 Plans to remove the cross from the vicinity of Auschwitz were indeed underway, as the presence of a Christian symbol at this important site of the Shoah generated significant protests from Jewish communities in Europe, North America and Israel. The cross was originally part of an altar used during a Mass John Paul II celebrated at Birkenau, Auschwitz's sister camp, during the pontiff's first pilgrimage to Poland in 1979 – hence its popular designation as the "papal cross." After being stored in a local church's basement for a decade, the parish priest and a group of former (Polish Catholic) Auschwitz prisoners planted the cross in the convent's backyard. Although religious considerations may have played a role, it is clear that the act was also, and perhaps primarily, politically motivated: it was a gesture of protest against efforts to relocate the Carmelite convent away from Auschwitz. For detailed accounts of the convent dispute, see Bartoszewski (1991), Głownia and Wilkanowicz (1998), Rittner and Roth (1991); for a pro-Polish, conservative view that includes several documents, see Raina (1991).

3 Born in 1931, Świtoń organized the first Committee of Free Professional Unions in the People's Republic of Poland (Komitet Wolnych Związków Zawodowych) in 1978. He was a member of Solidarity between 1980 and 1989 and a deputy in the Sejm from 1991 to 1993. During the later 1970s and throughout the 1980s, he participated in a number of hunger strikes.

4 Pronounced Osh-VYEN-chim. Oświęcim is a small town of approximately 50,000 people in southwestern Poland, about 75 kilometers from Cracow. It could not be distinguished from myriad other small Polish towns, were it not for the fact that this is where the Nazis built the world's most notorious concentration and death camp, Auschwitz. If "humanity's largest cemetery" is known in the world by its German designation, in Poland it is known as and referred to as Oświęcim. The use of different names for the same site is related to Auschwitz's respective meanings for the different parties involved. Whereas "Auschwitz" is, for Jews and the world, the symbol of the Holocaust and now of universal evil, "Oświęcim" is for Poles the symbol of their martyrdom during World War II. The symbolic representations of the site and the events that took place there should not be conflated with the site itself. I therefore use quotation marks to emphasize the construction and porousness of "Oświęcim" and "Auschwitz" as meaningful symbols. The names without the quotation marks refer to physical sites: Auschwitz is the former camp and current museum, while Oświęcim is the small town where Auschwitz is located. Although Poles only very rarely use the name Auschwitz to denote the former camp and current museum, this is the term I privilege to reflect the historical record. When quoting someone, I keep the term used in the original language in which the allocution was made. For an analysis of the historically constituted and multilayered meaning of "Oświęcim" in Poland, see chapter 3 of my book (2006). On the duality of "Oświęcim"/"Auschwitz" more broadly, see Tanay (1991); Goban-Klas (1995); Sułek (1998); Novick (2000); Kucia (2001, 2005); Alexander (2002); and Huener (2003). For an excellent analysis of the meaning of Auschwitz and its mythologization by Israeli and diaspora Jews, Soviet Russians and Poles, as well as the multiple and often contradictory philosophical preoccupations raised by Auschwitz, see Webber (1992). On Holocaust memorial sites in Communist and post-Communist Poland, see Young (1993).

5 Radio Maryja was established in 1991 as a local radio station in Toruń, and has since expanded into a nationwide network with an estimated six million listeners. In addition to its radio network and a television station, Radio Maryja has developed into a genuine social movement, with various religious and social

organizations, political groups and publications more or less loosely affiliated with it (Jasiewicz 1999).

6 The crown is not the symbol of royalty, but that of sovereignty. See Zdzisław Mach's interesting article on the Polish coat-of-arms (1992).

7 Poland was thrice partitioned between Russia, Prussia and Austria: in 1772, 1793 and 1795. "The Partitions" refer to the period from 1795 to 1918, when the Polish state disappeared from the European map.

8 As a tradition from the baroque period, Easter sepulchers during Holy Week were elaborately decorated, complete with special effects (adornments, *trompe-l'oeil*, lights, etc.), often reflecting patriotic themes. On Good Friday, as Jesus-Poland lay in the tomb with guards keeping watch nearby, people prayed for his Resurrection and attended the mandatory confession. On Saturday night, during an evening service, Christ would symbolically be resurrected, and his tomb would be found empty the following morning. The tradition was revived during the World War II and remains to this day. Every church has its own sepulcher with its own scenographic style, and participates in an unofficial competition. People go from church to church to compare and evaluate the representations of the entombment. The Easter sepulchers of Father Henryk Jankowski (Solidarity's chaplain in the 1980s) in Saint Brygida's parish in Gdańsk are infamous for their controversial nationalist depictions, which are often anti-Semitic in content.

9 Maryjane Osa (1996) has shown that pastoral mobilization organized around Our Lady of Częstochowa in the 1960s provided solid foundations for the emergence of the Solidarity movement some 15 years later, and Renata Rogozińska demonstrated in her study of Paschal themes in Polish art in the period 1970–99 that Easter sepulchers in the 1980s were one of the most important places of patriotic manifestations (2002: 29–31).

10 Despite the socialist state's official atheism, in the 1980s even some state-sponsored commemorations used crosses on official monuments, attesting to the power of the symbol (and the relative weakness of the state). For example, the 1956 Poznań Uprising, during which several dozen people were killed, was commemorated with a monument constituted by two giant crosses. The first was engraved with the date 1956 and the other with 1968, 1970, 1976 and 1980, years of the other major uprisings in Communist Poland. The monument was unveiled in 1981 during celebrations that lasted three days.

11 On this narrative revision and its causes, see Kucia (2001) and Zubrzycki (2006).

12 Świtoń and his followers were not mainstream figures in the Polish sociopolitical landscape. Although the drama's main characters, they remained marginal. Their views are close to those expressed in the national Catholic daily *Nasz Dziennik*, tied to Radio Maryja, and to those of *Nasza Polska*, a far-Right weekly. For comparative purposes, *Gazeta Wyborcza*, Adam Michnik's center-Left daily, has a circulation of 570,000 (720,000 on Saturdays). It has an Average Issue Readership (AIR) of two million; it is read by 7.2 percent of Poles above 15 years of age. It has consistently been the most popular and influential nation-wide daily since the fall of Communism (its circulation is actually higher than any other paper in Eastern Europe (Ekiert and Kubik 1999: 15)). *Nasz Dziennik*, on the other hand, has a circulation of 300,000 and an AIR of 170,000 (0.6 percent) according to research conducted by OBOP in February 1999 ($n = 2,931$; $+/-1.2$ percent). (See Ośrodek Badań Prasoznawczych [2000], and Ośrodek Badania Opinii Publicznej (1999)). Even though marginal, Świtoń *did* mobilize support for his war of the crosses, and the issues the event raised were not themselves peripheral, but rather became a lightning rod for mainstream commentary and discussion.

13 Dawid Warszawski is the pen-name of Konstanty Gebert, public intellectual, editor of the Jewish monthly *Midrasz*, and frequent contributor to *Gazeta Wyborcza*.

14 One of the main protagonists of the Carmelite convent controversy, Rabbi Avraham Weiss from New York, Kalman Sultanik, vice-president of the World Jewish Congress during the war of the crosses, and Menachem Pinchas Joskow-icz, then head rabbi in Poland, independently suggested that Auschwitz-Birkenau be removed from the Polish nation-state to become "extra-territorial." Sultanik proposed that the former camp be under the joint jurisdiction of UNESCO, Jewish organizations and the Polish government (*Polska Agencja Prasowa*, June 4, 1998), while Rabbis Weiss and Joskowicz suggested that it be under Israeli control.

15 The Molotov–Ribentropp pact, which divided Poland between Nazi Germany and the Soviet Union, and the conferences of Potsdam and Yalta are commonly referred to as the fourth Partition of Poland.

16 Świtoń also explained to me why the hierarchy was neither truly Polish nor truly Catholic: according to him, the Church's hierarchy is controlled by crypto-Jews; children who had been saved from the Holocaust by nuns and priests, converted to Catholicism and were now out to destroy the Church from within (Interview, April 25, 2001). This view is commonly reported in newspapers and publications of the far-Right, like *Nasz Dziennik* and *Nasza Polska*.

17 See Czarnowski ([1934] 1988) for a classical ethnography of the Polak-katolik stereotype; Zawadzki (1996) for an analysis of the Catholicization of the national tie, a process which was accentuated and generalized only under socialism; and Nowicka (1991) for an analysis of the contemporary significance of the Polak-katolik stereotype in processes of inclusion and exclusion.

18 This does not mean that the state was not shaping subjects, for it obviously was. But subjects did not *identify* with the state, and instead built their national identity through the Church.

19 The term "civil religion" was first coined by Jean-Jacques Rousseau in the *Social Contract*. It is mostly associated with Durkheim and Durkheimian perspectives. It was popularized in the United States in the late 1960s with Robert Bellah's article "Civil Religion in America" (1967), on the heels of which a veritable sociological industry grew up before again receding by the 1990s. For an interesting resurrection of the concept after the events of September 11, 2001, see Johnson (2005).

20 This is far from the perennialist model of the relationship between nationalism and religion, which claims that the modern nation grew out of already existing religious communities. I show elsewhere (2006), in contradistinction to that view, that the association between Catholicism and Polishness was not natural but historically specific. It is the result of a hard process of construction that is never totally completed and that requires extensive maintenance and upkeep in institutions of social reproduction – pedagogy, law, the state, the Church – and by public leaders through speeches, publication, political mobilization and ritual performance.

References

Primary sources

Newspapers and magazines: *Gazeta Polska, Gazeta Wyborcza*, Katolicka Agencja Informacyjna's *Biuletyn Prasowy, Midrasz, Nasz Dziennik, Nasza Polska, Nie, Polityka, Polska Agencja Prasowa, Rzeczpospolita, Słowo Żydowskie, Tygodnik Powszechny, Więź, Wprost, Zawsze Wierni, Znak*.

Ośrodek Badania Opinii Publicznej (1999) *Index Polska-Badania czytelnictwa prasy*.
Ośrodek Badań Prasoznawczych (2000) *Katalog Mediów polskich 1999/2000*, Cracow: Jagiellonian University Press.

Secondary sources

Alexander, J.C. (2002) "On the Social Construction of Moral Universals: The 'Holocaust' from War Crime to Trauma Drama," *European Journal of Social Theory*, 5(1): 5–86.
Bartoszewski, W.T. (1991) *The Convent at Auschwitz*, New York: George Braziller Inc.
Bourdieu, P. (1991) *Language and Symbolic Power*, Cambridge: Harvard University Press.
—— (1991) "Genesis and Structure of the Religious Field," *Comparative Social Research*, 13: 1–44.
Brubaker, R. (1996) *Nationalism Reframed: Nationhood and the National Question in the New Europe*, Cambridge: Cambridge University Press.
Cała, A. (1995) *The Image of the Jew in Polish Folk Culture*, Jerusalem: Magnes Press, Hebrew University.
Czarnowski, S. ([1934] 1988) "La culture religieuse des paysans polonais," *Archives des Sciences sociales des Religions*, 65(1): 7–23.
Durkheim, É. ([1912] 1995) *The Elementary Forms of Religious Life*, translated by K. Fields, New York: Free Press.
Ekiert, G. and Kubik, J. (1999) *Rebellious Civil Society: Popular Protest and Democratic Consolidation in Poland, 1989–1993*, Ann Arbor: University of Michigan Press.
Głownia, M. and Wilkanowicz, S. (eds) (1998) *Auschwitz: Konflikty i dialog*, Cracow: Wydawnictwo Św. Stanisława.
Goban-Klas, T. (1995) "Pamięć podzielona, pamięć urażona: Oświęcim i Auschwitz w polskiej i żydowskiej pamięci zbiorowej," in Z. Mach (ed.) *Europa po Auschwitz*, Cracow: Universitas: 71–91.
Graczyk, R. (1999) *Polski Kościół-polska demokracja*, Cracow: Universitas.
Greenfeld, L. (1996) "Is Nationalism the Modern Religion?," *Critical Review*, 10(2): 169–91.
Hayes, C. (1960) *Nationalism: A Religion*, New York: Macmillan.
Huener, J. (2003) *Auschwitz, Poland, and the Politics of Commemoration, 1945–1979*, Athens: Ohio University Press.
Irwin-Zarecka, I. (1989a) *Neutralizing Memory: The Jew in Contemporary Poland*, New Brunswick: Transaction Publishers.
—— (1989b) "Poland after the Holocaust," in Y. Bauer, Alice L. Eckardt, F.H. Littell, E. Maxwell, R. Maxwell and D. Patterson (eds) *Remembering for the Future: Working Papers and Addenda*, vol. 1, New York: Pergamon Press: 143–55.
Janion, M. and Żmigrodzka, M. (1978) *Romantyzm i historia*, Warsaw: Państwowy Instytut Wydawniczy.
Jasiewicz, K. (1999) "Democratic Transition and Social Movements in Poland: From Solidarność to Rodzina Radia Maryja," presented at the annual meeting of the American Association for the Advancement of Slavic Studies, November 18, St Louis, MO.
Johnson, P.C. (2005), "Savage Civil Religion," *Numen*, 52: 289–324.

Kapralski, S. (2001) "Battlefields of Memory: Landscape and Identity in Polish–Jewish Relations," *History and Memory*, 13(2): 35–58.

Krajewski, S. (1997) *Żydzi, Judaism, Polska*, Warsaw: Vocatio.

Krzemiński, I. (2002) "Polish–Jewish Relations, Anti-Semitism and National Identity," *Polish Sociological Review*, 137: 25–51.

Kubik, J. (1994) *The Power of Symbols against the Symbols of Power: The Rise of Solidarity and the Fall of State Socialism in Poland*, University Park: Pennsylvania State University Press.

Kucia, M. (2001) "KL Auschwitz in the Social Consciousness of Poles, AD 2000," in E. Maxwell and J.K. Roth (eds) *Remembering for the Future: The Holocaust in an Age of Genocide*, New York: Palgrave: 632–51.

—— (2005) *Auschwitz jako fakt społeczny: Historia, współczesność i świadomość społeczna KL Auschwitz w Polsce*, Cracow: Universitas.

Llobera, J. (1996) *The God of Modernity: The Development of Nationalism in Western Europe*, Oxford-Washington: Berg.

Mach, Z. (1992) "National Symbols in Politics: The Polish Case," *Etnologia europea*, 22: 89–107.

—— (1993) *Symbols, Conflict and Identity, Essays in Political Anthropology*, Albany: State University of New York Press.

Marvin, C. and Ingle, D.W. (1999) *Blood Sacrifice and the Nation: Totem Rituals and the American Flag*, Cambridge: Cambridge University Press.

Marszałek, J. (1998) *Broniąc Krzyża Polski bronimy*, vol. 2, *Opis wielkiej żydowskiej krucjaty wojennej przeciwko katolicyzmowi na przykładzie Papieskiego Krzyża w hitlerowskim obozie zagłady Birkenau-Auschwitz w Oświęcimiu*, Warsaw: Polska Oficyna Wydawnicza.

Novick, P. (2000) *The Holocaust in American Life*, New York: Mariner Books.

Nowicka, E. (1991) "Polak-katolik: O związkach polskości z katolicyzmem w społecznej świadomości Polaków." in E. Nowicka (ed.) *Religia a obcość*, Cracow: Nomos: 117–38.

Osa, M. (1996) "Pastoral Mobilization and Contention: The Religious Foundations of the Solidarity Movement in Poland." in C. Smith (ed.) *Disruptive Religion: The Force of Faith in Social-Movement Activism*, New York: Routledge: 67–85.

Raina, P. (1991) *Spór o klasztor sióstr karmelitanek bosych w Oświęcimiu*, Olsztyn: Warmińskie Wydawnictwo Diecezjalne.

Rittner, C. and Roth, J.K. (eds) (1991) *Memory Offended: The Auschwitz Convent Controversy*, New York: Praeger.

Rogozińska, R. (2002) *W stronę Golgoty: inspiracje pasyjne w sztuce polskiej w latach 1970–1999*, Poznań: Księgarnia Św. Wojciecha.

Smith, A.D. (1986) *The Ethnic Origins of Nations*, New York: Blackwell.

—— (2003) *Chosen Peoples: Sacred Sources of National Identity*, New York: Oxford University Press.

Sułek, A. (1998) "Wokół Oświęcimia: Spór o krzyże na tle wyobrażeń Polaków o sobie i Żydach," *Więź*, November: 61–70.

Tamir, Y. (1995) "The Enigma of Nationalism," *World Politics*, 47: 418–40.

Tanay, E. (1991) "Auschwitz and Oświęcim: One Location, Two Symbols," in C. Rittner and J.K. Roth (eds) *Memory Offended: The Auschwitz Convent Controversy*, New York: Praeger: 99–112.

Turner, V. (1967) *The Forest of Symbols: Aspects of Ndembu Ritual*, Ithaca and London: Cornell University Press.

—— (1974) *Dramas, Fields and Metaphors: Symbolic Action in Human Society*, Ithaca and London: Cornell University Press.

Webber, J. (1992) "The Future of Auschwitz: Some Personal Reflections," The First Frank Green Lecture, Oxford Centre for Postgraduate Hebrew Studies.

Weber, M. (1978) *Economy and Society*, vols 1 and 2, Berkeley–Los Angeles–London, University of California Press.

Young, J.E. (1993) *The Texture of Memory: Holocaust Memorials and Meaning*, New Haven: Yale University Press.

Zawadzki, P. (1996) "Le nationalisme contre la citoyenneté," *L'année sociologique* 46(1): 169–85.

Zubrzycki, G. (2001) "'We, the Polish Nation': Ethnic and Civic Visions of Nationhood in Post-Communist Constitutional Debates," *Theory and Society*, 30(5): 629–69.

—— (2005) "'Poles-Catholics' and 'Symbolic Jews': Jewishness as Social Closure in Poland," *Studies in Contemporary Jewry*, vol. 21 ("Jews, Catholics, and the Burden of History," E. Lederhendler (ed.)), New York: Oxford University Press: 65–87.

—— (2006) *The Crosses of Auschwitz: Nationalism and Religion in Post-Communist Poland*, Chicago: University of Chicago Press.

9 National identity and tourism in twentieth-century Ireland
The role of collective re-imagining

Eric Zuelow

In recent years many commentators have declared nations to be either dying or dead; globalization has "deterritorialized" nations, they claim, and created a planet populated with increasingly cosmopolitan *citoyens du monde*. Yet there are significant indications that such pronouncements are premature. Americans, for example, whose nationalism usually goes undeclared, reacted to the September 11, 2001 terrorist attacks in an unabashedly nationalist fashion that was exemplified by the nearly ubiquitous display of flags. Likewise, the end of the Cold War has done little to change the amount of violent nationalist conflict around the globe (Ayres 2000). Instead, Michael Billig's notion of "banal nationalism," in which nationalism is hidden behind other identities until a moment of crisis, appears accurate (Billig 1995). Nations do not die but persist, often hidden from view, until circumstances make them necessary. The problem, which Billig does not solve, is to explain this persistence and why it is that, when needed, nations possess the remarkable ability to be both current and relevant.

Consider the example of nineteenth- and twentieth-century Ireland. Prior to independence, Irish nationalism was largely predicated on the need to define Ireland in opposition to England. Gaelic language and culture provided a powerful contrast with English culture. Rugged west coast scenery offered a striking "other" to the landscape of England's Home Counties. Irish political groups, ranging from the Fenians to the Irish Parliamentary Party, strove to separate Ireland from Britain – either through independence or devolution. Once Ireland gained its independence, needs changed. Irish leaders now faced a series of daunting challenges that included the formation of functioning political institutions, a housing crisis, poverty and disease, a woefully inadequate criminal justice system, damagingly high emigration, and more. These challenges were themselves chronologically contingent. The problems of the 1920s were different from those of the 1950s. Yet change did not diminish the salience of national identity. This chapter is concerned with one major question: how and why did the nation remain important despite such widely varying circumstances?

Such an exploration is made difficult because scholars commonly disagree about precisely what a nation is, and currently existing definitions fail to fully describe the realities of "nationness." For example, Miroslav Hroch claims that nations are composed of memories of a common past, "a density of linguistic or cultural ties," and "a conception of the equality of all members of the group organized as a civil society" (Hroch 1996: 79). There are two closely related problems with this suggestion. First, such a description demands that members of the nation share memories of a common past – a demand that is problematic because memories are often hotly contested. Monuments may certainly reflect common myths, but their meanings tend to be read differently within a given society.[1] At the same time linguistic and cultural ties are also contested. In Scotland, for example, there are no fewer than three linguistic traditions (English, Scots and Gaelic), yet this diversity has not limited the development of a common national identity. Likewise, in Ireland, the primacy given to the Gaelic language in the nationalist mythology is largely the domain of a small segment of the intelligentsia and Gaelic-speaking areas themselves traditionally showed little commitment to language preservation, putting more importance on economic development (see below).

Others have presented more subjective definitions for the nation, defining it as a psychological phenomenon rather than a collection of objective criteria. Walker Connor contends that nations are units composed of specific ethnic groups, and that nationalism, which he prefers to call "ethnonationalism," is defined as loyalty to one's ethnic group (Connor 2002: 25). People are members of the nation because they *believe* that they have common ancestral ties with their fellow members (Smith 2002: 63). Connor's characterization has definite benefits. In particular, it explains why different people within a nation might believe widely varying things about their common ancestry and so interpret the past differently. Yet Connor's emphasis on ethnic ties is problematic because not all nations are defined in ethnic terms. While identity may certainly be based on an ancestral principle (*ius sanguinis*) – as in Germany from 1842 to 2000 – it might also be built on an older territorial principle (*ius soli*), which is prominent in countries created by a history of immigration such as in the United States (Kurthen and Minkenberg 1995: 181).

Benedict Anderson extends the idea that nations are primarily psychological constructions by defining them as "imagined communities" (Anderson 1991: 6–7). His definition is hugely popular for a variety of very solid reasons, the most important of which is that it is flexible enough to explain the existence of virtually all nations, while specific enough to distinguish nations from other communities. However, Rick Altman correctly points out that this definition fails to provide any means of explaining how nations change, how they are re-imagined. He argues:

> Anderson concentrates on the moment when a nation was formed and stops there, failing to acknowledge the ongoing nature of the process he has described. Nationhood, in other words, is not merely established, it

must be *maintained*; its definition, therefore, will inevitably shift over time.

(quoted in Williams 2002: 3)

This paper builds on Altman's critique by arguing that nations are not static, but instead constantly evolve to meet changing demands. Michael Billig is correct when he argues that nations are embodied in the "habits of social life" and he is right to point out that established nations maintain their nationalism through a "continual 'flagging,' or reminding, of nation-hood," but there is more going on (Billig 1995: 8–9). Nations are not main-tained strictly through the occasional unrolling of a flag or a burst of inflamed rhetoric. Instead, older traditions, symbols and memories are con-stantly altered to serve successive generations, while at the same time new traditions are created to meet new demands. Neither a perennial reality nor an entirely modern creation, nations are actually an ongoing process that assures continued relevance. More than an "imagined community," the nation is perpetually *re-imagined* through an ongoing exchange of ideas. The challenge is to uncover how this exchange of ideas actually functions.

Viewing nations as a process of debate renders discussion concerning whether nations were created from the top down or the bottom up largely superfluous. Consider the great pageant promoted by Sir Walter Scott in 1822 upon the occasion of George IV's visit to Scotland. This event is often cited as the moment, if there was a single moment, when Highland dress became the national dress of Scotland (Prebble 1988: 103). It is very clear that Scott stage-managed the entire visit; he even went so far as to compose a letter to the Scottish people teaching them how to dress and behave at each stage of the royal tour. Indeed, it is true that of the thousands who flocked to Edinburgh, many accepted Scott's directions. Yet many others voiced their contempt for the affair. One Highlander thundered that he had never seen "so much tartan before ... with so little Highland material" (*Black-wood's Edinburgh Magazine*, September 1822: 359–68). Another commenta-tor complained that Highlanders, "a small part of the Scottish population in number ... had more than their share of the royal notice" (*Letters to Sir Walter Scott* 1822: 74–6). Newspapers described the situation as "kilts versus breeches" and one newspaper expressed concern that Lowlanders, so unaccus-tomed to the draftiness of the soon-to-be national dress, might be "killed by the kilt" because they would be ill prepared to suffer the vicious Scottish wind (*Blackwood's Edinburgh Magazine*, September 1822: 359–68). In short, George IV's visit certainly spawned a renewed interest in Highland dress, but it did so both in positive and negative respects. Scott may have created events for consumption, but individuals made a choice about whether the Highland symbolism was *their* symbolism. What happened, in other words, was that the event spawned a dialogue about whether or not Scottishness was synonymous with the Highlands.[2]

National dialogue is not the monopoly of an elite but instead takes place among both insiders and outsiders; national members drawn horizontally from across society join with foreign governments, and others whose expectations help shape the nation. This ongoing process both defines the nation and accounts for its continued relevance. The challenge is to reconcile the reality of personal choice, the notion of nationalism as a perpetual process, and the need to make sense of ever-changing and largely individual identities, which, somehow, coalesce into a collective identity, in order to produce a workable research methodology.

This chapter attempts to offer an understanding by using tourism as a window into the evolution of Irish national identity in the years following independence. The underlying assumption is that nations are negotiated at specific "nexus" where dialogue about the nation is inspired and carried out. Although tourism is certainly not the only such meeting point, it represents a particularly useful nexus for several reasons. First, tourism is often identified as a national interest because it is able to offer benefits to many different groups within the national community, while at the same time these groups often have disparate concerns in mind; the result is an immediate dialogue about exactly what the nation's priorities should be. Second, tourism, at least national tourism, requires consideration of precisely what it means to be part of the nation being promoted, its defining characteristics, history and geographic space. There is not always consensus about the best image to present to the tourist gaze, and thus tourism quite naturally prompts discussion about the nature of national identity (Zuelow 2005: 189–204). Finally, tourism involves the movement of people both within their own nation and between nations, and it places a premium on the interaction of people from different geographic spaces. The result of this contact is a continual exchange of ideas about mutual identities and "a dynamic between previous understanding and expectations and new observations and experiences" (Schwartz 1994: 3).

This chapter traces the role played by tourism in the ongoing process of redefining Irish nationalism and national identity following the Irish Civil War (June 1922–April 1923). The following pages offer a roughly chronological account of successive challenges and adaptations, beginning with discussion of a debate that began in the wake of the Civil War about precisely what Ireland's national goals should be. Once widespread agreement emerged concerning the national interest in promoting tourism, attention shifted toward the question of precisely how Ireland should be represented, both to insiders and outsiders. At each stage, I have endeavored to show at least a few of the differing poles of debate. Although an article of this length cannot possibly be comprehensive, the following pages nevertheless demonstrate the notion of the nation as the product of ongoing debate, able to perpetually change shape to match new demands.

The national interest debate

When Dáil Eireann (Irish parliament) ratified the Anglo–Irish Treaty on January 7, 1922, Ireland gained, in the words of revolutionary leader Michael Collins, "not the ultimate freedom that all nations desire and develop to, but the freedom to achieve it" (quoted in Coogan 1992: 301). The Irish tourist industry was one important beneficiary of this new independence while at the same time the process of developing tourism played a vital role in helping to define Irish identity in the new state. Shortly after the conclusion of the Civil War, the Irish Tourist Association (ITA) was launched in Cork and by June 1924 the group emerged as the only national tourism body of the Irish Free State.[3] Initially, the ITA was not alone – at least two other tourism associations were also founded in the immediate aftermath of the Irish Civil War: the Tourist Organisation Society of Ireland (TOSI) and the West of Ireland Tourist Development Association. Unlike nineteenth-century tourism development efforts, the new bodies were comprised mainly of *Irish* tourism advocates. In fact, following a merger of the three tourism organizations, the Irish Tourist Association employed a staff that was almost entirely comprised of republican nationalists who once fought for an Irish Republic, first against the British and then against their own countrymen. For some, tourism simply equaled employment, but for others, such as former IRA man turned ITA secretary J.P. O'Brien, it was an all-consuming passion, an opportunity to celebrate all that was best about Ireland and a chance to show the world that Ireland could be economically successful. O'Brien pored over the tourism literature from countries such as France, Switzerland and England; he traveled widely to observe European tourism programs firsthand; and he dreamed about an Emerald Isle that would be a mecca for sportsmen, a destination for golfers and even an international culinary center. For O'Brien, and others like him, tourism superseded political disputes over the type of government Ireland should have; tourism was a powerful vehicle for helping Irish men raise their status, and thus it bolstered an already strong sense of nationalism (Andrews 1982: 66 and 71; Zuelow 2004b: 37–8).

Between roughly 1924 and 1952, the Irish engaged in an extended debate about whether tourism ought to be considered a national interest. Those who opposed tourism can be easily forgiven for their lack of foresight. In the wake of the Irish Civil War, the new government had serious problems to address. Transportation networks were hopelessly disrupted. Dublin was seriously overcrowded. Infant mortality was appalling. Worse, a significant portion of the citizenry did not support the new state and government institutions were too weak to seriously challenge opposition.[4] At a time when the very existence of the state was in question, most wondered how anybody could seriously advocate spending money to entice tourists – most of them English – to visit Ireland.

Yet that is precisely what the Irish Tourist Association advocated. For the

ITA, tourism was not just a national interest, it was a nationalist obligation and should "appeal to every patriotic Irishman" (*Kerryman*, January 26, 1924). Tourism represented not only a way to bring in much needed income, it was also a means of teaching both visitors and the Irish themselves about the country's unique geography, history and culture (*Kerryman*, August 21, 1926). Equally important, a successful tourist development program would help establish Ireland as a notable European nation-state by placing the country into the company of other states who were just then launching their own nationalist tourism movements. Since the turn of the century, Spain, France, Austria and Italy initiated major tourism promotion efforts. In Spain, for example, advocates insisted that "those anxious for progress and for our country to figure among the most prosperous, patriots in general" should take the initiative by furthering tourism development (Pack 2004: 56). Tourism was a pan-European movement and Ireland's tourism advocates were both aware of their neighbors' activities and anxious to take part themselves. Not surprisingly, ITA representatives visited the Continent in order to discover "the French method of catering for tourists" (*Kerryman*, January 15, 1927).

Others were not so sure. Some Dáil ministers argued that the Irish should focus on making Ireland a place worth living in and the government should not be "so very keen on making this country an attractive place for tourists" (Dáil Debate, November 20, 1924: 1322). Was the welfare of the Irish people not the nation's primary concern, especially in a time of crisis? As one newspaper put it:

> If it can be found possible to provide building materials for the erection or reconstruction of hotels for wealthy foreigners, many of whom are as mythical as their wealth, it ought to be possible to provide some materials for the more urgent need of housing our own people.
>
> (*Kilkenny People*, June 15, 1946)

On a similar note, why should money be given to tourist development when tuberculosis was rampant and infant mortality appalling (*Kilkenny People*, July 24, 1943)?

There were cultural objections to tourism as well. Since the development of the Irish-Ireland movement in the 1880s, Gaelic culture was widely believed to be a fundamental marker of Irish identity. Gaelic sport, dance and language distinguished Ireland from England and exemplified a significant justification for independence. Now that the country was independent, the actual significance of Gaelic culture to the Irish people was being tested. On one hand, many language enthusiasts felt that the introduction of tourism represented a "deadly threat" to the Irish language revival and so to the heart of the country itself. It was feared that if a large number of Anglophone tourists descended on Ireland's already shrinking Gaeltachts (Irish-speaking districts), the native language would die out. One cabinet minister went so far as to urge development of a new policy that would balance economics with the urgent cause of language preservation. He suggested "a drastic re-organization of the whole [Gaeltacht] area" in which holiday villages would be constructed and staffed with Irish-speakers employed to talk with tourists, while English-speakers would be banned from entering Irish homes outside special tourist areas. Local disciplinarians backed with government support would enforce the scheme (MacEntee, November 20, 1934).

Letter-writers protested emphatically against tourist development and the expenditure of public moneys thereon, "while no effective steps [were] being taken to protect the Gaeltacht from *such a formidable influx of foreignism. For it is a deadly threat to the Gaeltacht, if not to the whole Gaelic revival movement*" (*Irish Press*, September 30, 1938; emphasis mine). Not only would tourists inspire Gaelic-speakers to abandon Irish in favor of English, they were synonymous with hedonism and waste, with modernity. There was nothing *Irish* about luxury, jazz and trash. Nothing Irish about reshaping the country to fit foreign tastes. Developing tourism, at least for those who spoke out about the Tourist Traffic Act, represented a betrayal of all that was fundamentally Irish (*Irish Press*, October 3, 1938).

On the other hand, those in the ITA and even a substantial number of rural Gaelic speakers were anxious to promote tourism. These groups believed that increased tourist traffic would assure "increased employment in the Gaeltacht, thereby helping to stop emigration of Irish speakers and [to] preserve the language," not to mention increasing the amount of farm produce consumed, much of it grown by Gaelic-speaking farmers. Both sides of the debate were careful to support the preservation of the language, but they adopted quite different approaches to doing so. One stressed radical conservatism, the other advocated a leap into the modern age. One group emphasized the importance of an identity based upon a timeless and (hopefully) unchanging set of cultural and linguistic practices, the other favored a forward-looking Ireland that was not afraid to adapt itself to changing realities.

From the 1920s to the early 1950s, tourism prompted debate about the very nature of Ireland's national interest. Should Ireland be modern or traditional? Should outsiders be welcomed or turned away? It was more than a debate about economic policy; it was a debate about what the "Irish people" wanted now that the Anglo–Irish Treaty freed them to decide matters for themselves. More importantly, as long as the debate raged in Ireland's newspapers, pubs and halls of government, it was never possible to escape both the idea that Ireland was a nation, despite the recent lesion of Civil War, and that this nation had to collectively work out what it wanted from independence. In other words, the national interest debate assured a transition from an older separatist identity to a newer state-building one; Irish identity could no longer be defined in opposition to England, now it needed to draw people together and focus them on the task of building a unified state.

By 1952, there was finally widespread agreement that tourism development was in the national interest. There were several reasons for the shift but the single most important was that the Irish Tourist Association and its supporters finally convinced those in power, as well as a variety of others, including many local entrepreneurs, parish priests and community groups, that tourism development was a good idea. Rural communities now held tourism as a curative to the high emigration that threatened to wipe them from the map. County councils believed that tourism would bring vital infrastructural improvements and tourist dollars. The Department of Industry and Commerce dreamed of an improved balance of payments. The Department of External Affairs believed that tourism would provide an important form of "cultural propaganda" that would raise Ireland's diplomatic and economic profile with foreign powers – especially with those who were angered by Ireland's neutrality during World War II (Zuelow 2005: 189–204). Even so, tourism still did not enjoy universal support. Previously expressed anguish over the tourism-inspired demise of the Gaelic language diminished though it did not disappear. Others doubted whether tourism would ever bring its promised benefits and angrily attacked pro-tourism schemes that might detract from other forms of development (*Irish Times*, January 18, 1961). There were even those who did not relish an influx of tourists and who were willing to threaten visitors, especially English ones (Lemass 1964).

Defining Ireland

Once the decision was made to take tourism seriously, tourism developers faced a new problem hinted at by the modernization/traditionalist clash outlined above: what exactly did the Irish people think of themselves and how did they want to present that identity to the world at large?

In many ways it was easier to say what Ireland was not. In December 1949, *Holiday Magazine*, an American publication, issued an extensive article written by Frank O'Connor, a major twentieth-century Irish short-story writer. Although the article, which featured many beautiful color photographs, looked fantastic, O'Connor's story was more problematic. He drew attention to Ireland's terrible slums, described the country's sick and poorly dressed children, spoke of disease and unemployment, and painted a picture of an oppressive society in which boys and girls were rigorously separated and an omnipresent clergy ruled all.

Much of O'Connor's account was correct. Dublin's overcrowding was notorious. Poverty was widespread and tuberculosis was all too common. The Church was extraordinarily powerful and could be frighteningly oppressive. Yet *Holiday*'s Ireland was not the Ireland imagined by the Irish themselves and public outcry was immediate and vociferous. There were protests, complaints and demanded apologies (*Irish Press*, January 21, 1950; Byrne 1949; *Irish Independent*, January 7, 1950; Killarney Urban District Council

1950). Even the Catholic press, which seldom commented on tourism-related issues, condemned the piece as a "grave mistake" (*Catholic News*, November 26, 1949). But what did the Irish people as a group want Ireland to be? In 1943, long-time Prime Minister Eamon De Valera, offered a utopian vision in which Ireland would

> be the home of a people who valued material wealth only as a basis of right living, of a people who were satisfied with frugal comfort and devoted their leisure to things of the spirit; a land whose countryside would be bright with cosy homesteads, whose fields and villages would be joyous with sounds of industry, the romping of sturdy children, the contests of athletic youths, the laughter of comely maidens; whose fire-sides would be the forums of the wisdom of serene old age.
>
> (Brown 1985: 113)

Yet the people themselves largely rejected this view through their actions and instead moved in large numbers to Dublin or further afield. Apparently the people did not relish the idea of living in rural poverty; they did not want to be frugal nor to accept the truth of what O'Connor had written.

Once more, tourism provided a fertile soil for the creation of something new, a fresh Ireland that would expunge the unsavory smells of rural poverty. The alternate Ireland that was developed and marketed reflected a combination of the older symbols of the Irish *ethnie* and more recent creations that together reflected an overwhelmingly positive vision of Ireland and Irish identity. This new identity, while initially created for tourists, played another role as well. Not only did the process of debating it draw a substantial cross-section of the population into a dialogue about Irishness, but the resulting products – new family-friendly festivals, a kinder and gentler history and an equally attractive landscape – were inescapable. They *became* reality. Three short vignettes can stand as examples of the larger process.

New festivals: An Tóstal

Until quite recently, Ireland was overwhelmingly agricultural and rural. Although Ireland did not undergo the kind of industrial revolution that swept Britain, Germany and France, there were changes during the late nineteenth and early twentieth centuries. Many moved to Dublin and Cork or emigrated. Industrialization was attempted. The network of country fairs that once dominated country life were rendered obsolete by improved transportation networks (Cronin *et al.* 2001: 14).

By the 1950s, few "traditional" fairs remained and those that did sparked feelings of deep ambivalence. Puck Fair was by far the most important surviving fair and it featured drinking and dancing, animal filth, Traveller encampments and brawls. More notable, however, was the crowning of a goat as king by a young girl queen – an act that carried a faint suggestion of sexual bestiality. While hundreds continued to attend the fair, others had objections that were not dissimilar from those voiced regarding the depiction of Ireland in *Holiday* magazine. Beyond the obvious symbolic problem with the goat, those opposed to Puck believed that it was "all about drinking" (Rukeyser 1965: 25) and therefore offered an image of the Irish as drunken. The fair was also marked by "hatred and dreariness" and "long, slow, slugging fighting, breaking everything it passes through" (ibid: 28) – a fact which might remind visitors of Ireland's long and bloody history of both internal and external conflict.

Tourist authorities were well aware of the symbolic problems exemplified by Puck. The editor of the Tourist Board's *Ireland of the Welcomes* magazine, for example, informed one Puck-enthused travel writer that he should "only stress those aspects of Puck Fair which are universally acceptable as attractions" (Gorman September 4, 1959). Where the Fair's participants saw Puck as something uniquely Irish, the authorities saw Dionysian excess filled with drinking and fighting as well as veiled sexuality. One group embraced tradition while another feared what this tradition said about modern Ireland. Which was it to be? Was Ireland going to be violent and drunken or welcoming?

The solution to the dilemma posed by Ireland's traditional fairs was to create new events that were acceptable to a wide audience. "An Tóstal, Ireland at Home," the first of these new tourist festivals, was held between 1953 and 1958. Although the Tóstal was completely modern, it was firmly rooted in memory of Ireland's past; it was presented as a vestige of Irish history. Organizers proudly claimed that An Tóstal was a direct descendant of "great festivals of long ago – Tara, Tailteann, Carmain, Uisneach and all the rest" (*An Tóstal Programme*, 1953). Of course, in reality, Tailteann, a sort of medieval Olympic Games, had not been held since 1169 (with the exception of a shortlived revival in the 1920s), Tara was more associated with medieval governance than hedonistic enjoyment; and the other two events were pagan religious holidays and bore virtually no similarity to the very modern and mostly secular An Tóstal (Joyce 1912). Even the Gaelic name chosen for the festival was meant to inspire memories of "Ireland's earliest national assemblages" (An Bord Fáilte, June 1952: 96). "Ireland at Home" was offered to visitors as being just as traditional as Puck Fair, if not more so, yet An Tóstal lacked the ambivalence attached to the more traditional Irish fair.

Organizers further stressed the historical antecedents of An Tóstal through the choice of events. This choice was not made at national level, but rather was left to local organizing committees. The "strongest possible emphasis" was placed on Gaelic life, history, language and culture. General themes included "nationality," "culture" and "constitutional and civic life." National traditions, language, music, art, drama, folklore, recreation and leisure were given precedence (An Bord Fáilte, June 1952: 3).

But An Tóstal did not solely emphasize the past, the event also spanned the divide between tradition and modernity. Amid the theatre and music festivals, Gaelic games and historical pageants, organizers also included industrial expositions and parades while the Tóstal guidebook stressed the country's modern industry (Fógra Fáilte 1953). Far from providing an image of the idle Irish, the festival presented work as a vital window into the Irish soul. The failure to industrialize the country was not the fault of the Irish. Organizers argued that, although no systematic effort to develop manufacturing was attempted until independence, since that time "substantial advances have been made towards effecting a satisfactory economic balance between agricultural and manufacturing enterprise" (ibid: 53). For organizers, it was a matter of significant pride that "considerable progress" was made in a short period of time toward industrializing Ireland (ibid: 56).

It would have been possible to create a tourist festival without reference to the past – the 1951 Festival of Britain, for example, predominantly focused on the present and future (Conekin 2003) – but from local councils to central authorities there was a strong desire to place An Tóstal into historical context and to draw on preexisting traditions as markers of authentic Irishness. Timeless culture was reformatted and reformed to match new demands. Poverty, alcoholism and emigration were replaced by productivity, joyfulness and strength. There was both an invention of tradition and a perpetuation of older *ethnie*. The national past persisted through change.

Yet, despite all of this, An Tóstal was not universally welcomed. For example, the satirical magazine *Dublin Opinion* printed a series of cartoons criticizing the unreality of the affair. One cartoon depicted a Tóstal committee asking two homeless men to disappear from view, "just until after the Tóstal." Another image made light of the exaggerated importance assigned the event as a farmer implored his daughter not to emigrate because the Tóstal was bringing along guests and deserting them would be counter to stereotypes of Irish friendliness and hospitality. Newspaper reports were often similarly grim, especially after few tourists ultimately traveled to Ireland to participate in the early spring event. The *Leinster Express*, for example, lamented that the Tóstal scene was one of "flags and bunting bedraggled, bands playing bravely, no sign of tourists, and ministers of state standing under umbrellas saying their piece" (*Leinster Express* August 2, 1958). Many argued about the timing of the event, noting that Irish weather is not always conducive to tourism during the rainy season. Did the country really want to emphasize its frequently damp weather?

Despite the criticism, An Tóstal lasted through 1958 and, once cancelled, many of the local festivals created for the larger national event persisted as new traditions for a new Ireland. There were culinary festivals (never mind that the quality of Irish cuisine was long an issue among tourism developers and that training schemes were necessary to improve the quality of Irish cooking (Taoiseach's speech 1960)), theatre festivals, opera festivals and more – all of which avoided the challenges posed by "authentic" Irish events. The dialogue concerning what Irishness should entail created revised traditions to replace older, more troubling versions while, at the same time, creating a dialogue about Irishness that almost unavoidably drew people from across Ireland into the discussion. Tóstal publicity was everywhere, as was pressure to conform to the high standards of aesthetic and corporeal behavior demanded by festival organizers.

A renewed history: the restoration of Kilmainham Jail[5]

Past and present were connected using more than just festivals. Historical sites could also be utilized as a means of informing a new generation about the heroism of the past, while at the same time creating a more recent mythology. The restoration of Kilmainham Jail represents a classic example of how this process worked.

The British opened Kilmainham Jail just in time to accept rebel prisoners captured during the United Irishmen Uprising of 1798. Thereafter, the prison held virtually every major Irish revolutionary figure from Robert Emmet to Charles Stuart Parnell, the Fenian William Smith O'Brien to republican Eamon De Valera. Furthermore, Kilmainham was the site of infamous events including the execution of major 1916 Rising leaders and of the first irregular prisoners executed by the Free State during the Irish Civil War. Even so, the overwhelming majority of prisoners at Kilmainham were not nationalist heroes, but ordinary men and women driven to crime by poverty and hunger.

Prior to the late 1950s, Kilmainham Jail fell increasingly into ruin, a victim of memory. Who wanted to celebrate the Civil War or the horrors of colonial oppression? During the late 1950s the ambivalence lifted. The immediate cause was the zeal of a handful of nationalists who worried that the revolutionary past might be forgotten. These men, led by a largely forgotten Lorcan C.G. Leonard, created the Kilmainham Jail Restoration Society and composed a proposal that called for the restoration of the prison through voluntary effort. The government, pleased to be rid of the rotting structure, was quick to provide the Society with the keys at a nominal one-penny rent.

There are two particularly salient points to be made about the restoration effort. First, the Society was able to generate interest in its project because it reformulated memory of the prison. During its first meeting, the group agreed to simply forget everything that occurred after 1921 (Leonard 1960). Memory of the Civil War was simply ignored, cleverly erasing conflict that would otherwise have derailed the group's plans. Indeed, the only memory that had any place at Kilmainham was that of unified struggle. Yet this does not mean that all debate was avoided. In 1966, just as the restoration project was reaching its conclusion, the Labour Party proposed the erection of a special memorial to the Marxist leader of the Citizen Army, James Connolly, in the prison yard where he had been executed in 1916. The Restoration

Society rejected the proposal, however, saying, "James Connolly belonged to the whole Irish people and not to any political party, not even to the one he founded" (Dowling 1966). Without exception, Kilmainham was reconstructed as a symbol of a *unified* sense of Irish identity, not a political tribute to one party or another.

Second, the restoration was significant because the message of political and social unity offered by the Society helped create widespread public awareness of and favor for the project. Overwhelmingly, the costs of restoration were met through voluntary contributions from individuals, businesses and other organizations willing to support the effort. Not only did the voluntary nature of the project allow the Restoration Society to work around unpleasant memories, but it also reshaped the central memory of the prison into that of a site representing the *whole* of Ireland. The restoration would not have been possible without government approval, but it was everyday Irishmen and women who undertook the bodily memory work required to rebuild the site. The workers had taken aim at Ireland's problems, just as the revolutionaries had done, and stood as physical reminders of the country's improving fortunes during the early 1960s. While the 1950s were a time of declining industrial output and dropping GNP, to say nothing of climbing unemployment (O'Hearn 1998: 38), the 1960s represented a period of "remarkable growth" and the workers symbolized this reversal (ibid: 49). While those who emigrated had abandoned the nation and its problems, these volunteers reconstructed the jail as a totem of the national struggle, an Irish phoenix risen.

Just as with An Tóstal, the restoration of Kilmainham drew on history but altered it to meet new demands. Historical memory proved malleable, able, without difficulty, to transform to serve chronologically contingent needs.

A revived landscape: the Tidy Towns and Villages Competition

The process of renegotiating the past did not end with the creation of festivals or the restoration of the past but had to extend to the landscape as well. Between 1851 and 1921, more than 4.5 million Irish men and women emigrated overseas (Miller 1985: 569). Independence certainly did not end the evacuation. During the 1950s, for example, four of every five children born between 1931 and 1941 emigrated (Lee 1989: 379). The exodus transformed the landscape. Derelict sites and ramshackle structures pockmarked both urban and rural Ireland. Those buildings that remained were drab and grey with all the personality of "wet cement" (Zuelow 2002a). To gaze on an Irish townscape was to gaze upon a history of misfortune, not the joyful openness and growing prosperity that tourism proponents wanted to emphasize.

Efforts to reinvent the Irish landscape stretch to the very beginning of the post-independence tourist movement, but serious efforts at improvement only took flight during the 1950s. Even before the first An Tóstal planning efforts, officials urged the Irish people to plant colorful window boxes, repaint their homes, to trim unruly hedgerows, and to generally improve the appearance of both the Irish countryside and Irish townscapes (An Bord Fáilte June 1951: 4–5). Then, when the government announced the An Tóstal festival, the public was told:

> we must be proud of what we have to show and therefore we must plan and prepare. Everyone can help, by decorating homes, by removing eyesores, by writing to friends abroad, by showing courtesy to our visitors, [and] by aiding in the setting up and activities of local Tóstal committees.
>
> (An Bord Fáilte, September 1952: 1)

Civic pride was essential and local committees were the "most effective weapon" for creating it (An Bord Fáilte August 1952: 2). Newspaper-readers were urged to "trim your lawns and plant flowers" (*Kilkenny People*, March 14, 1953), and were informed that An Tóstal would "result in the brightening up of towns and villages and the clearing away of eyesores" (*Kilkenny People*, March 21, 1953). In short, An Tóstal was an excuse for redefining aesthetic sensibilities and for teaching the Irish people to be better, more welcoming hosts.

A number of towns energetically adopted Tourist Board suggestions and the public-education component of An Tóstal was judged to be a resounding success. Bord Fáilte strove to expand the ability of the festival to promote civic pride and the implementation of local improvements (Memorandum, February 19, 1958; Zuelow 2002b). The result was a new "Tidy Towns and Villages Competition" inaugurated as part of the 1958 An Tóstal. There were no large prizes and little publicity, yet the idea was popular enough to attract 53 entries in the first year alone (Bord Fáilte 1958; Zuelow 2002a). Enthusiasm was infectious and spread like a pandemic of aestheticism.

The Tidy Towns and Villages initiative resonated at both the local and national levels. The Minister for Local Government was especially smitten by the idea and promptly encouraged "earnest consideration" of the project by each local authority and stressed "the desirability of taking part in the competition." Participation was "clearly in the national interest . . . so that there may be widespread awakening of civic consciousness in the direction of making and keeping towns clean, tidy, and generally attractive." In keeping with the Tidy Towns idea, the Department of Local Government urged measures to clear derelict sites, improve sanitary conditions, remove litter and otherwise embellish townscapes by providing litter receptacles, planting trees and shrubs, maintaining public sanitary conveniences and painting public buildings, to say nothing of working closely with shopkeepers to make further improvements (Department of Local Government 1959: 114–15).[6]

Backed by strong support, the Tidy Towns Competition quickly took hold. There were 82 entries in 1959, 213 in 1960, and an impressive 804 in 1984 (Bord Fáilte 1959; Bord Fáilte 1961; Bord Fáilte 1984). By 1964 Bord Fáilte reported that "Irish villages and towns looked markedly neater and more colorful than at any time in the past," and it attributed the improvement to the Tidy Towns Competition (Bord Fáilte 1964). Soon, the competition was expanded by the addition of new categories, including one for rural roadside properties – an interesting category because "contestants" did not register to compete, as was the case in the other categories; rather, Tourist Board officials simply noted particularly attractive properties "which set an example to others in the district" while driving around the country (ibid.). It was a less than subtle way of encouraging rural dwellers, using peer pressure and competition, to maintain their land and houses in a manner acceptable to tourists and the tourist authorities.

Tidy Towns was a top–down program; however, the actual implementation of change was often carried out by grassroots organizations. Local church leaders frequently conducted the campaigns. Even more often, Tidy Town efforts were the domain of women anxious to demonstrate their organizational abilities on a public stage. They sought to show Ireland that its women were far more than just good housekeepers; they were stewards of Irish places and spaces, with control over the aesthetic appeal of their country. It was a way for women to express both local and national pride and to be rewarded accordingly (Zuelow 2002a).

The end result of the Tidy Towns effort was the complete redefinition of Irish land and townscapes. Where once Irish scenery reflected a legacy of poverty, now Irish places and spaces symbolized friendliness, warmth and economic growth. In effect, markers of unpleasant memory were removed, providing symbols of a new version of the past that exemplified all that was best about the Irish character. As above, Tidy Towns did not entirely reinvent Irishness, nor did the Competition draw extensively (if at all) on past models. Instead, it drew together a combination of people from across society and prompted a dialogue about what Ireland should look like, how the past should be imagined, and what the present would mean for the Irish nation.

Conclusions

Throughout the history of independent Ireland, tourism functioned as a nexus for debate about the very meanings and collective goals of Irish nationhood. The change engendered by tourism was everywhere. Schoolchildren visited historical sites such as Kilmainham Jail; more Irish people traveled within their own country; drivers traveled roadways repaved and signed for tourists; tourist festivals took place everywhere; and people from across the society contributed to debate concerning the national interest by offering their thoughts in letters to the editor and to government officials, as well as during discussions held at pubs, council meetings and public debates. Even homeowners who cared little about the appearance of their homes could not escape public pressure to improve the aesthetics of their buildings and yards. In short, it was difficult if not impossible to escape the tourism-inspired debate and this debate, in turn, was closely tied to the question of Irish national identity. What was the nation's past? What was the national landscape? What traditions made the country unique? What interests did members of the Irish nation have in common? As long as the assumption of national unity was combined with concern about what was fundamentally "Irish," national identity was perpetuated and altered to meet new demands.

James E. Young, one of the leading scholars of Holocaust memory, makes a vital point when he writes that the most successful memorial is one that remains "unfinished, unbuilt, a forever unresolved process.... Instead of a fixed sculptural or architectural icon ... the debate itself – perpetually unresolved amid ever-changing conditions – might now be enshrined" (Young 1997: 879). The very moment that memory is marked by a fixed, unchanging memorial is the moment that it will be forgotten. The same thing is true of nations. The moment that people stop imagining the existence of nations (complete with the "interests" members of these nations believe they have in common) is the moment that nations will cease to be important.

Nations persist not because their members have a series of *ethnie* in common, but because there is *disagreement* about the relative importance of these various markers. Resulting debate assures that aspects of nationness are almost always in the public eye and are frequently discussed. Likewise, globalization does not weaken nations as many suggest, it generates renewed debate about how the nation fits into a larger world of other nations. The proliferation of American culture, McDonaldization and Disneyfication, for example, creates another nexus for debate because it raises the question: what impact will Ronald and Mickey have on native culture (whatever that native culture might involve)?

The challenge for scholars is to locate nexus at which debate occurs. Such nexus might include political issues such as immigration/emigration, cultural questions such as the precise nature of national festivals, or geographic challenges such as the preservation of symbolic landscapes. These debates may actually appear quite banal and need not be prompted by any external threat or challenge; those engaged in these discussions may not even realize that they are helping to perpetuate the nation. Irish tourism planners, for example, did not believe they were fundamentally defining Irishness, but their day-to-day concern with assigning primacy to one cultural marker or another, with shaping landscapes to attract tourists, and with stressing all that was best about Irishness meant that they perpetuated dialogue with every initiative they proposed or considered.

Nations persist and change as a result of mundane, everyday discussion that is, in turn, shaped by changing contingencies; then, as Michael Billig argues, nations are ready to rise from banality, in an up-to-date form, when circumstances demand. Only by understanding the dynamic nature of nations can we ever hope to understand their persistence.

Notes

1 Much of the literature on monuments has focused on Holocaust memorials that often reflect national mythologies while recalling Nazi atrocities. James Young's *The Texture of Memory* (1993) goes a long way toward showing both how Holocaust memorials reflect national myths and also how they are variously interpreted within a given national community.

2 Readers interested in a more complete discussion of the royal visit should see Eric Zuelow, " 'Kilts *versus* Breeches': The Royal Visit, Tourism, and Scottish National Memory," *Journeys: The International Journal of Travel and Travel Writing* 7.2 (Fall 2006).

3 An earlier Irish Tourist Association was active in the 1890s under the direction of an Englishman named Frederick W. Crossley. See Furlong (2003).

4 At the conclusion of the Irish Civil War in 1923, the Irish Republican Army (IRA) merely dumped arms and did not offer an unconditional surrender to the Free State government against whom they had fought. Many IRA men continued to carry out attacks on both the Irish government and English servicemen (who were stationed at several English "Treaty Ports" as per the terms of the Anglo–Irish Treaty of 1921). The most famous of these attacks was the assassination of the Minister for Justice and Home Affairs, Kevin O'Higgins, in 1927. The government used a variety of tactics to stem the IRA threat, but the process of reconciliation and recovery took time. Indeed, social and political divisions left by the Civil War affected Irish life in one way or another into at least the 1950s and early 1960s.

5 Readers interested in a more complete account of the restoration should consult: Eric Zuelow, "Enshrining Ireland's Nationalist History Inside Prison Walls: The Restoration of Kilmainham Jail," *Eire-Ireland* Vol. 39, Nos. 3 & 4, Fall/Winter 2004, 180–201. The author is grateful to the Irish American Cultural Institute for permission to reuse material from this article: Copyright © 2004: Irish American Cultural Institute, 1 Lackawanna Place, Morristown, NJ, 07960. Reproduced by permission of the publisher, the Irish American Cultural Institute.

6 The author would like to thank Dr Aoife Bhreatnach for bringing this reference to his attention.

References

Newspapers and periodicals

Blackwood's Edinburgh Magazine
Catholic News
Irish Independent
Irish Press
Irish Times
Kerryman
Kilkenny People
Leinster Express

Published primary sources

(1822) *Letters to Sir Walter Scott, Bart., On the Moral and Political Character and Effects of the Visit to Scotland of His Majesty King George IV*, Edinburgh: Waugh and Innes.

"An Tóstal" (Ireland at Home) (1953) April 5–26. National Archives Ireland (NAI), Tourism, Transport and Communications (TTA) 12/1.

An Bord Fáilte (1951) *Irish Tourist Bulletin*, June, NAI, Department of the Taoiseach (DT), S14995A.

—— (1952) *Irish Tourist Bulletin*, June, NAI, DT, S14995A.

—— (1952) *Irish Tourist Bulletin*, August, NAI, DT, S14995A.

—— (1952) *Irish Tourist Bulletin*, September, NAI, DT, S14995A.

Andrews, C.S. (1982) *Man of No Property*, vol. 2, Dublin and Cork: Mercier Press.

Bord Fáilte (1958) *Annual Report and Accounts, Year Ending 31st March 1958*, Dublin: Bord Fáilte.

—— (1959) *Annual Report and Accounts, Year Ending 31st March 1959*, Dublin: Bord Fáilte.

—— (1961) *Annual Report and Accounts, Year Ended 31st March 1961*, Dublin: Bord Fáilte.

—— (1964) *The Irish Tourist Board Report for the Year Ended March 31 1964*, Dublin: Bord Fáilte.

—— (1984) *Bord Failte Report and Accounts for the Year Ended December 1984*, Dublin: Bord Fáilte.

Dáil Debate, 9, November 20, 1924.

Department of Local Government (1959) *Department of Local Government Report, 1958–1959*, Dublin: Public Records Office.

Fógra Fáilte (1953) *An Tóstal: Official Souvenir Guide*, Dublin: Fógra Fáilte. Michael Gorman private collection.

Rukeyser, M. (1965) *The Orgy*, New York: Coward-McCann.

Unpublished primary sources

(1950) Letter from Killarney Urban District Council Resolution and Letter to the Taoiseach, January 23, NAI, DT, S14716A.

(1958) Confidential Memorandum on An Tóstal Review, February 19, NAI, TTA 12/5.

(1960) Taoiseach's speech at closing banquet of International Hotel Association Conference, April 2, NAI, DT, S13087F.

Byrne, J. (1949) Letter to [?], [?] December, NAI, DT, S14716A.

Dowling, S. (1966) Letter to *Irish Times*, October 27, Kilmainham Jail Archives (KJA).

Gorman, M. (1959) Letter to Leslie Daiken, September 4, National Library of Ireland, MS 33, 472 Box 3, Folder 11.

Lemass, S. (1964) Letter to Erskine Childers, August 6, NAI, DT, S13087H/95.

Leonard, L.C.G. (1960) Manuscript: "The Kilmainham Project as I Dreamt It and Lived It," KJA.

MacEntee, S. (1934) Memorandum: Development of the Tourist Industry in the Gaeltacht, November 20, NAI, DT, S7839A & B.

Zuelow, E.G.E. (2002a) Interview with Michael Kevin O'Doherty, July 30, Dublin, Ireland.

Zuelow, E.G.E. (2002b) Interview with Michael Gorman, October 11, Dublin, Ireland.

Unpublished dissertations

Pack, S.D. (2004) "Spain in the Age of Mass Tourism, Modernization, and Dictatorship, 1945–1975," Ph.D. thesis, University of Wisconsin–Madison.
Zuelow, E.G.E. (2004b) "The Tourism Nexus: Tourism and National Identity since the Irish Civil War," Ph.D. thesis, University of Wisconsin–Madison.

Published secondary sources

Anderson, B. (1991) *Imagined Communities: Reflections on the Origin and Spread of Nationalism*, London and New York: Verso.
Ayres, R.W. (2000) "A World Flying Apart? Violent Nationalist Conflict and the End of the Cold War," *Journal of Peace Research*, 37(1): 105–17.
Billig, M. (1995) *Banal Nationalism*, London: Sage Publications.
Brown, T. (1985) *Ireland: A Social and Cultural History, 1922 to the Present*, Ithaca and London: Cornell University Press.
Conekin, B.E. (2003) *"The Autobiography of a Nation": The 1951 Festival of Britain*, Manchester and New York: Manchester University Press.
Connor, W. (2002) "Nationalism and Political Illegitimacy," in D. Conversi (ed.) *Ethnonationalism in the Contemporary World: Walker Connor and the Study of Nationalism*, London and New York: Routledge.
Coogan, T.P. (1992) *The Man Who Made Ireland: The Life and Death of Michael Collins*, Niwot, CO: Roberts Rinehart Publishers.
Cronin, D.A., Gilligan, J. and Holton, K. (eds) (2001) *Irish Fairs and Markets*, Dublin: Four Courts Press.
Furlong, I. (2003) "Frederick W. Crossley: Irish Turn-of-the-Century Tourism Pioneer," *Irish History: A Research Yearbook*, 2: 162–76.
Hroch, M. (1996) "From National Movement to the Fully-Formed Nation: The Nation-Building Process in Europe," in G. Balakrishnan (ed.) *Mapping the Nation*, New York and London: Verso.
Joyce, P.W. (1912) *A Social History of Ancient Ireland*, vol. II, New York: B. Blom.
Kurthen, H. and Minkenberg, M (1995) "Germany in Transition: Immigration, Racism and the Extreme Right," *Nations and Nationalism*, 1(2): 175–96.
Lee, J.J. (1989) *Ireland 1912–1985: Politics and Society*, Cambridge and New York: Cambridge University Press.
Miller, K.A. (1985) *Emigrants and Exiles: Ireland and the Irish Exodus to North America*, Oxford and New York: Oxford University Press.
O'Hearn, D. (1998) *Inside the Celtic Tiger: The Irish Economy and the Asian Model*, London and Sterling, VA: Pluto Press.
Prebble, J. (1988) *The King's Jaunt: George IV in Scotland, 1822*, London: Collins Publishing Group.
Schwartz, S.B. (ed.) (1994) *Implicit Understandings: Observing, Reporting, and Reflecting on the Encounters between Europeans and Other Peoples in the Early Modern Era*, Cambridge: Cambridge University Press.
Smith, A.D. (2002) "Dating the Nation," in D. Conversi (ed.) *Ethnonationalism in the Contemporary World: Walker Connor and the Study of Nationalism*, London and New York: Routledge.
Williams, A. (ed.) (2002) *Film and Nationalism*, Newark: Rutgers University Press.
Young, J.E. (1993) *The Texture of Memory*, New Haven: Yale University Press.

—— (1997) "Germany's Memorial Question: Memory, Counter-Memory, and the End of the Monument," *South Atlantic Quarterly*, 96(4): 853–80.

Zuelow, E.G.E. (2004a) "Enshrining Ireland's Nationalist History inside Prison Walls: The Restoration of Kilmainham Jail," *Eire-Ireland*, 39(3 & 4): 180–201.

—— (2005) "The Tourism Nexus: National Identity and the Meanings of Tourism since the Irish Civil War" in M. McCarthy (ed.) *Ireland's Heritages: Cultural Perspectives on Memory and Identity*, Aldershot and Burlington: Ashgate.

Part III

Threat, response, re-emergence

10 The persistence of the Baltic nations under Soviet rule

An ethno-symbolist critique of modernist perspectives on the breakup of the USSR

Mark A. Jubulis

Introduction

How do we explain the rise of nationalism in the Soviet Union during the era of Gorbachev's reforms? Did the existing theoretical literature on nationalism provide an adequate framework for interpreting the events that led to the breakup of the Soviet Union? Reflecting the general modernist consensus, most scholars have begun with preconceived notions of the modern, artificially constructed nature of nations and have denied the persistence of pre-Soviet nations within the USSR. They have interpreted the rise of nationalism under Gorbachev as the result of Soviet nation-building policies and the institutional legacies of Soviet federalism (Suny 1993; Brubaker 1994). Other modernist accounts have neglected aspects of culture and identity in favor of an instrumentalist emphasis on elite interests (Gleason 1990; Laitin 1991; Roeder 1991). The insights of these modernist approaches are valid primarily with respect to the republics of Central Asia, where no clear nations had existed in the pre-Soviet past and where local elites belatedly adopted nationalist policies in response to the weakening of central control from Moscow. However, these modernist perspectives offer a flawed explanation of the breakup of the USSR because the "new" nations of Central Asia experienced little mass mobilization in favor of independence and played a minimal role in ending the Soviet regime.

A major flaw in the modernist analysis of nationalism in the USSR is the glossing over of differences among the 15 republics in an effort to fit reality into a single parsimonious theory. In particular, the idea that the Soviet Union created nations has absolutely no relevance for the Baltic republics of Lithuania, Latvia and Estonia, which were independent nation-states prior to their incorporation into the Soviet Union in 1940. It was the historic memory of this lost sovereignty and the sense of grievance towards the Soviet annexation and subsequent policies of cultural Russification that explains the emergence and intensity of the Baltic nationalist movements in the 1980s. This is significant for the story of Soviet collapse because the Baltics were the first to engage in nationalist mobilization for independence.

Their arguments then spread to other republics, thereby creating a crisis of legitimacy for the Soviet state (Muiznieks 1995).

The work of Anthony D. Smith and the ethno-symbolist approach to nationalism offers a useful corrective to the dominant modernist theories. The Baltic nationalist movements exemplified many of the themes emphasized in Smith's writings on nationalism and provide evidence for the persistence of nations within the USSR. National identities were sustained during the Soviet era through the endurance of historical memory and national myths. Under glasnost, the Baltic nations mobilized in the defense of their preexisting cultures and languages which were threatened by Russification in their historic homelands. The Baltic nationalist movements emphasized the historic continuity of their statehood by holding demonstrations on the anniversaries of important historic events and restoring old symbols of pre-Soviet national identity. They desired political sovereignty in order to protect their threatened cultures and prepare the way for national regeneration in the future.

The modernist consensus

A key holding of the modernist approach to nationalism is that nations are recent artificial constructions based on false myths of deep historical pedigree and continuity. Modernists generally assume that nationalists falsify history and create myths in order to manipulate the masses and gain political power (Eley and Suny 1996: 8). The main theoretical framework for this "constructivist" perspective was provided by Hobsbawm and Ranger in *The Invention of Tradition* (1983), and it has now become part of the dominant modernist consensus. In the words of Gellner, "Nationalism is not what it seems, and above all it is not what it seems to itself. The cultures it claims to defend and revive are often its own inventions" (1983: 56).

This assumption that nations are artificial constructs based on false premises creates expectations for the imminent deconstruction of nations. In some cases, modernists seem to take Renan's description of the nation as a "daily plebiscite" to an extreme and expect national identities to emerge and dissolve overnight. As Brubaker recommends,

> To make sense of the Soviet and Yugoslav collapse and their aftermaths, we need ... to think theoretically about relatively sudden fluctuations in the "nationness" of groups ... my argument is that we should ... refrain from using the analytically dubious notion of "nations" as substantial, enduring collectivities.
>
> (1996: 19–21)

The modernist approach is shaped by the belief that the "age of nationalism" has passed and that humanity is about to enter a "post-national" era. Marxist historians see nationalism as emerging during the industrial stage of historical development, but since nationalism no longer serves the same function in the post-industrial world of globalization, "It is no longer a major vector of human development" (Hobsbawm 1990: 163).

Modernist assumptions regarding the malleability of identities and the passing of the age of nationalism are responsible for the failure of many scholars to anticipate the rise of nationalism in the USSR in the late 1980s. For some, this meant expressing hostility to the term "empire" to describe the Soviet Union because the term implied the persistence of "captive nations." Instead, modernists expected identities to shift in new directions, perhaps in the direction of a "Soviet" identity. As David Laitin wrote,

> the problem with calling the Soviet Union an empire today is that . . . it allows one to assume its ultimate decomposition. I do not want to suppose the collapse of the Soviet Union. I want to analyze those factors that can enhance the integrity of the Union.
>
> (Laitin 1991: 143)

Laitin adopts the constructivist view of nationhood which implies the possibility of deconstruction, but rejects the term "empire" because it implies decomposition. With this rather arbitrary position as his starting point, it becomes difficult to disentangle Laitin's conclusion that "the center will hold" (1991: 175) from his original assumption.

Despite the failure of modernism to anticipate the rise of nationalism in the final years of the Soviet Union, the modernist assumptions were adopted unquestionably and enthusiastically after the breakup of the Soviet Union in 1991. A major conclusion of much of this work is that the nationalism which emerged in the Soviet Union during the Gorbachev years did not represent the interests of preexisting nations forcibly submerged within the Soviet "empire." Rather, the nations that became politicized in the late 1980s were the creation of Soviet nationalities policy and were subsequently nurtured, consolidated and strengthened by the institutional framework of Soviet federalism. In the words of Suny:

> The story of Soviet nationalities can be characterized as one of a state making nations. . . . Rather than primordial nations slumbering for 74 years, waiting to be aroused by Gorbachev's embrace, the nationalities of the USSR were constantly being shaped by the state-initiated transformation of the Soviet years.
>
> (Suny 1993: 159–60)

Brubaker also doubts that preexisting nations "somehow survived despite Soviet attempts to crush them . . ." and concludes that: "Nationhood and nationalism flourish today largely because of the regime's policies. . . . Far from ruthlessly suppressing nationhood, the Soviet regime pervasively institutionalized it" (1996: 17).

The notion that the Soviet Union created nations comes from the policy pursued in the late 1920s known as *korenizatsiia* ("nativization"). Following the Russian Civil War and the creation of the Soviet Union, the new state found itself in control of non-Russian territories with large uneducated peasant populations, but no native Communist cadres. Korenizatsiia was adopted in order to train local cadres and bring Communist ideology to the masses in their native languages. The Bolsheviks also adopted the slogan of "national self-determination" and adopted federalism so that non-Russian nationalities would not fear "Great Russian Chauvinism." However, it is important to note that the Bolsheviks turned to federalism as a means of accommodating national differences which were already evident, as several nationalities, including Ukrainians and Georgians, had engaged in failed efforts to secure independence as the Tsarist regime crumbled. In order to make Soviet rule appear less threatening to these groups that had already achieved national consciousness, the Soviet constitution enshrined special rights for Union republics, including the right of secession. Real national autonomy was nonexistent, however, given the Communist Party's absolute monopoly on power. No decisions of substance could be made by local elites without the approval of Moscow. Ultimately, the "fraternal friendship" of Union republics was supposed to lead to their eventual "drawing together" into a single "Soviet people."

The institutional framework of Soviet federalism has been central to most of the recent studies of the rise of nationalism in the USSR (Beissinger 2002; Walker 2003). The main argument is that federalism served to consolidate nationhood in the Union republics and provided a readymade platform for nationalist mobilization when Gorbachev began to liberalize the Soviet Union. This institutionalist approach builds on the assumptions of the constructivist school of thought by suggesting that Union republic status caused residents of the republic to "imagine" themselves as part of the titular nation (Brubaker 1994: 65). Furthermore, since these approaches emphasize the malleability of identities and argue that they are shaped by political institutions, then they can also be reshaped by new institutional arrangements. For example, Linz and Stepan (1992) made the argument that the USSR could have remained intact had all-Union elections been held before republican-level elections. This simple change of sequence would have drastically altered identities by channeling participation and a sense of collective identity toward the all-Union level, thereby creating disincentives for political elites to appeal to nationalism.

Flaws in the modernist explanation of Soviet dissolution

To evaluate the argument that federalism was responsible for the rise of nations and nationalism, one has to ask which nations of the USSR were "created" by the Soviet leaders? The policy of korenizatsiia and impact of federalism had the greatest impact on the ethnic groups of Central Asia, which had not yet been consolidated as nations, but we cannot speak of Soviet "nation-building" in the Baltic republics where national conscious-ness had already developed during a period of independent statehood (1918–40). The Balts were "state nations" to use John Armstrong's (1968) terminology. There, the Soviets faced the problem of too many national elites and they deported many of them to Siberia.

These different historical backgrounds led to different levels of national-ism in the 1980s. As Vujacic and Zaslavsky observed, "In stark contrast to the Baltics, . . . ethnic mobilization in Central Asia lacks secessionist inter-ests . . . local intelligentsias have failed to elaborate clear nationalist or pan-Islamic programs" (1991: 134). Ray Taras also noted that "Case studies of the Central Asian republics suggest the involuntary nature of statehood that arrived in the region" (1993: 528). Indeed, the leaders of the Central Asian republics were left out in the cold when Yeltsin and the leaders of Belarus and Ukraine effectively killed the USSR by forming the Commonwealth of Independent States. The Central Asian republics rushed to join the new Commonwealth because they feared being left on their own. Thus, mod-ernist approaches have the most to say about the republics which experi-enced the least amount of nationalist mobilization and weakest desire for separation (Central Asia), and the least to say about the republics that had the strongest nationalist movements and desire for independence (the Baltics). We cannot simply write the Baltics off as an exception and main-tain the modernist thesis because the Baltics were so central to the drama of national revival and Soviet collapse.

A similar flaw can be found in Mark Beissinger's *Nationalist Mobilization and the Collapse of the Soviet State* (2002). While Beissinger does an excellent job of explaining the contagious nature of nationalism in the USSR as it spread like a tidal wave from the "early risers" to the "late risers," he does not adequately explain why nationalism emerged in the first place in the early risers (the Baltic republics). His main thesis is that the "contentious event" (period of flux) forced people to reconsider their identities and loyal-ties. Beissinger's approach applies to the late risers like Russia, where many people transferred their loyalty from the Soviet state to Russia as a distinct nation. However, we need to remember that the "late risers" learned sub-stantially from the initial rise of nationalism in the Baltics. As Beissinger notes,

> Secessionist mobilization emerged in the Soviet Union as a transnational tidal force . . . developing first in the Baltic in the summer and fall of 1988 and then spreading in a massive way to Georgia, Armenia, Azer-baijan, Moldova, Ukraine, and even eventually Russia itself.
>
> (2002: 160)

Beissinger recognizes the centrality of the Baltics to the story of Soviet col-lapse by suggesting that the tidal wave of nationalism could have been stopped had Gorbachev recognized Baltic independence in 1989 (2002: 9). This would seem to warrant an explanation of why nationalism emerged in the early risers in the first place. He does admit that the Baltics possessed a "latent nationalist frame [of discourse]" and "Resistance to Soviet occupation never entirely ceased among the Balts" (2002: 167, 168). However, he refuses to alter his modernist assumptions in light of this evidence concerning the persistence of pre-Soviet national identities. Instead of recognizing the strong grip of national identities on the Baltic popular consciousness, he says that they enjoyed a "preexisting structural advantage" compared to other republics.

The content of this "structural advantage" includes things stressed by the ethno-symbolist approach, which I examine below, such as historical myths and memories, a rich heritage of ethnic symbols and traditions, and an emotional attachment to an historic homeland, but these things are not stressed by Beissinger because they conflict with his initial modernist assumptions regarding the "ambiguous, arbitrary, and constructed character of nationalist claims" (2002: 9). Furthermore, Beissinger struggles to fit the Baltics into his modernist framework of "identities in flux" by pointing out that the goals of the nationalist movements in the Baltics shifted from a demand for greater sovereignty in 1988 to a demand for full independence in 1989–90. However, a shift in political goals or strategy is not the same thing as a shift in national identity.

Other modernists have viewed nationalism primarily as an instrumentalist political strategy for regional elites to enhance their power at the expense of the center. For Gleason (1990) and Roeder (1991), nationalism in the Soviet republics was a cover for the efforts of local Communist elites to secure control over the economic resources of their republics. According to Gleason, the struggle for republican rights is best seen as a form of "bureaucratic nationalism" designed to achieve sovereignty, which is "defined in terms of the ability of the republic to exercise its prerogatives by means of generating its own sources of revenue" (1990: 132). He claims that "The nativization policies combine with the natural identification of the members of the native elite with their ethnic brethren, traditions, and homelands to produce a 'national climate' among the leadership in the republics" (1990: 99). Roeder also focuses on the economic interests of the "ethnic cadres" in his analysis and goes so far as to portray the local Communist elites as the primary leaders of nationalist mobilization (1991: 211–13, 229–31).

The main problem with the instrumentalist approach is that, rather than explaining the rise of nationalism, it directs our attention away from nationalism. It has absolutely no explanation for why the nationalist appeals of elites would elicit such a strong emotional response among the masses. Moreover, the instrumentalist approach ignores the way that glasnost permitted the emergence of nationalist pressure from below. It is simply not true, as claimed by Roeder and Gleason, that the well-established Communist cadres led the efforts of nationalist mobilization in the Baltics. Rather, the local Communist parties resisted the emergence of popular movements, realizing sooner than Gorbachev that they would espouse radical nationalist agendas that would threaten the integrity of the Soviet Union. For example, the head of the Latvian Communist Party at the time was Boris Pugo, a hardliner who would later become one of the eight conspirators against Gorbachev in the 1991 August coup. Many of the so-called "native cadres" were not perceived as "native" by the local populations because they were actually born in Russia and then transferred to the republic. Instead of sharing the interests of the local populations, these imported cadres tended to be hardline Communists and "internationalist" in outlook (Šilde 1987).

As a result of this resistance on the part of local elites, Gorbachev had to intervene directly by replacing the reactionary Brezhnev-era holdovers in the local party establishments with new reform-minded Communists. He then sent his deputy Alexander Yakovlev to the Baltics in the summer of 1988 to encourage the local Communists to support deeper glasnost and perestroika. Only after these changes and this pressure from the center did some local Communists openly support the new popular fronts, while others continued to resist, forming their own "interfront" organizations and aligning themselves with the Soyuz faction in the USSR Congress of People's Deputies. In Lithuania, Algirdas Brazauskas became First Secretary of the Lithuanian Communist Party on 20 October 1988, replacing hardliner Ringaudas Songaila, and the popular front Sajudis held its founding congress on the same day, having done all of the planning long before Brazauskas was in control. Brazauskas later became a well-known Communist supporter of nationalist demands, but he was merely reacting to the rise of popular nationalism from below (see Vardys 1989).

Modernists also provide a distorted view of Soviet history by downplaying the role of national grievances against the oppressive side of Soviet nationality policy. Since Brubaker's argument is that the institutional arrangements of federalism contributed to the "crystallization of nationhood," he concludes that the Soviet regime had no systematic policy of "nation-destroying" (1994: 58). This view ignores the powerful role of "internationalist" ideology in the Soviet system and leaves out too much of Soviet history, from the demographic impact of collectivization in Ukraine and Kazakhstan to the deportation of entire nations after World War II. It also ignores the mass immigration of millions of Russians into the non-Russian republics. For example, by 1989 the Latvian share of the population of Latvia had decreased to 52 percent (down from 77 percent in 1940) and Russian had become the majority language in all of Latvia's major cities (Mežs 1992 and Zīle 1991). Rather than "flourishing," native cultures were distorted by imposed guidelines of "socialist realism" and atheism, the brutal destruction of traditional peasant traditions in the countryside, and falsified versions of national history which were written by Party propagandists (Tillett 1969).

Finally, we should note two chronological problems associated with the modernist explanations discussed above. First of all, the totalitarian aspects of Stalinism and the return of "Great-Russian Chauvinism" after victory in the "Great Patriotic War" came after the period of korenizatsiia. Therefore, by the 1980s, memories of suffering were far more recent than memories of advance made earlier in the 1920s. For most of the national groups of the USSR, Soviet history does not represent a happy time of "nation-building." Rather, their historic memories are more likely to center on themes of terror, deportations, repression, censorship, the immigration of Russians and cultural Russification. Second, the argument of Linz and Stepan that all-Union elections could have diffused nationalist sentiment ignores the fact that nationalism was in full bloom before the pivotal election cycle of 1990. As early as 1988, the popular fronts in the Baltics were challenging the legitimacy of Soviet rule by drawing attention to the secret protocols of the Molotov–Ribbentrop Pact of 1939 and the illegal occupation and annexation of the Baltics by the Soviet Union in 1940. It was the policy of glasnost which allowed these deeply rooted resentments to be expressed, and glasnost was part of the early liberalization phase of Gorbachev's reforms rather than the later democratization phase, which is the focus of the article by Linz and Stepan.

Smith's ethno-symbolist approach applied to the Baltics

Most of the authors reviewed above are trapped in a dichotomous mode of thought, in which one is either a modernist or a primordialist. This has led to the unfortunate mistake of dismissing all cultural arguments as forms of discredited "primordialism." By contrast, Anthony D. Smith's approach, "ethno-symbolism," offers a more sophisticated "middle way" which acknowledges some of the points made by modernists, yet also recognizes the salience of national identities which have developed over long periods. I concur with Smith when he states that

> the continuing power of myths, symbols, and memories of ethnic chosenness, golden ages and historic homelands has been largely responsible for the mass appeal of ethnic nationalism in the aftermath of the Cold War and the demise of the Soviet empire...
>
> (Smith 1999: 19)

Smith's view of nationalism presents a direct challenge to the modernist consensus and corrects many of its serious flaws. In particular, Smith draws our attention to modernism's "failure to accord any weight to the pre-existing cultures and ethnic ties of the nations that emerged in the modern epoch, thereby precluding any understanding of the popular roots and widespread appeal of nationalism" (Smith 1999: 9). He warns against some of the key limitations of modernism, which include its stark instrumentalism, excessive focus on elites, and the "failure to distinguish genuine constructs from long-term processes and structures in which successive generations have been socialized" (Smith 1999: 9). For "Constructing the nation away misses the central point about historical nations: their powerfully felt and willed presence, the feeling shared among so many people of belonging to a transgenerational community of history and destiny" (Smith 2000: 57).

In contrast to the dominant modernist paradigm, Smith's work places much more emphasis on history, culture and continuity in the formation of nations. In place of "creation" and "invention," Smith speaks of rediscovery, reinterpretation and regeneration (Smith 1999: 177–9). Whereas modernists avoid the "resonance" problem altogether, Smith explains that nationalists appeal to shared historical experiences, myths, symbols, traditions and visions of the homeland which are instantly recognizable to the masses who have received these pieces of ethno-history from previous generations. When such "generational linkages" are combined with a rich cultural heritage, people develop a strong sense of "spiritual kinship" with their ancestors who shared the same "distinctive cultural qualities" (Smith 1999: 58; 2000: 55). This process goes far towards explaining the continuity and durability of many particular national identities.

Modernists have accurately emphasized the contingency of nationhood throughout history. However, a key aspect of the ethno-symbolist approach is that "contingent" does not necessarily mean arbitrary. According to Smith, nationalists do not create nations *ex nihilo*, but rather build upon pre-existing cultural materials that have gradually formed over the *longue durée* (Smith 1999: 3–24, 175; 2001: 20, 57–61, 77, and 83). Modern nation-builders are forced to work within a specific historic and cultural context and they are therefore limited in their ability to fabricate entirely new identities (Smith 2001: 20, 77). This is why it was so difficult for the Soviet leaders to impose a uniform "Soviet" identity on peoples as diverse as Estonians and Uzbeks. They simply lacked the necessary common cultural traits and historic experiences and memories which would allow them to view themselves as belonging to the same "imagined community." When we apply this ethno-symbolist approach to the rise of nationalism in the Baltic republics in the 1980s, we find that Smith's approach is superior to the modernists in terms of capturing the true nature of the nationalist struggles, both in terms of the content of the nationalist claims and the emotional response of the masses.

Pre-modern *ethnie* and their cultures

The great debate in the study of nationalism concerns the origins of nations. According to the ethno-symbolist approach, a modern national identity is forged out of preexisting ethnic identities and cultural materials and there is much less emphasis on invention and fabrication. In the case of the Baltic nations, this transformation from pre-modern *ethnie* to modern nationhood began in the 1850s through a process of "vernacular mobilization" led by nationalist intelligentsias (Smith 1991: 61–8; Raun 1986; Plakans 1974). During the latter half of the nineteenth century, the Baltic languages were standardized; oral traditions and folk songs were collected and published, national literary traditions blossomed, and the local populations became more literate and urbanized. The Baltic peoples at the time were ruled by Russia, but in Latvia and Estonia the local economic and cultural elites were predominantly German. Thus, nationalist mobilization involved the elevation of Baltic "low cultures" to the status of "high cultures," and the displacement of German cultural dominance.

The decision to hold annual song festivals in the 1870s was similar to the stories of the "invention of tradition" discussed by Hobsbawm and Ranger (1983). However, it must be stressed that the songs themselves were truly ancient, surviving as an oral tradition for hundreds of years. The oldest Latvian folk songs (*dainas*) were first sung over 1,000 years ago. Therefore, the "inventors" of these traditions (song festivals) were working with a deeply rooted cultural heritage (ancient folk songs). As Smith argues, "Clearly there is more to the formations of nations than nationalist fabrication, and 'invention' must be understood in its other sense of a novel recombination of existing elements" (Smith 1999: 46).

Significantly, the consolidation of national consciousness occurred prior to the policies of cultural Russification imposed by the Tsarist regime in the 1880s (Plakans 1981). As Toivo Raun explains, "cultural Russification was a complete failure because Estonian national identity was already too strongly developed, and, if anything, the attempted cultural pressure actually served to promote Estonian national consolidation" (Raun 2003: 139). Once the cultural process of nation-building had been accomplished, the Baltic nations were prepared to engage in a political struggle for autonomy, which began during the 1905 Revolution and eventually culminated in the achievement of independence in the aftermath of World War I. The Baltic nations then enjoyed independent statehood from 1918 to 1940 and this experience greatly consolidated their strong sense of national identity before they were forcibly incorporated into the Soviet Union. It was the historical memory of this period more than the institutions of Soviet federalism, which allowed the Baltic nations to endure despite their loss of statehood.

Given this prior development of nationhood, the entire Soviet experience is perceived by the Baltic peoples to be a tragic story of decline from their previous status. Soviet nationality policies directly threatened the cultures of the Baltic nations through censorship and the imposition of an alien Communist ideology, the deportation of local populations and immigration of non-Baltic peoples, and linguistic Russification. It is therefore perplexing that Suny could make the sweeping claim that "*all* [emphasis added] non-Russians in the Soviet Union experienced to a greater or lesser degree a gain in their potential capacity to represent themselves as nations" (Suny 1993: 159). By 1989, the immigration of Soviet settlers turned the native Baltic nationalities into minorities in many of their largest cities and these urban

Balts were forced to conduct their daily lives in a Russian cultural environment (Dreifelds 1996: 148). Thus, the struggle for independence in the late 1980s was defensive in nature, motivated by a desire for cultural and national preservation. This explains the prominent role of intellectuals and cultural figures in the Baltic nationalist movements (Dreifelds 1989). Rather than opportunistically turning to nationalism for instrumentalist reasons, the goal of these leaders was to preserve their "fund of irreplaceable culture values" for posterity (Smith 1991: 84).

Shared historical experiences and memories

The ethno-symbolist approach places great emphasis on the role of shared historical experiences and memories in the formation of nations. Such memories forge the nation into a single community with a "collective mission and national destiny" (Smith 1996: 384). Historical memories connect the members of the nation to their historic homeland and provide models for emulation in the present. Without this historic perspective, it is impossible to maintain a sense of continuity across generations or to form myths of "golden ages" that inspire nations towards regeneration. Ethno-symbolists believe that nations are inherently historic formations, created over the *longue durée*, and that the past contributes to our understanding of the present. By contrast, modernists treat the past as something created to suit the needs of the present.

In the late 1980s, Mikhail Gorbachev introduced reforms that allowed Soviet historians to reexamine the past. His goal was to allow criticism of past mistakes in order to justify economic reforms (Sherlock 1988). However, in the Baltic republics, the green light to allow a reexamination of the past led directly to demands for national independence. When Baltic historians turned their attention to the Stalinist era, they exposed the fiction of the Communist myth of "socialist revolution" in 1940 and uncovered the true nature of the illegal annexation and occupation of their countries. Most debates in the press focused on the existence of the secret protocols of the Molotov–Ribbentrop Pact of 23 August 1939, which assigned spheres of influence in Eastern Europe between Hitler and Stalin. This revelation (the existence of the secret protocols had always been denied by the Communists) inspired demands for national independence because it struck at the heart of the legitimacy of Soviet rule in the Baltic. Soviet legitimacy was further undermined by additional historical inquiries into the brutality of the Stalinist regime and the deportation and murder of thousands of Baltic civilians during the occupation in 1940, the reoccupation of 1944, and the collectivization of agriculture in 1948–9.

The nationalist reaction to these revelations shows that, contrary to Suny and Brubaker, the Balts were motivated by resentments towards Soviet oppression of their preexisting nations. This is why the commemoration of the Molotov–Ribbentrop Pact (MRP) became one of the central historical motifs of the Baltic nationalist struggles. Baltic attitudes towards the MRP highlight the symbolism inherent in historical memory. The Baltic interpretation that the MRP led directly to Soviet occupation ran contrary to the publicly ordained Communist view, and therefore the subject had a particular meaning for Balts that it did not have for Russians. In other words, the denunciation of the MRP represented a coded message for the Balts. When they said in 1988 that they wanted to "undo the consequences" of the MRP, they were telling each other that their goal should be to regain their lost independence. This is why it is not accurate to speak of a change in identity as the Baltic nationalist movements shifted from demanding "sovereignty" to demanding "independence." The subject of independence was on the table the second that the MRP was denounced, even though it was still too risky to publicly proclaim the goal of seceding from the USSR in 1988.

The symbolic significance of reclaiming the past also explains the high levels of mass mobilization achieved by the Baltic nationalists when they staged annual "calendar demonstrations" to commemorate significant events in their history. In Riga, these demonstrations took place at important sites in Latvia's history, such as the freedom monument erected in 1935, the National Theater where independence was proclaimed in 1918, and the Cemetery of the Brethren where many national heroes are buried. The first demonstrations were held in 1987 in a tense atmosphere, but they increased in size in 1988 and 1989 as the limits of glasnost expanded. At these demonstrations, people carried the pre-Soviet flags of the independent Baltic states, which were national symbols instantly recognized by all of the participants. These pre-Soviet national flags reflected the power of symbols to exert a coded meaning which is intelligible only to members of the group. One does not carry a pre-Soviet national flag to demand "limited sovereignty" within a "renewed Soviet federation." The obvious and direct message was that we should regain our lost statehood.

Compared to modernism, the ethno-symbolist approach emphasizes the power of historic memories and traditional ethnic symbols to "resonate" with the people. In a short time, the Baltic popular fronts were able to attract hundreds of thousands of people to their demonstrations. These events were liberating for the participants, who were not able to express their true feelings before glasnost, and they also served to strengthen the communal bonds of the Baltic nations (see Īvāns 1995). The 1989 demonstration commemorating the MRP took the form of a human chain uniting over 2 million people from Tallin to Vilnius. Candles were also placed in the path in order to represent ancestors who perished under Stalinism. In January of 1991, many Balts showed that they were willing to die to defend their national freedoms in their historic homelands. Thousands of people in Vilnius and Riga erected barricades and formed human chains around their parliaments in order to defend them from Soviet attack. Fourteen people were killed by Soviet troops in Vilnius and five in Riga.

In Latvia, the period of the late 1980s was referred to as the "Third

Awakening" to establish continuity with the first national "awakening" of the nineteenth century and the second of the pre-Soviet era of independence (Stradiņš 1992). As they regained independence in 1991, the Balts reestablished continuity with the past by replacing the Soviet street names with their pre-Soviet names. Thus, "Lenin street" in Riga was renamed Brivibas iela ("Freedom street"). This process of reestablishing continuity with pre-Soviet nationhood was also followed in matters of politics and citizenship. The Balts did not claim to be creating new states in 1991. Rather, the constitutions and government institutions of the interwar era were "restored," as was the body of citizenry in Latvia and Estonia (Jubulis 2001). This restorationist approach was aided by the non-recognition policy of the West in regard to the Soviet annexation of the Baltics in 1940, which maintained the *de jure* continuity of the three Baltic states in international law (Hough 1985).

Of course the newly regenerated Baltic nations would not be the same as those that lost their statehood in 1940. Indeed, much had happened to alter the demographic and cultural makeup of the Baltics during the Soviet era. But the generational and cultural links that did in fact remain between the Baltic nations of 1940 and 1988 did much to inspire the Baltic nations to regain their statehood. Furthermore, nationalists appeals resonated with the people because they tapped collective historic memories that were relatively recent. People were still alive in the 1980s who were born in the independent Baltic states before the Soviet occupation. Most others had heard stories about the pre-Soviet era from their parents or grandparents. Historical continuity did not have to be "invented" by nationalist elites because it was already remembered by the people. Instead, nationalists rediscovered and reinterpreted a "popular living past" (Smith 1999: 9).

This brief overview of the prominence of history in the Baltic nationalist movements challenges the dominant modernist assumptions regarding the invention of tradition and the fabrication of history by nationalist elites. To be sure, many nationalist myths do represent distortions of the past and it is the duty of professional historians to uncover the truth. But it would be wrong to leap from the realization that nationalists have often falsified history to the blanket assumption that all nationalist histories are based on blatant falsehood (Archard 1995). In the Baltics, nationalists were defending historical truth against false Communist propaganda. Responding to pressure from the Baltic nationalists, a special commission set up by Gorbachev in 1989 verified the existence of the secret protocols of the MRP. Therefore, the total skepticism of modernists towards the claims of nationalists is not warranted. To be sure, Baltic nationalists were not 100 percent objective, being prone to glorify national accomplishments and downplay national failures, but on balance their version of history was far closer to any reasonable standard of objective truth than that of the ruling Communist Party. The Baltic nationalists were rediscovering an authentic past; restoring state symbols that existed in the pre-Soviet past; and remembering ancestors who actually lived and died as a result of Soviet policies. The Baltic nationalists were reconstituting a single historic narrative that established continuity with the past and pointed towards a renewal of independent statehood in the future.

Myths as a source of national revival

Shared historical experiences contribute to the formation of national myths, and myths in turn reinforce historical memory and help to maintain and perpetuate national identities (Schöpflin 1997). In particular, myths of origin, "golden ages," decline and regeneration provide nations with a sense of authenticity, collective dignity, historical continuity and future destiny, as well as hope for a "restoration of the community to its former high estate and true mission" (Smith 1997: 48–51). For the Baltics, the important point about myths of origin is that the Soviet myth of how the Baltics voluntarily joined the Soviet Union and experienced "socialist revolutions" was absolutely rejected by the Balts themselves. Baltic nationalists in the 1980s were most concerned with myths of a "golden age" (1918–40) when their nations flourished and experienced freedom from outside interference; a myth of decline (referring to the Soviet era) when the welfare of their nations was imperiled by harsh external forces; and myths of regeneration (the message crafted by nationalists that all will be well again once we regain our political independence).

The nationalist emphasis on myths of "golden ages" has caused modernist critics to condemn nationalism as reactionary for seeking a "return to the past." However, while nationalists are indeed inspired by the myth of the "golden age," this does not signify a desire to return to the past. Rather, they become inspired to work towards regeneration in the future, and this is fully compatible with "progressive" agendas such as economic modernization. As Smith notes, the "nation" can often be viewed as a "faith-achievement" group (Smith 1991: 17). The function of myth in the Baltic cases has convinced the Baltic peoples that they belong in the European West (as in the "golden age" of independence) rather than in the Russian East (the "dark age" of Soviet rule). This has meant that they have exerted tremendous efforts in the post-Soviet era to reform their countries in order to meet the standards for EU and NATO membership (Jubulis 1996).

According to Smith, "The creation and dissemination . . . of the belief that 'we are a "chosen people"' has been crucial for ensuring long-term ethnic survival" (1999: 130). As the easternmost nation of Catholic Europe, Lithuanians have long viewed their nation as having a special mission to defend the values of the "West" against hostile invaders, as it did in the time of the Grand Duchy of Lithuania (1253–1572), or against anti-Western ideologies, as in the struggle against Communism in the twentieth century (Packer and Furmonavicius 2000). In Siauliai, Lithuania, there is a "Hill of Crosses" where Catholic Lithuanians have placed hundreds of thousands of crosses in memory of relatives lost or killed in struggles to defend Lithuania from foreign occupation. The religious significance of the site dates from medieval times and it has become a symbol of the persistence of national identity and spiritual resistance to foreign rule. Several times during the Soviet era the KGB bulldozed the hill, yet each time Lithuanians returned to replace the crosses. Furthermore, one of the most successful pieces of samizdat resistance literature in the Soviet Union was the Chronicle of the Lithuanian Catholic Church. As in Poland, the importance of the Catholic faith persisted in Soviet-controlled Lithuania and provided strength and hope to Lithuanians living under Communism.

Homelands and sacred ethnoscapes

Nations must possess a unique historic homeland, which "becomes a repository of historic memories and associations, the place where 'our' sages, saints and heroes lived, worked, prayed and fought" (Smith 1991: 9). Over the *longue durée* there develops "a close association between a given landscape and a particular community, such that a people is felt to belong to a specific territory and a territory to a particular people" (Smith 1999: 151). Modernists downplay the emotional attachment that a people may have towards its homeland as well as the reinforcing role that homelands play in the maintenance of national identity. However, as Smith points out, the ancestral homeland, or "ethnoscape," becomes "an intrinsic part of the character, history and destiny of the culture community, to be commemorated regularly and defended at all costs, lest the 'personality' of the ethnic or regional community be impugned" (Smith 1999: 151).

The notion of "defending the homeland" was another key feature of Baltic nationalism in the late 1980s. During the initial stages of glasnost, Baltic nationalists focused on environmental concerns and objected to Soviet industrial policies on the grounds that they were spoiling the homeland. In Latvia, the first evidence of mass mobilization during the Gorbachev era took the form of protest against Soviet plans to build a hydroelectric dam on the Daugava River (Muiznieks 1987). Also, themes about nature and references to specific places in Latvia figure prominently in the vast collection of Latvian folk songs. Baltic nationalists also defended the policies designed to protect their languages, arguing that Lithuania, Latvia and Estonia were the only places in the world where those languages were spoken in public. If they fell out of use in their historic homelands, these languages would die out completely. The symbolic significance of homelands in nationalist struggles also helps to explain the contrast between the very high level of nationalist mobilization among the Baltic national groups compared with the very low level of counter-mobilization among Russian-speaking immigrant minority groups in the Baltic, who were not engaged in a defense of their own historic homelands (Jubulis 2001: 27–30).

The political implications of ethno-symbolism

Smith's writings do not often deal with the political aspects of nationalism, but he does offer a few comments on the political goals of nationalist movements and we can extrapolate further from the ethno-symbolist issues we have discussed so far. Politically, the concept of homeland is central to the nationalist struggle for territorial autonomy. Smith defines "nationalism" as "an ideological movement for attaining and maintaining autonomy, unity and identity for a population which some of its members deem to constitute an actual or potential 'nation'" (Smith 2001: 9). We saw above that nations desire autonomy to protect and promote their "irreplaceable culture values," but whether this autonomy requires independent statehood or can be accommodated within a federalist framework depends on the specific circumstances of each particular nation. In the Baltic cases, historical memory and a desire to reestablish continuity with the past pointed in the direction of restored statehood (Hroch 1996). In the modern era, nationalism has become a doctrine of political legitimacy and the historical debate over the Molotov–Ribbentrop Pact and the forcible annexation of the Baltics in 1940 destroyed the legitimacy of Soviet rule in the Baltic. As Smith explains, ethno-history can often give rise to a

> claim to a specific autonomy, in virtue of a previous, distant era of liberty, the heroic, golden age now lost through oppression and neglect. . . . Such quests for autonomy are often felt to represent merely a "restoration" of ancient, lost rights and freedoms.
>
> (Smith 1999: 70)

The restoration of statehood was also deemed necessary according to the Baltic national myths of regeneration. No new institutional arrangement could have changed these perceptions, which were based on the power of myth, historical memory and national identity. Moreover, Baltic nationalists perceived the Soviet Union as an illegitimate empire, and they argued that all of the Soviet nations should exercise their right to national self-determination. This is one of the reasons why the Baltic nationalist message spread so quickly to other parts of the Soviet Union (Muiznieks 1995: 4). The ethno-symbolist concerns of the Baltic nationalists gave rise to demands for sovereignty and independence which were then adopted by other Soviet republics, leading to a "parade of sovereignties" and the breakup of the Soviet state. As Roman Szporluk has argued (2000), a fatal flaw in the Soviet empire was that it became overextended when it annexed the Baltics and other parts of the "Soviet West," territories where national identity was already strong and cultural values were very different from those of the Russian/Soviet East. After 50 years of Soviet oppression, Gorbachev's reforms allowed the Baltics to reclaim their national histories, reassert their pre-Soviet cultural values, and regain their place in Europe.

Conclusion

The emergence of nationalism in the Baltics and the demands for independence were directly related to the ethnic, cultural and historical issues emphasized by the ethno-symbolist approach to nationalism. They were not based on the instrumentalist calculations of the ruling local Communist parties. To the extent that Baltic nationalism was shaped by the Soviet experience, it was a response to Soviet repression rather than the positive outcome of Soviet nation-building. The nationalism that first emerged in the Baltics and ultimately threatened the integrity of the Soviet state was characterized by the expression of pent-up grievances against Soviet rule on the part of nations that had substantial historical continuity and deeply rooted cultures and traditions. Contrary to the modernist view, the Baltic nations preceded the rise of Baltic nationalism in the 1980s. Modernists overlook the fact that once a nation is created, the resulting collective identity becomes an important and enduring part of the lives of its members and that it is successfully passed down from generation to generation. Even when the culture and characteristics of the nation change, its members may retain their particular national identity. One need not assume that collective identities are "immutable" or that they have existed for all time in order to recognize that they do in fact exist, can become rather stable over time, and shape the behavior of individuals.

References

Archard, D. (1995) "Myths, Lies and Historical Truth: A Defence of Nationalism," *Political Studies*, 43: 472–81.

Armstrong, J. (1968) "The Ethnic Scene in the Soviet Union: The View of the Dictatorship," in E. Goldhagen (ed.) *Ethnic Minorities in the Soviet Union*, New York: Praeger.

Beissinger, M. (2002) *Nationalist Mobilization and the Collapse of the Soviet State*, Cambridge: Cambridge University Press.

Brubaker, R. (1994) "Nationhood and the National Question in the Soviet Union and post-Soviet Eurasia: An Institutionalist Account," *Theory and Society*, 23: 47–78.

—— (1996) "Rethinking Nationhood: Nation as Institutionalized Form, Practical Category, Contingent Event," in R. Brubaker, *Nationalism Reframed*, Cambridge: Cambridge University Press: 13–22.

Dreifelds, J. (1989) "Latvian National Rebirth," *Problems of Communism*, 38(4): 77–94.

—— (1996) *Latvia in Transition*. Cambridge: Cambridge University Press.

Eley, G. and Suny, R. (1996) "Introduction: From the Moment of Social History to the Work of Cultural Representation," in G. Eley and R. Suny (eds) *Becoming National: A Reader*, Oxford: Oxford University Press.

Gellner, E. (1983) *Nations and Nationalism*, Ithaca: Cornell University Press.

Gleason, G. (1990) *Federalism and Nationalism: The Struggle for Republican Rights in the USSR*, Boulder: Westview Press.

Hobsbawm, E. (1983) "Introduction: Inventing Traditions," in E. Hobsbawm and T. Ranger (eds) *The Invention of Tradition*, Cambridge: Cambridge University Press.

—— (1990) *Nations and Nationalism since 1780*, Cambridge: Cambridge University Press.

Hough, W. (1985) "The Annexation of the Baltic States and Its Effect on the Development of Law Prohibiting the Forcible Seizure of Territory," *New York Law School Journal of International and Comparative Law*, 6(2): 303–533.

Hroch, M. (1996) "Nationalism and National Movements: Comparing the Past and the Present of Central and Eastern Europe," *Nations and Nationalism*, 2(1): 35–44.

Īvāns, D. (1995) *Gadījuma Karakalps*, Riga: Veida.

Jubulis, M. (1996) "The External Dimension of Democratization in Latvia: The Impact of European Institutions," *International Relations*, 13(3): 59–73.

—— (2001) *Nationalism and Democratic Transition: The Politics of Citizenship and Language in Post-Soviet Latvia*, Lanham: University Press of America.

Laitin, D. (1991) "The National Uprisings in the Soviet Union," *World Politics*, 44(1): 139–77.

Linz, J. and Stepan, A. (1992) "Political Identities and Electoral Sequences: Spain, the Soviet Union, and Yugoslavia," *Daedalus*, 121(2): 123–39.

Mežs, I. (1992) *Latvieši Latvijā: Etnodemogrāfisks Apskats*, Kalamazoo: LSC Apgads.

Muiznieks, N. (1987) "The Daugaupils Hydro Station and Glasnost in Latvia," *Journal of Baltic Studies*, 18(1): 63–70.

—— (1995) "The Influence of the Baltic Popular Movements on the Process of Soviet Disintegration," *Europe-Asia Studies*, 47(1): 3–25.

Packer, A. and Furmonavicius, D. (2000) "A Brief History of Lithuania," in V. Landsbergis, *Lithuania Independent Again*, trans. A. Packer, Seattle: University of Washington Press.

Plakans, A. (1974) "Peasants, Intellectuals, and Nationalism in the Russian Baltic Provinces, 1820–90," *Journal of Modern History*, 46(3): 445–75.

—— (1981) "Russification Policy in the 1880s," in E. Thaden (ed.) *Russification in the Baltic Provinces and Finland, 1855–1914*, Princeton: Princeton University Press.

Raun, T. (1986) "The Latvian and Estonian National Movements, 1860–1914," *Slavonic and East European Review*, 64(1): 66–80.

—— (2003) "Nineteenth- and Early Twentieth-Century Estonian Nationalism Revisited," *Nations and Nationalism*, 9(1): 129–47.

Roeder, P. (1991) "Soviet Federalism and Ethnic Mobilization," *World Politics*, 43: 196–232.

Schöpflin, G. (1997) "The Functions of Myth and a Taxonomy of Myths," in G. Hosking and G. Schöpflin (eds) *Myths and Nationhood*, New York: Routledge.

Sherlock, T. (1988) "Politics and History under Gorbachev," *Problems of Communism*, 37(3–4): 16–42.

Šilde, A. (1987) "The Role of Russian-Latvians in the Sovietization of Latvia," *Journal of Baltic Studies*, 18(2): 191–208.

Smith, A. (1991) *National Identity*, Reno: University of Nevada Press.

—— (1996) "Memory and Modernity: Reflections on Ernest Gellner's Theory of Nationalism," *Nations and Nationalism*, 2(3): 371–88.

—— (1997) "The 'Golden Age' and National Renewal," in G. Hosking and G. Schöpflin (eds) *Myths and Nationhood*, New York: Routledge.

—— (1999) *Myths and Memories of the Nation*, Oxford: Oxford University Press.

—— (2000) *The Nation in History*, Hanover: University Press of New England.

—— (2001) *Nationalism: Theory, Ideology, History*, Cambridge: Polity Press.

Stradiņš, J. (1992) *Trešā Atmoda*, Riga: Zinātne.

Suny, R. (1993) *The Revenge of the Past: Nationalism, Revolution, and the Collapse of the Soviet Union*, Stanford: Stanford University Press.

Szporluk, R. (2000) *Russia, Ukraine, and the Breakup of the Soviet Union*, Stanford: Hoover Institution Press.

Taras, R. (1993) "Making Sense of Matrioshka Nationalism," in I. Bremmer and R. Taras (eds) *Nations and Politics in the Soviet Successor States*. Cambridge: Cambridge University Press.

Tillett, L. (1969) *The Great Friendship: Soviet Historians on the Non-Russian Nationalities*, Chapel Hill: University of North Carolina Press.

Vardys, V.S. (1989) "Lithuanian National Politics," *Problems of Communism*, 38(4): 53–76.

Vujacic, V. and Zaslavsky, V. (1991) "The Causes of Disintegration in the USSR and Yugoslavia," *Telos*, 88: 120–40.

Walker, E. (2003) *Dissolution: Sovereignty and the Breakup of the Soviet Union*, Lanham: Rowman & Littlefield.

Zīle, L. (1991) "Latvijās rusifikācija 1940–1990," *Latvijas Vēsture*, 1(1): 31–6.

11 Croatian language policy

Establishing national identity in the era of globalization

Mitchell Young

Since their country's independence in 1991, Croatian linguists and policy makers have faced the challenge of asserting a linguistic identity for the new nation while adapting to the economic and political realities of a globalizing era. In 1850 an agreement linking Croatian with Serbian – for both political and linguistic reasons – was concluded in Vienna. For nearly a century and a half afterwards some Croatians advocated a distinct Croatian while "unitarists" sought to merge the languages completely. The controversy intensified in the 1980s, becoming a factor in the centrifugal politics of that era (Bugarski 1989, quoted in Bugarski 1995). Upon independence, a primary goal of many Croatian scholars and some Croatian officials was to undo the marriage of the two South Slavic languages (Kačić 2001; Pavletić 1997).

Language's role in national identity formation has long attracted the notice of scholars. Early writers on nationalism, such as Gellner and Deutsch, focused on language's role in communication (Deutsch 1966; Gellner 1964). Later works by sociolinguists have emphasized its symbolic role in creating ethnic or national identity (Ferguson 1968). Nationalist language planning programs typically seek to preserve or restore an "authentic" language of the past; such activity accords with Anthony Smith's emphasis on ethnic symbols being important for development of national identity over the *longue durée* (Fishman 2004; Smith 1991). In the Croatian case the attempted merger with Serbian is blamed for interfering with Croatian authenticity. In such situations planners often attempt to create linguistic distance from rival groups by means of changes in grammar or lexicon, especially by resurrecting archaic words or coining "authentic" neologisms (Kloss 1967; Fishman 2004).

However, the aim of intentionally creating (or broadening) the language barrier between two peoples would seem to go against the global *Zeitgeist* of recent decades which celebrates transnational integration and is skeptical of nationalist activities. In order to meet the challenge of asserting a unique identity in a global era, Croatian language planning has developed along two levels.[1] Corpus planning – the reform of the language itself to create an authentic and unique Croatian – is carried out indirectly via state support of scholarly institutions, as is the related activity of constructing a nationally oriented narrative of the language's history. In contrast, status planning – the policies which denote when and where the various languages of Croatia can be used – is determined by legislation. Here the government acts directly to assure Croatian's central place while at the same time meeting international and European norms on the treatment of language minorities. I argue that this two-level process allows the Croatian republic to gain international approval and to avoid international criticism for being excessively nationalistic, while at the same time it asserts a unique linguistic identity that shows it to be part of the historic West.

I base my claims on data from the history of Croatia linguistics, Croatian language-related laws passed since independence, and recent writings on language issues in Croatia. The first section of the paper puts the potential conflict between Croatian linguistic identity and globalization in historical context. I then show how corpus-planning efforts, including interpretation of the history of the language, both establish a unique Croatian identity and link Croatia with the West. Next I focus on government legislation and Croatian language status policy. I conclude the chapter with a review and interpretation of the data.

Globalization versus history

With the concept of sovereignty of nations being eroded by technological, economic and ideological forces, Croatia's independence could be seen as a cul-de-sac, rather than a milepost along the major thoroughfare of historical development (Hobsbawm 1992: 163–83). According to this view, the main line of historical development is globalization, the growing transnational integration of economies, cultures and political systems. This tightening integration would seem to be the opposite of the emergence of small, independent states in the post-Communist space–states which often based their legitimacy on a historical legacy of sovereignty (Hroch 1993).

The paradox of globalization

Popular accounts of globalization hold that increasing ties across national boundaries have drastically limited the policy options of modern states in a variety of spheres. In this model, nation-states are now strictly limited to a neoliberal model of limited government intervention. The columnist Thomas Friedman calls this the "Golden Straitjacket" – a situation where a national economy can prosper only by playing according to the rules of the global market system, a system which will lead – to some extent – to global cultural homogenization (Friedman 1999: ch. 6).

The extension of the golden straitjacket will (and should) lead to the demise of the nation-state, according to writer Kenichi Ohmae. He asks "[i]n a world where economic borders are progressively disappearing, are [nation-states'] arbitrary, historically accidental boundaries genuinely meaningful in economic terms?" (1995: 2). Ohmae's answer is a resounding "no." Unlike Friedman, his vision is not one of gigantic corporations homogenizing world culture. Rather, he sees regions, typically based on geographic-economic considerations, replacing the nation-state as a primary means of organizing social relations.

Ironically, Ohmae notes that the demise of larger nation-states has often been the result of something that looks like ethno-nationalism (though he does not use that term). He notes that Quebec has been moving away from English-speaking Canada, that Catalonia, with its "deeply entrenched historical identity," is a prime beneficiary of Spain's devolution of power, and most pertinent to the present essay, he decries the "noxious brew of ancient hatred, more recent antagonism, and unbridled ambition in what used to be Yugoslavia" (Ohmae 1995: 8–9). Ohmae recognizes that his regionalization scheme can serve as a cover for ethno-national interests:

> It is one thing for faction leaders in Northern Ireland, say, to call for independence as a means of ensuring less cumbersome linkages with the global economy. But is quite another if their underlying motive is to use that greater independence to fulfill their own, highly sectarian agendas.
>
> (1995: 119)

There is something of a paradox here. The victory of the market may lead to cultural homogenization and even the demise of the nation-state. Yet in the relatively rare cases of state disintegration or devolution of power the faultlines are along lines of "deeply rooted historical identity." Economic forces may be causing a relative decline in state power, but prima-facie evidence shows that new states form along cultural, not economic, lines. Or more exactly, new states form along previous sub-state boundaries (republic boundaries in the case of ex-Yugoslavia) and then experience population movements which make the cultural-historical nation and the political state more congruent.

Croatia experienced this process of disintegration followed by population movements. Many Croatians considered their culture distinct from Serbs and other South Slavs. Part of the reason for the independence movement was to preserve Croatian distinctiveness, a difficult task in a global era. A large number of those who did not consider themselves part of the historical and cultural Croatian nation, in particular the Krajina Serbs, rebelled and eventually fled the state. The Croatian republic became a more homogeneous, more distinctly Croatian polity, despite being born in a global era.

Language historically has been a large part of Croatian distinctiveness, despite its close linguistic relationship to other South Slav tongues. To understand the continuing importance of language as a marker of Croatian identity, and the response of Croatian language planners to the pressures of globalization, it is necessary to review the historical connection between language and various national movements in Croatia.

Language and history in Croatia

Language issues were at the root of the movement for South Slav unification. Unification with the Serbs was based on linguistic similarity; the association of the two languages (1850) came nearly 70 years before the creation of the Kingdom of Serbs, Croats and Slovenians (1918). Yet the language merger was met with long-term opposition that persisted – with varying intensity – until Croatian independence. Political independence brought an opportunity to reestablish linguistic identity, but this particularistic concern had the potential to clash with the globalizing spirit of the age.

The first Croatian national movement was founded by the lawyer, publisher and amateur linguist Ljudevit Gaj (1809–72). Influenced by pan-Slavic ideas while a student in Pest, Gaj returned to Croatia determined to start a South Slav national movement (Despalatovic 1975). His political ideas were reinforced by his ideas about language. "Gaj and his associates were first of all national awakeners whose aims were served – but not exhausted – by their admittedly important linguistic innovations" (Banac 1984: 216). Gaj created a standardized orthography for Croatian which would serve to connect Croatian with other Slavic languages: "an orthography worth its name, through which we can more closely connect ourselves with our brother Slavs, those educated in the Latin script" (Gaj 1830).

To promote a linguistic base for political unification, Gaj embraced the widespread Stokavian dialect (spoken in Bosnia, Herzegovina, Serbia and Slavonia), creating a composite language which would include aspects of all Croatian dialects: "[G]aj brought centuries-old trends to a victorious conclusion by bridging the linguistic gap between Kajkavian Croatia and the rest of the Croat lands" (Banac 1984: 216).[2]

However, Gaj's Illyrian project went beyond the traditional Croatian cultural area; he sought to unify South Slavs on a linguistic basis. This meant reckoning with the work of the Serb linguist Vuk Karadžić (1787–1864) who also used Stokavian as a basis for a standardized and modernized Serbian. The 1850 Vienna Agreement between Serb and Croat linguists led to the construction of a standard literary language – Serbo-Croatian – based on Stokavian.

The agreement met fundamental opposition almost immediately. Writer and politician Ante Starčević (1823–96), among others, wished to maintain a separate Croatian language (Pavletić *et al.* 1997: 80). Starčević saw no need for a common South Slav language; he sought to create a modern standard for Croatian that differed from the Vukovian system. This matched his program of pressing for Croatian rights within the Hapsburg Empire rather than pursuing unification with other South Slavs.

Starčević's ideas did not prevail in his lifetime. At the turn of the twentieth century linguists favoring unification with the Serbs seemed to have won the battle (Babić 1992; Kačić 2001: 45–9). Yet this victory was temporary; Croatian resistance to a unitary Serbo-Croatian would arise repeatedly in conjunction with political struggles in the twentieth century.

The creation of Yugoslavia (known as the Kingdom of Serbs, Croats and Slovenians until 1929) following World War I saw the continuation of the trend towards tight linguistic unification. Croatian writers went so far as to adopt Serbian "ekavian," the sub-dialect of the Belgrade area, for their work (Anić 1998: 29). However, this trend was brought to an abrupt halt by the assassination of the Croatian Peasant Party leader Stjepan Radić (b. 1871) in 1928 and the ensuing political conflict. Throughout the 1930s tense political relations between Zagreb and Belgrade were reflected in language controversies.

World War II brought the fascist regime of the Independent State of Croatia (*Nesavisna Država Hrvatska* – NDH) to power. It set up an Office for Language (*Ured za Jezik*) specifically to "purify" the Croatian language. A system of "root" orthography was introduced, mirroring the attempts of Starčević and other "national" linguists of the nineteenth century (Leskovar 1942).[3]

The defeat of the fascist Croatian regime discredited the movement for a separate Croatian. While the 1945 constitution of the Federal People's Republic of Yugoslavia guaranteed the equality of Serbian, Croatian, Slovenian and Macedonian, the tendency toward unification of Serbian and Croatian resumed (Babić 1969). In 1956 Serbian and Croatian linguists reached the Novi Sad Agreement, which unified literary Serbo-Croatian with two "variants" representing Serb and Croat. The Croatian linguist Ljudovit Jonke later claimed that the device of eastern and western "variants" served as cover under which the entire Croatian language was saved (Babić 1992).

In the mid-1960s space opened up for dissent on political issues, including language. Croatian linguists and literary figures publicly made the case that language unitarism was going too far; in 1967 the Croatian cultural organization *Matica Hrvatska* published the "Declaration on the Name and Situation of the Croatian Language" which demanded that Croatian be recognized as its own language and that it be protected from the continuing influence of Serbian (Hekman 1997).

The Croatian spring of 1971 saw the culmination of demands of Croatia politicians and cultural leaders for national recognition. Their demands were too much for the Titoist system; movement leaders were purged, jailed or exiled. *Matica Hrvatska* was banned and an orthography of Croatian (not Serbo-Croatian) was withdrawn from public circulation (Bratulić 2003; Babić *et al.* 1971).[4]

The crackdown temporarily halted agitation for linguistic independence. However, the constitution of the Croatian Socialist Republic acknowledged Croatian as the official language (Anon 1974). With the deterioration of the political situation in Yugoslavia as a whole in the 1980s, linguistic controversies resumed. The linguist Ranko Bugarski noted that, in the course of the decade, language had become a proxy for conflicts in politics and economics. "It is little wonder that among our [the Yugoslav] public there is increasing consciousness that language is more than grammar" (1995: 46).

As Bugarski's quote indicates, these debates were not confined to linguists or language "gatekeepers." Liberalization in Yugoslavia allowed the reestablishment of *Matica Hrvatska* and its membership grew rapidly – standing at between 7,000 and 8,000 individuals and institutions by the late 1990s. Its flagship publication, *Vijenac*, had a print run of around 15,000 copies (Dugandzija 1999).[5] *Matica* thus disseminated the ideas and debates of scholars to the general Croatian public. The journal *Jezik* ("*Language*"), with a subscriber base of 2,000–3,000, performed a similar role, particularly among educators (Anon 2000). Finally, the public was exposed to language politics as the differences between Serbian and Croatian were intentionally preserved by "publishing houses and the media . . . and were often invested with political meaning" (Kalogjera 1989: 171).

This brief history shows that language issues have long been important to Croatian nationalists. "Serbianization" in the guise of imposed linguistic unity, itself the result of Serbian dominance in Yugoslavia, was considered an existential threat to the distinct Croatian nation. The historical evidence shows language policy was tied to the fate of the state, with periods of political and linguistic centralization corresponding with political centralization, yet with a persisting element of resistance.

With independence, there were demands on the government to assert a unique linguistic identity for Croatia. Yet worldwide economic, cultural and political trends all worked against particularistic programs (at least according to globalization theorists). The next sections will show that Croatians were able to negotiate a path between particularistic sentiment and the political and economic demands of globalization. Existing cultural institutions working with indirect government support built up a separate Croatian linguistic identity. Direct legislation satisfied international norms – especially in the area of language minority rights – in language status planning while at the same time making Croatian central to political and economic life in the Republic.

Corpus planning and the historical narrative

Croatia's 1991 independence meant that its language planners were free to make policy. One of the first questions they faced was: What is Croatian? Given Croatian history, it is not surprising that linguists and lay people should be concerned about the nature of the language. Nevertheless there is no evidence of direct government action concerning the lexicon or grammar of the language. This is surprising given the struggle to preserve a Croatian linguistic identity in the Yugoslav era. It is also in sharp contrast to the radical language reform and "purification" instituted by the World War II-era fascist NDH regime (see above).

The Croatian government did support – through financing, official status or both – an expert community of linguists and institutions performing the work of establishing Croatian linguistic identity. By leaving internal reform of the language to these institutions, the Croatian government avoided unpleasant connotations of the NDH's Office for Language and its drastic measures (Anić 1998). As linguist Josip Silić has stated: "Such an office, which we had in other times, turns out to be useless or even damaging" (Hekman 1996). Moreover, the Croatian government avoided the appearance of being excessively nationalistic in an era which looked unfavorably on nationalism.

Below I explain these institutions and their role in Croatian language planning. Then I detail how these organizations have gone about reshaping Croatian itself. Finally, I examine how the reworking of the historical narrative of language development has portrayed Croatia and Croatian as a participant in the main intellectual events in the development of Western Europe.

Institutions

One of the legacies of the Croatian national movement's historic connection with language issues is a strong collection of institutions outside government that were (and are) capable of formulating and disseminating ideas about language and language policy. These organizations include "popular" cultural groups as well as small associations of scholars. Because these institutions existed prior to independence, and because the linguists who work in them are generally committed to a separate Croatian linguistic identity,[6] there was no need for the Croatian government to establish a separate "Office of Language" as the World War II era government had done.

Instead, these quasi- and non-governmental institutions helped both to reshape language as a marker of Croatian identity – connected with Croatian history and capable of functioning in the modern world – without the need for direct government intervention. The model is close to an ideal described by Josip Silić:

> I am for the "hand" of the state, but in the sense of [it] offering help to experts and expert bodies to continue their study of linguistic communication sufficiently.... Language policy planning needs the equally weighted participation of government and institutions which work with the language.
>
> (Hekman 1996)

The work of these expert bodies is manifold. The cultural group *Matica Hrvatska* disseminates ideas about Croatian through its publication *Vijenac* as well as its widespread chapters throughout Croatia and beyond (Bratulić 2003).[7] The Croatian Philological Society (HFD) performs a similar role by publishing the journal *Jezik*, written by linguists for an interested lay audience (Babić 1997).

The ideas promoted in *Vijenac* and *Jezik* often originate with scholars associated with the Croatian Academy of Science and Art (HAZU), which is tasked with promoting "Croatian cultural heritage and its affirmation throughout the world" (HAZU 2001) or the Miroslav Krleža Lexicographical Institute, which concentrates on Croatian language and literary history as well as producing new standard lexicons (Krleža Institute 2002). The Institute for Croatian Language and Linguistics (IHJJ) is involved with establishing norms for Croatian via traditional linguistic activities such as the compilation of dictionaries, lexicons and grammars (Rončević 2004). The linguistics department at the University of Zagreb is more forward-looking; it focuses on preparing the Croatian language for use with modern technology, including compiling Croatian corpora as well as improving software to enable use of Croatian in modern communications networks and information systems (Institute for Linguistics 2002).

There is a close relation, though not always a harmonious one, between the Croatian government and the above institutions. Most get a significant amount of state funding: for example, the Krleža Institute received approximately US$2.85 million from the state in 1999 (Sabor 1999a). The state recognizes the "special significance" of institutes like Krleža and HAZU for the republic, devoting special legislation to their governance (Sabor 2003c). According to a former editor of the *Matica Hrvatska* publication *Vijenac*, dependence on the state makes it possible for political parties to "penetrate" cultural organizations. *Matica Hrvatska* itself has been subject to political pressures, including pressure to dismiss editorial staff (Dugandzija 1999).

Reshaping the Croatian language

The close relations with the state meant government could rely on these institutions to produce work which supported a unique Croatian national identity on the language front. Most linguists working in the institutions were devoted to the idea that Croatian is a independent language (Greenberg 2001; Pulig 2001). Their output of new dictionaries and orthographies, technologies to integrate Croatian with modern information processing systems, and historical narratives of the language have helped Croatian claim a distinct linguistic identity.

Dictionaries and orthographies

The creation of orthographies and dictionaries are traditional functions of language planning; sociolinguist Charles Ferguson denoted the process as graphicization and linked it with development of national and/or religious identity (1968: 31–2). The products of graphicization offer tangible proof of a language's unique identity and reflect a new political order (Weinstein 1983: 11). In Croatia the government has funded existing institutions to produce these works. For example, from 1996–2001 the Ministry of Science, Education and Sport (MZOS) funded the production of several dictionaries of modern Croatian and its dialects through the Institute for Croatian Language and Linguistics (IHJJ) (MZOS 2001). The project director was Miro Kačić, a main proponent of differentiating Croatian from Serbian (Kačić 1997). It is likely that the dictionaries reflected his ideas, helping to create maximum difference between Croatian and Serbian and reflecting the language purism he saw as essential to the Croatian linguistic system (Kačić 2001).

Croatian orthography (spelling rules) has been a controversial area since the first modern efforts at systemization in the eighteenth century. Some Croatians supported the so-called "root" orthography (see note 3 below) as opposed to the phonetic system devised by the Vuk Karadžić (Budak 1941). During World War II, the NDH regime promoted the "root" system. The *Londonac* was influenced by the root orthography (see above and Babić *et al.* 1971); its direct descendant is one of two rival orthographies produced after independence (Babić *et al.* 1994) (the other being a phonetic orthography in the Vukovian tradition). The new system, which created separation from the old Serbo-Croatian standard, has met with considerable resistance on the part of the Croatian literary community but has had the support of important political figures (Anon 1999; Bajrusi 2005).

Technical aspects of corpus planning

The traditional creation of orthographies and dictionaries has been supplemented in recent years by advances in computational linguistics, especially the compilation of corpora – scientifically gathered samples of language. Corpora are used to aid lexicographical activities and to develop modern informatics systems.

The Croatian government has invested in developing two corpora, a million-word corpus completed in 2002 and a 30 million-word corpus currently in progress (the million and 30 million refer to the number of words sampled, not the number of entries in the corpus). The 30 million-word corpus will be sampled from older works of Croatian, for example those of Croatian Renaissance writers. More modern texts will be drawn from the period since 1991, that is, post independence. Goals of the 30 million-corpus project are to facilitate research into Croatian linguistics, the standardization of orthography, and study of the formation of neologisms in Croatian. The work has been carried out by the University of Zagreb's department of linguistics, supported by the Ministry of Science, Education and Sport (formerly the Ministry of Science and Technology) (MZT 1995).[8]

The development of these computer-based corpora seems to go against the belief that electronic communications networks necessarily erode national cultures. In the Croatian case, making the language compatible with modern communications and informatics has led planners to attempt to develop the language. This includes developing software to handle unique characteristics of Croatian. Perhaps paying heed to the sociolinguist Hans

Kloss's observation (1967: 41) that the creation of words for technical concepts had become more important for language survival than literature or poetry, the Croatian language community has responded to the threat of English-language domination in technological areas by modernizing their idiom (Hekman 1996; see also note 8).

The history and politics of Croatian

The Croatian corpus project has looked forward, embracing modern technology. The reworking of the historical narrative looks backward to establish Croatian's authenticity by emphasizing the continuity of language's development before the merger with Serbian. Historians and lexicographers have stressed the progress of Croatian, especially its literature, from the Middle Ages. That progress is framed in the context of Western European developments in language, thought and politics.

Historical links with the West

Placing Croatian language and literature in a Western context is part of a more general portrayal of Croatia as a Western European nation. By putting Croatian language and literature firmly in the mainstream of Western historical development, the country's scholars create distance from Serbia and Serbian while promoting the idea that Croatia is a natural member of Western groupings like the European Union.

Textbooks convey these ideas to students. In a high school (upper form) grammar book, Stjepko Težak and Stjepan Babić present Croatian literary and linguistic history as a seamless progression from the late Middle Ages onward (1996: 14–19). They hold that the language's standardization progressed continuously from the Renaissance through Gaj's nineteenth-century reforms. In contrast, they view developments at the end of the nineteenth century and early twentieth century, specifically moves to merge the language with Serbian, as a break with the normal development of the Croatian language. Once Croatia achieved independence, according to the textbook authors, it was:

> in once sense as if we have returned before 1918 to continue from that era where, because of the Serbian dominance in the first Yugoslavia, the Croatian linguistic tradition was broken; and in another to before 1945, in that those linguistic characteristics which were suppressed or eliminated are now returning.
>
> (Težak and Babić 1996: 18)

This sentiment is typical of the consensus in Croatian linguistics circles. The linguist Miro Kačić held that normal standardization of Croatian began in the eighteenth century. However, this process was interrupted at the turn of the nineteenth century by "breaking points" – such as the adoption of a Vukovian grammar for Croatian schools in 1899 or the 1956 Novi Sad agreement – which interfered with the language's proper course (Kačić 2001).

The Miroslav Krleža Institute – mandated to compile the Croatian Encyclopedia and promote Croatian intellectual culture (Sabor 2003d) – is another main proponent of the view that the history of Croatian language and literature is continuous except for the attempted merger with Serbian. The institute also stresses Croatian language and literature's links with intellectual developments in Western Europe. Its webpage on the history of Croatian encyclopedia-making extols the work of Croatians such as Jakov Mikalja (1601–54), the compiler of an Italian–Croatian dictionary; Juraj Habdelić (1609–78), who wrote a Croatian (Kajkavian)–Latin lexicon; and Faust Vrancić (1551–1617), who wrote a work containing 5,000 terms from each of four major European languages and Dalmatian (i.e. a Croatian dialect) (Krleža Institute 1998).

Language and politics

The Croatian historian Anđelko Mijatović has also written of the place of Croatia in the European system. Mijatović, a long-time cultural advisor to Franjo Tudjman and member of his cabinet (Vuković 2005; Sadkovich 2005) wrote: "Croats had always been aware of their own statehood and had developed their cultural identity parallel with the other advanced European nations" (Mijatović 2000: 52). He claims that by AD 879 "Croats were already completely included into the Christian community and cultural life of Western Europe, not only by having been converted to Christianity but also by building churches." Despite being geographically situated between large empires, the "Croats achieved great political and other successes and managed to consolidate their national identity, their statehood and to follow the civilized achievements of the contemporary Europe." (2000: 53).

The bilingual work by Vlatko Pavletić, Milan Moguš and Niksa Stancić *Hrvatski jezik u Hrvatskom Saboru/The Croatian Language in the Croatian Parliament* (1997) emphasizes even more strongly the connection between the development of the language and Croatian politics in the Western cultural milieu.[9] Written by authors who have held relatively high political appointments and published by the Croatian government's official press, the work traces Croatian participation in Western culture to the early Middle Ages – specifically to the Croat political leaders adopting Latin language as a medium of communication: "The role of Latin is important as evidence of centuries of Croatian involvement in Western civilization and culture" (Pavletić 1997: 11). While national movements often seek legitimacy by portraying continuity with a real or imaginary past, the Croatian case is unique in the emphasis that the scholars and politicians have placed on the language and culture being part of the more general development of Western intellectual and social history.

This section has shown that Croatia possessed a set of quasi-governmental or independent language institutions that were capable of performing the work of corpus reform as well as rewriting the historical narrative of the language. Their scholarship helped establish a unique linguistic identity for Croatia, one that portrayed the country as a long-time participant in Western European culture. It was carried out without direct government action, but with government financial support. In an era celebrating globalization, this policy helped to avoid the appearance of excessive nationalism while still building a Croatian linguistic identity.

Language status planning in a global era

In contrast to the indirect nature of Croatian corpus planning, Croatian language status planning has been conducted largely through legislation. In this section I highlight laws regarding Croatian and minority languages that are spoken in Croatia.[10] I then explore two controversies arising from language policy, bilingualism in Istria and education in minority languages (particularly Serbian). Finally I turn to laws requiring use of Croatian or another language for specific functions. Taken together, the data show that Croatian language planners have made concessions both to the political reality of developing norms on treatment of language minorities and to the economic reality of the necessity of the use of "world languages" in some activities.

Language laws and the Croatian constitution

Language-related legislation in Croatia is relatively scarce. Between December 1990 and July 2005, 223 laws with an explicit language component were promulgated, excluding laws regarding international treaties and standardization of weights and measures.[11] This amount is not impressive considering the total volume of Croatian legislation. Moreover, there are no laws which focus specifically on the Croatian language itself or promote language reform. These facts serve to support a comment by a Croatian linguist that the government of Croatia under the nationalistic Franjo Tudjman regime and still less under Stjepan Mesić did not put much priority on language issues.[12]

However, there has been a *de facto* language status policy. The first constitution, adopted in 1990, explicitly puts Croatian in the center of the linguistic ecology of the Croatian republic. "In the Republic of Croatia the Croatian language and Latin script is in official use" (Sabor 1990: Article 12). Other languages may be declared official in specific localities, but only *along with* Croatian (Sabor 1990: Article 12). Croatian is clearly the only official language throughout the republic and has retained this status through four substantial revisions (in 1997, 1998, 2000 and 2001) of the Croatian constitution (Sabor 2001a).

Although Croatian is official throughout the republic, the constitution of 1990 and successive revisions have contained provisions guaranteeing rights to non-Croatian speakers. Article 14 of the constitution protects individuals against discrimination based on – amongst other things – language. Article 15 guarantees members of "nations and minorities free expression of belonging to a nationality, free use of their own language and script, and cultural autonomy" (Sabor 1990: Articles 14–15). There is a slight but significant change to Article 15 in subsequent revisions to the constitution – "nations and minorities" (*narodi i manjine*) is changed to "national minorities" (*nacionalne manjine*) (Sabor 2001a: Article 15). In the context of former Yugoslavia, this has implications of a demotion from the status of a constituent nation to that of a national minority.

Articles 12, 14 and 15 taken together imply that Croatian is central to the state. Linguistic minorities, while guaranteed rights as individuals and as group members, are peripheral in the republic. This parallels the statement in the preamble to the constitution that "The Republic of Croatia is constituted as the national state of the Croatian people and the state of members of autochthonous national minorities" (Sabor 1990: Preamble). The constitution sets up a situation where both the Croatian people and the Croatian language are central to the state, while guaranteeing peripheral groups (and their languages) certain rights. This situation was solidified, but not significantly altered, in 2000 when the Croatian parliament passed laws specifically addressing language minority rights (Sabor 2000).

Conflict over minority language rights

The rights of peripheral groups found in the constitution and other laws have not been respected to the fullest. During the 1990s the Croatian government was prepared to defend the favored status of Croatian to the fullest and only slowly granted concessions to minority language groups. While international pressure and internal political change have moderated the central government's stance somewhat, the Zagreb regime still resists erosion of Croatian's central position.

Istria: conflict over bilingualism

From the end of World War I and earlier, Italian and Croatian language identities have clashed in Istria, the historical region and administrative division comprising the peninsula at the top of the Adriatic Sea. In 1994 the region adopted official bilingualism (Italian and Croatian) in its foundational law. This particular aspect of the law was based on several bilateral and European conventions, including the Osim agreement (1975) which settled territorial issues between Italy and the then Socialist Federal Republic of Yugoslavia. The Croatian government challenged this law in the Constitutional Court particularly because of "the equality in law between Italian and Croatian" put forth by the policy (Ustavni Sud 1995). The Constitutional Court decision backed the central government, but on the technical grounds that only municipalities had the right to decide local language policy, and only the central Croatian government could interpret treaties (Ustavni Sud 1995). This policy still holds, despite greater recognition of language minority rights granted with an eye towards European integration (Sabor 2004: Section 1.3.2).

Even though there are no irredentist claims on Croatian territory, the government saw Istrian bilingualism as a challenge to the cultural integrity of the state and actively sought to end that challenge. Past struggles over language in the region also occupied the mind of at least one judge on the Croatian Supreme Court. The struggle between the central government and Istrian bilingualism continues. The issue came up in the 2001 elections and, as late as 2003, the Croatian central government was seeking to remove bilingual signs on government offices in Istria (Žužić 2003).

Serbs and Serbian language education

While the Croatian government was worried about official bilingualism in Istria, it also had to deal with the problem of linguistic minorities – in particular the Serbs of eastern Slavonia – who desired education in their own language and script. Their complaints about the lack of such education attracted the attention of the United States State Department, which included language issues in its 1998 report on human rights issues in Croatia. The Croatian government – according to the United States – had failed to live up to an agreement to provide textbooks or instruction in Serbian.[13] In addition, a number of Serb teachers were dismissed under pressure from Croats who had been resettled in the area (State Department 1998). The Croatian government responded, denying some charges and putting others in mitigating context (Croatian Government 1999).

Lessening of language conflicts

With time and continuing pressure from the Council of Europe and the United States, schools for the Serbian minority were established in eastern Slavonia and other measures were taken to promote minority language instruction. As of August 2003, there were 31 schools in which Serbian was the language of instruction in Croatia, and another 31 schools in which another minority language was the language of instruction (Spajić-Vrkaš 2003).

In both cases – the Italians in Istria and the Serbs in eastern Slavonia – it seems that a stable situation has been reached. The government of the republic has pointed out progress made in granting language rights in conformance with European norms (Sabor 2004: Section 1.3.2). The concessions seem enough to satisfy minority groups. Yet much legislation actually promotes Croatian as the central language of the country. In the following section I show how laws primarily addressing non-language-related topics promote a Croatian linguistic identity via status planning.

Croatian in economic and political life

Croatian legislation is often concerned with establishing Croatian as the central language of the state's economic and political life. Regulations in these spheres do not prohibit the use of other languages, but do give Croatian the central place by requiring its use in many situations.

Croatian and the economy

The regulation of banks and businesses provides examples of the government's insistence on Croatian in economic activity. For foreign banks, at least one member of the local board of directors most speak Croatian. Financial reports must be completed in Croatian (Sabor 2002). Applications for mergers of businesses must be submitted in Croatian, as must applications for leasing part of the radio spectrum (Sabor 2001b; Sabor 2003b). Firms' tax documents and any evidence of income and expenses of businesses must be submitted in Croatian (Sabor 1999b).

These and similar laws show that Croatian is the language in which business with the state must be conducted. They govern the language of economic activity. Each has an article dealing with language issues, and they all specify Croatian as the official means of communicating with the government. This did not necessarily have to be the case. For example, options for keeping business records or submitting bids in English – the lingua franca of business today – might have been instituted, especially for international firms. Yet the Croatian legislature insists on requiring the national language for official communications with the government.

Croatian in politics and civil society

Perhaps more telling are language restrictions on names of foundations, societies and political parties operating in Croatia. According to a 1993 law, charitable foundations must have a Croatian name, although foundations set up to benefit a minority group can also have a name in the minority group language (Sabor 1993d). Societies such as human rights organizations, business associations and educational groups must have a Croatian name as their official title while operating in Croatia (Sabor 1997; Sabor 2001c). Political parties too must have a Croatian name, although they may have a minority language name *along with* the Croatian name. However, in party logos, the Croatian name must be written in letters at least as large as the foreign name of the party and in the top position (Sabor 1993c). There is no sign of the relaxation of these regulations; the law governing political parties was amended in 1998 and again in 2001, but the language provisions were left intact (Sabor 2001c).

These laws show that the Croatian parliament has legislated the use of Croatian in the business, political and non-profit spheres in laws whose primary focus is not language. Croatian is the language of the state, of the economy and of civil society. Other language groups are granted limited language rights, but Croatia is following a model which explicitly and implicitly puts Croatian in the center of important sectors of activity. Minority languages, on the other hand, are marginalized.

Preparing for globalization: Croatian and "world languages"

While minority languages have been regulated to their various geographical niches and Croatian has been given a central place in economic, political and civic life, there is a third class of language that appears in legislation and is directly related to globalization, the so-called "world languages." The term "world language" is not clearly defined in Croatian law but, according to customs service regulations, they are French, German, Italian and English (Financija 2004).

Laws requiring use of world languages are generally practical. A few require high officials to be proficient in a world language; the Croatian government recognizes that its officials must operate in these languages in the larger world. Other laws requiring knowledge or use of world languages are concentrated in fields such as transport and navigation – where language issues could affect safety – and in obvious areas like tourism administration.

Some examples of practical laws are qualifications which require sea pilots to be able to communicate in English and Italian, especially in the terms relating to their trade. On land, hazardous cargo must be accompanied by documentation in Croatian and a world language such as English, German or French (Sabor 1993b). Laws require signage in national parks to be in English (as well as Croatian) (Okoliša 1998). Proficiency in a world language is a requirement for many jobs from tour guide to the president of the Croatian Telecom board (Sabor 2001b; Turizma 1999). Croatia is also training its officials in world languages in order to prepare for entry into the EU (Sabor 2003a).

Such laws show that Croatia is devising a language policy which meets the needs of the globalized economy. There is nothing particularly surprising in this data. The unexpected result is that *both* preparations for globalization and the assertion of Croatian as central to economic, political and civil life have been established in law. This is an indication that the practical need to deal with globalization does not necessarily put an end to attempts to forge a linguistic identity.

Conclusion

When it achieved independence in 1991, the Croatian government faced pit-falls in attempting to establish a linguistic identity apart from Serbian. Language issues concerned a significant segment of the population, many of which pressed for government action to separate Croatian from the hybrid Serbo-Croatian. At the same time, the practical realities of globalization as well as the development of transnational norms on the treatment of linguistic minorities meant that Croatia could not appear to be radically nationalistic.

Despite these constraints, Croatia has been able to maintain, and even restore, a separate linguistic identity. It has done this in law, by pursuing a strategy of regulating minority languages to specific niches, while asserting the dominance of Croatian throughout the territory of the country. At the same time, a set of government-supported institutions capable of carrying out language planning allowed an indirect role for government in shaping Croatian linguistic identity.

Conforming to international (or Western) norms has not stopped the development of a unique Croatian linguistic identity. Indeed, in looking back to a past in which the language and its literature participated fully in Western intellectual developments, the reworked historical narrative about the language is complementary to Croatian desires to integrate into Western institutions. It shows, in a sense, that Croatia is a fit member of "the club."

Nor are the extension of global communications networks necessarily a death knell for a small language like Croatian. Rather, the efforts of linguists to develop the language itself and associated technology so that Croatian can be used in modern informatics systems and is capable of expressing technological concepts themselves become a project of reinforcing national identity.

Despite the tendency toward globalization, Croatia has put effort into establishing a unique and, in the view of many Croatians, authentic linguistic identity. Indeed the Republic has had some success in this project. This case should give pause to the prophets of globalization who see a world in which nations erode in the face of worldwide communication and economic networks. At least in the case of Croatian language policy, planners have shown the ability to adapt to the global era while still asserting national identity. The Croatian language persists as a symbol of the Croatian nation.

Notes

1 Language planning has been defined as "a government authorized, long term sustained and conscious effort to alter a language itself or to change a language's functions in a society for the purpose of solving communications problems" (Weinstein 1983: 37) or "the authoritative assigning of scarce resources to language" (Fishman 2004: 79). Fishman (2004: 79–94) also describes the corpus and status aspects of language planning and their relation to each other.
2 Croatian has three historical dialects, Kajkavian, Cakavian and Stokavian, so-called for their word for "What." Kajkavian is spoken around Zagreb and the

mountains to the north, Cakavian is centered on the central Dalmatian coast and islands, and Stokavian is spoken in southern Dalmatia and Slavonia, as well as by inhabitants of Bosnia and Herzegovina, Serbia and Montenegro.

3 In the "root" (*korijenski*) or morphological orthography, word roots tend to remain unchanged despite phonetic changes they undergo in combination with other elements of the word. This contradicts the Vukovian injunction to "write as it is spoken."

4 A single complete copy found its way to London. Printed in the exile *samizdat* press 1972; it came to be known as the *Londonac* (*Londoner*). It served as the basis for post-independence orthographies by the same linguists (Babić *et al.* 1994).

5 The population of Croatia is about 4.5 million. Per capita, 7,000 members in Croatia would equate to about 93,000 members in the United Kingdom or 450,000 members in the United States.

6 There are exceptions, but they prove the rule. The linguist Dubrovko Skiljan proclaimed the situation was so biased to the nationalist side that "it was impossible to do scholarly work in Zagreb" because of the climate of nationalism. Skiljan left Croatia for Slovenia (Pulig 2001). The late linguist Vladimir Anić too felt that politics were intruding on language policy, and that language norms created for political reasons would fail over the long run. Anić engaged in a polemic against those who sought a radical reform to Croatian (Anić 1998: 43; Mostarkić 2001).

7 Interview with Croatian linguist Anton Knezović, May 25, 2002, Monterey, California, in addition to published sources.

8 Interview with linguist Marko Tadić, June 5, 2002, Zagreb, in addition to published sources.

9 The authors of this work have held various governmental positions, either as political appointees or as elected officials. The work itself was produced by the official publisher of the Croatian parliament, *Narodne Novine*.

10 That is, laws, policies and court decisions which have a clause or provision related to language status or use. Examples include laws establishing a language as official, requiring its use or affirming rights to use a language. Such clauses appear in legislation covering many types of activity.

11 I used two internet search engines, Google (www.google.com) and Altavista (www.altavista.com). A search of the form "jezi* site:www.nn.hr" where jezi* is a declined form of the word *jezik* was conducted repeatedly in June, July and August 2005. "Hits" were aggregated and checked for duplicates. Only HTML documents with a title of the form xx-dd-mm-yyyy "Title" (e.g. 117-23-07-2003 "Zakon o Hrani," a law found *Narodne Novine* no. 117 for 2003, published 23 July) were examined, as inspection showed each individual law was represented by a document meeting this criteria. Laws about treaty ratifications and laws concerning standardization of measures, judged to bear little relation to language planning, were excluded.

12 Interview with linguist Marko Tadić, June 5, 2002, Zagreb.

13 There is a certain irony in that by insisting that Croatian was a separate language from Serbian, the Croatian government essentially created its largest linguistic minority.

References

Croatian legislation

All legislation referenced as "Sabor" in the text is published online by the official gazette, *Narodne Novine*, at www.nn.hr/sluzbeni-list/sluzbeni/index.asp.

Sabor (1990) "Ustav Republike Hrvatske [Constitution of the Croatian Republic]," No. 56/90, (December 22) (accessed March 16, 2005).

—— (1991) "Uredba o Leksikografskom Zavodu 'Miroslav Krleža' [Decree on Lexicography Institute 'Miroslav Krleža']," No. 6/91 (February 13) (accessed October 17, 2005).

—— (1993a) "Razrješenje Pomoćnika Ministra Znanosti [Decision on the Appointment of Assistant Minister of Science]," No. 41/93 (May 7) (accessed August 26, 2005).

—— (1993b) "Zakon o Prijevozu Opasnih Tvari [Law on the Transport of Dangerous Cargo]," No. 97/93 (October 26) (accessed August 5, 2005).

—— (1993c) "Zakon o Političkim Strankama [Law on Political Parties]," No. 76/93 (August 7) (accessed August 26, 2005).

—— (1993d) "Zakon o Ustanovama [Law on Foundations]," No. 76/93 (August 16) (accessed August 5, 2005).

—— (1997) "Zakon o Udrugama [Law on Associations]," No. 70/97 (July 7) (accessed August 5, 2005).

—— (1998) "Odluka o Dodjeli Državnih Nagrada Za Znanost [Decision on Granting State Medal for Science]," No. 95/98 (May 7) (accessed June 20, 2005).

—— (1999a) "Izmjene I Dopune Državnog Proračuna Republike Hrvatske za 1999. Godinu [Changes and Additions to the State Budget of the Republic of Croatia for 1999]," No. 70/99 (July 7), (accessed September 4, 2005).

—— (1999b) "Zakon o Izmjenama i Dopunama Zakona o Osiguranju [Changes and Additions to the Insurance Law]," No. 116/99 (October 27) (accessed June 23, 2003).

—— (2000) "Zakon o Uporabi Jezika i Pisma Nacionalnih Manjina u Republici Hrvatskoj [Law on the Use of the Languages and Scripts of National Minorities]," No. 51/00 (May 19) (accessed June 24, 2005).

—— (2001a) "Ustav Republike Hrvatski [Constitution of the Croatian Republic]," No. 41/01 (May 7) (accessed May 1, 2005).

—— (2001b) "Zakon o Izmjenama i Dopunama Zakona o Telekomunikacijama [Amendments and Additions to the Telecommunications Law]," No. 68/01 (July 27) (accessed June 22, 2005).

—— (2001c) "Zakon o Udrugama [Law on Associations]," No. 88/01 (October 11) (accessed June 23, 2005).

—— (2002) "Zakon o Bankama [Law on Banking]," No. 84/02 (July 17, 2002) (accessed June 23, 2005).

—— (2003a) "Program Stručnog Usavrsavanja Državnih Službenika za 2003 Godinu [Program of Professional Education for State Officials for the Year 2003]," No. 78/03 (May 14) (accessed June 22, 2005).

—— (2003b) "Zakon o Hrvatskoj Radioteleviziji [Law on Croatian Radio and Television]," No. 25/03 (February 19) (accessed June 22, 2005).

—— (2003c) "Zakon o Znanstvenoj Djelatnosti i Visokom Obrazovanju [Law on

Scientific Activity and Higher Education]," No. 123/03 (July 31), available online at www.nn.hr/sluzbeni-list/sluzbeni/index.asp/ (accessed July 18, 2005).

—— (2003d) "Zakon o Leksikografskom Zavodu Miroslav Krleža [Law on the Miroslav Krleža Lexicographical Institute]," No. 96/03 (June 10) (accessed June 18, 2005).

—— (2004) "Nacionalni Program Republike Hrvatske za Pridruživanje Europskoj Uniji – 2004 Godina [National Program of the Croatian Republic for Association with the European Union – 2004]," No. 37/04 (March 23) (accessed June 28, 2005).

Primary and secondary sources

Anić, V. (1998) *Jezik i Slaboda (Language and Freedom)*, Zagreb: Matica Hrvatska.

Anon (1974) "Jezične Odredbe u Ustavu SFRJ i SRH [Language Regulations in the Constitutions of the Socialist Federal Republic of Yugoslavia and the Socialist Republic of Croatia]," *Jezik*, 21: 65–7.

Anon (1999) "Anketa," *Vijenac*, 136 (20 May), available online at www.matica. hr/MH_Periodika/vijenac/1999/136/Vijenac136.htm (accessed July 12, 2005).

Anon (2000) "Dani Hrvatskoga Jezika I Casopis Jezik," *Jezik*, 47: inside back cover.

Babić, S. (1969) "Hrvatski Knjizevni Jezik I Pitanje Varianta [The Croatian Literary Language and the Variant Question]," *Kritika*, special edition.

—— (1992) "O Hrvatskom Prilogu Unitaristickim Nastojanjima [On the Croatian Role in the Unitary Movement (in Yugoslavia)]," *Jezik*, 39: 68–73.

—— (1997) "Suradnicima Jezika [To Colleagues of *Jezik*]," *Jezik*, 44: 117–18.

Babić, S., Finka, B. and Moguš, M. (1994) *Hrvatski Pravopis (Croatian Orthography)*, Zagreb: Školska Knjiga.

—— (1971) "Predgovor [Introduction]," *Hrvatski Pravopis*, London.

Bajrusi, R. (2005) "Sanader Glavni Lobist za Novi Pravopis [(Prime Minister) Sanader is the Chief Lobbyist for the New Orthography]," *Nacional*, February 22, available online at www.nacional.hr/articles/view/11303/27/ (accessed December 19, 2005).

Banac, I. (1984) "The Croat Language Question," in R. Picchio and H. Goldblatt (eds) *Aspects of the Slavic Language Question, Vol 1 Church Slavonic–South Slavic–West Slavic*, New Haven: Yale Concilium on International and Area Studies.

Bratulić, J. (2003) Excerpt from "Matica Hrvatska 1842–1997," *Matica Hrvatska*, available online at www.matica.hr/www/mhwww.nsf/english.htm#5 (accessed July 5, 2005).

Budak, M. (1941) Decree Regarding the Croatian Language, Its Purity and Spelling, trans. S. Djurić, in *Zločini Na Jugoslovenskim Prostorima u Prvom i Drugom Svetskom Ratu, Zbornik Documenata. (Crimes in Yugoslav Territories in the First and Second World Wars, A Collection of Documents)*, Beograd: Vojnoistorijski Institut, available online at www.pavelicpapers.com/documents/budak/mbu0003.html (accessed September 22, 2005).

Bugarski, R. (1989) "O Jezičkoj Problemi Kod Nas [On Our Language Problem]," *Politika* (March 2).

Bugarski, R. (1995) *Jezik od Mira do Rata*, 2nd revised edn, Beograd: Slovograf.

Croatian Government (1999) *Očitovanje Vlade Republike Hrvatske na Izvješće Državnog Tajništva SAD-a o Poštivanju Ljudskih Prava u Republici Hrvatskoj (Response of the Croatian Government to the Report of the United States State Department on the Human*

Rights Situation in the Republic of Croatia in 1998}, available online at www.vlada.hr (accessed December 18, 2004).

Despalatovic, E. (1975) *Ljudevit Gaj and the Illyrian Movement*, Boulder: East European Quarterly.

Deutsch, K.W. (1966) *Nationalism and Social Communication: An Inquiry into the Foundation of Nationality*, Cambridge: MIT Press.

Dugandzija, M. (1999) "Interview with Andrea Zlatar, Former Editor-in-Chief of *Vijenac*," *Nacional*, March 10, trans. ex-Yu Press, available online at www.exyupress.com/nacional/nacional2.html (accessed June 28, 2005).

Ferguson, C.A. (1968) "Language Development," in J.A. Fishman, C.A. Ferguson and J. Das Gupta (eds) *Language Problems of Developing Nations*, New York: John Wiley & Sons.

Financija [Ministry of Finance] (2004) "Pravilnik o Pologanju Stručnog Ispita za Ovlastenoga Carinskog Zastupnika [Directive on the Administration of the Professional Test for Authorized Customs Deputies]," No. 92/04 (July 7), available online at www.nn.hr/sluzbeni-list/sluzbeni/index.asp/ (accessed August 5, 2005).

Fishman, J.A. (2004) "Ethnicity and Supra-Ethnicity in Corpus Planning: The Hidden Status Agenda in Corpus Planning," in M. Guibernau and J. Hutchinson (eds) *History and National Destiny: Ethnosymbolism and Its Critics*, Oxford: Blackwell.

Friedman, T. (1999) *The Lexis and the Olive Tree*, New York: Farrar, Strauss & Giroux.

Gaj, L. (1830) [1983] *Kratka Osnova Horvatsko-Slavenskoga Pravopisanja, Poleg Modroljubneh, Narodneh i Prigospodarneh Telemov i Zrokov {A Short, Basic Croato-Slavic Orthography Based on Philosophical, National and Economic Grounds}*, Buda: Royal University of Buda Press [(facsimile edition) Zagreb: Cymelia Croatica].

Gellner, E. (1964) "Nationalism," in E. Gellner, *Thought and Change*, London: Weidenfeld & Nicolson.

Greenberg, R.D. (2001) *Language, Nationalism and the Yugoslav Successor States*, in C.C. O'Reilly (ed.) *Minority Languages, Ethnicity and the State: Minority Languages in Eastern Europe Post-1989*, London: Palgrave.

Gutterman, D. (2005) "Croatia – Other Proposals and Unofficial Variations," *Flags of the World*, available online at www.atlasgeo.net/fotw/flags/hr!.html (accessed June 21, 2005).

HAZU (Hrvatska Akademija Znanosti I Umjetnosti) (2001) "Main Tasks of the Croatian Academy for Science and the Arts," available online at mahazu.hazu.hr/ENG/mt.html (accessed February 8, 2006).

—— (2005) "Full Member Milan Moguš – Biography," available online at mahazu.hazu.hr/Akademici/MMoguš_bio.html (accessed May 17, 2005).

Hekman, J. (1996) "Razgovori: Josipom Silićem – Hrvatski iz Računala [Conversations: Josip Silic – Croatian from the Computer]," *Vijenac*, 78, available online at wap.macedonia.org/vijenac/stari/broj77-78/77-11.html (accessed June 5, 2005).

—— (1997) *Deklaracija o Nazivu i Polozaju Hrvatskog Knjizevnog Jezika {Declaration on the Name and Situation of the Croatian Literary Language}*, Zagreb: Matica Hrvatska.

Hobsbawm, E.J. (1992) *Nations and Nationalism since 1780: Programme, Myth, Reality*, Cambridge: Cambridge University Press.

Hroch, M. (1993) "From National Movement to the Fully Formed Nation: The Nation Building Process in Europe," *New Left Review*, 198: 3–20.

Institute for Linguistics [University of Zagreb] (2002) "Aims of the Institute," available online at www.ffzg.hr/zzl/ (accessed September 18, 2005).

Kačić, M. (2001) *Jezikoslovna Promišljanja {Thoughts about Language}*, Zagreb: Pergamena.

—— (1997) *Croatian and Serbian: Delusions and Distortions*, Zagreb: Novi Most.

Kalogjera, D. (1989) "Prescriptivism in Serbo-Croatian," in M. Radovanović (ed.) *Yugoslav General Linguistics*, Amsterdam: John Benjamins.

Kloss, H. (1967) "*Abstand* Languages and *Ausbau* Languages," *Anthropological Linguistics*, 9: 29–41.

Krleža Institute (1998) "A Short Survey of Encyclopaedia Making in Croatia," *Leksikografski Zavod Miroslav Krleža*, Zagreb, available online at www.hlz.hr/povijest.html (accessed March 13, 2005).

—— (2002) "Organization of the Miroslav Krleža Institute," available online at www.lzmk.hr/Zavod.aspx (accessed June 17, 2006).

Leskovar, B. (1942) *Koriensko Pisanje {Root Orthography}*, Zagreb: Hrvatski Državni Ured za Jezik.

Mijatović, A. (2000) *The Croats in Time and Space*, Zagreb: Školska Knjiga.

Mostarkić, S. (2001) "Vladimir Anić [Obituary]," *Jezik* 48: 82–4.

MZOS [Ministry for Science, Education and Sport] (2001) "Projekt: Rječnici Suvremenoga Hrvatskoga Jezika [Project: Dictionaries of Modern Croatian]," *zProjekti*, available online at www.mzos.hr/zProjekti (accessed June 22, 2004).

MZT [Ministry for Science and Technology] (1995) "Kompjutorska Obrada Hrvatskoga Književnog Jezika [Computer Processing of the Croatian Language]," 6-03-048, Zagreb, October 22, available online at www.mzos.hr/svibor/6/03/048/proj_e.htm (accessed June 21, 2004).

Ohmae, K. (1995) *The End of the Nation-state: The Rise of Regional Economies*, New York: Free Press.

Okoliša [Minister for the Environment] (1998) "Pravilnik o Unutarnjem Redu u Parku Prirode "Kopački Rit" [Internal Regulations for the Nature Park Kopacki Rit]," Zagreb: *Narodne Novine*, 84/98 (June 16), available online at www.nn.hr/sluzbeni-list/sluzbeni/index.asp (accessed August 5, 2005).

Pavletić, V. (2004) "Vlatko Pavletić – Biography," available online at www.vlatko Pavletić.com.hr/engl/biography.htm (accessed June 21, 2005).

Pavletić, V., Stancić, N. and Moguš, M. (1997) *Hrvatski Jezik u Hrvatskom Saboru {The Croatian Language in the Croatian Parliament}*, Zagreb: Narodne Novine.

Pulig, S. (2001) "Kako Jezik Postaje Nacionalnim Simbolom: Dubravko Skiljan [How Language Becomes a National Symbol: (Interview with) Dubravko Skiljan]," *Zarez*, 59 (July 5).

Rončević, D.B. (2004) "Institut [Description of the Institute]," *Institut za Hrvatski Jezik i Jezikoslovlje*, Zagreb, available online at www.ihjj.hr/institut.htm (accessed February 5, 2006).

Sadkovich, J. (2005) "Franjo Tudjman, a Political and Intellectual Biography [Research Outline]," IREX, available online at www.irex.org/programs/stg/research/05/sadkovich.pdf (accessed July 8, 2005).

Smith, A.D. (1991) *National Identity*, Reno: University of Nevada Press.

Spajić-Vrkaš, V. (2003) *Education for Democratic Citizenship 2001–2004*, Council of Europe, Zagreb, available online at www.ffzg.hr/hre-edc/hr/index.php?mmIID=/58/77/&main_search=education%20for%20democratic&cntID=74&l_over=1 (accessed September 17, 2005).

State Department (United States Department of State, Bureau of Democracy, Human Rights, and Labor) (1998) *Croatia Country Report on Human Rights Practices for 1998*, Washington, DC, February 26, available online at www.hri.org/docs/USSD-Rights/1998/Croatia.html (accessed December 15, 2004).

Težak, S. and Babić, S. (1996) *Gramatika Hrvatskoga Jezika*, Zagreb: Školska Knjiga.

Turizma (Minister of Tourism) (1999) "Pravilinik o Izmjenama i Dopunama Pravilnika o Razvrstavanju, Minimalnim Uvjetima i Kategorizaciji Ugostiteljskih Objekata [Amendments to Directives on the Categorization and Minimal Conditions for (Tourist) Accommodations]," Zagreb: *Narodne Novine*, 39/99, April 23, available online at www.nn.hr/sluzbeni-list/sluzbeni/index.asp (accessed August 5, 2005).

Ustavni Sud (1995) *Broj U-II-433/1994 {Case Number U-II-433/1994}*, Ustavni Sud Republike Hrvatske, Zagreb, February 2, 1995: *Narodne Novine*, 9/95, available online at www.nn.hr/sluzbeni-list/sluzbeni/index.asp (accessed June 29, 2005).

Vuković, M. (1996) *Broj U-III-938/1995 {Case Number U-III-938/1995} Dissenting Opinion*, Ustavni Sud Republike Hrvatske, Zagreb, April 3, 1996, *Narodne Novine*, 30/96, available online at www.nn.hr/sluzbeni-list/sluzbeni/index.asp (accessed June 28, 1995).

Vuković, T. (2005) "Razgovor: Dr Andjelko Mijatović, Povjesničar [Conversation Dr. Anđjelko Mijatovic, Historian]," Zagreb, *Glas Koncila*, November 6, available online at www.glas-koncila.hr/rubrike_interview.html?news_ID=5377 (accessed December 15, 2005).

Weinstein, B. (1983) *The Civic Tongue: Political Consequences of Language Choices*, New York: Longman.

Žužić, B. (2003) "Dvojezični Duh Istre Nitko Neće Pokoriti [No One Will Conquer the Bilingual Spirit of Istria]," Pula, Slobodna Dalmacija, February 18, available online atarhiv.slobodnadalmacija.hr/20030218/novosti08.asp (accessed June 20, 2005).

12 National identity in the Hashemite Kingdom of Jordan

State made, still durable

Stefanie Nanes

Inspired by Anthony Smith's work on the continuing importance of national identity in the contemporary world, this volume attempts to answer the question "why do nations continue to be relevant in today's globalized society." My contribution addresses this question using the case of Jordan. Although Smith prefers Egypt and Israel as his primary Middle Eastern examples of the longstanding existence of *ethnies*, Jordan offers an excellent opportunity to study the strength of even the most recent national creations. Jordanian identity has proven particularly resilient, despite its recent genesis, because Jordanian leaders have effectively coopted regional "myths, memories, values and symbols" to produce a durable national identity.

Jordanian national identity is a *mélange* of pre-state identities: Islam, Arab nationalism and tribalism. Jordan's royal family, the Hashemites, justified their rule by reference to their Islamic credentials, namely their descent from the Prophet Muhammad's family and their traditional responsibility to guard the Muslim holy places, Mecca and Medina. The Hashemites also used Arab nationalism, an ideology beginning to percolate through the region in the early twentieth century, to bolster their claim to govern. Bowing to local political demands, the Hashemites integrated existing power structures and organizations, i.e. tribes and tribal leaders (*shaykhs*). Although initially facing opposition from tribes accustomed to avoiding state control, the state was able to meld the tribal ethos into loyalty to the state. In sum, the particular demands of the Jordanian state-building experience produced Jordan's current national identity.

Today, this national identity is firmly identified with "the tribes" and tribalism. Even many citizens whom this identity excludes, i.e. Jordanians of Palestinian origin, associate Jordanian national identity with a tribal character. The two other strands, Islam and Arab nationalism, have not disappeared entirely, but have been made subservient to the tribal feature. The first section of this chapter explores the central myth symbol of Jordanian nationalism: the Arab Revolt, which established the pre-state threads of contemporary Jordanian national identity. The second section explains how the emergence of this identity was closely tied to the political exigencies of establishing a modern centralized state in a region where none had previously existed. The third section briefly discusses some of the contemporary ways these early inputs remain the key features of Jordanian national identity. The chapter closes with some reflections on implications for the future.

The Arab Revolt: the early foundation of Jordanian nationalism

Today's Hashemite Kingdom of Jordan had its beginnings in imperial maneuverings during World War I. By 1915, trench warfare had bogged down the Allied war effort in Europe, so Britain began to seek out a weaker flank of the Ottoman Empire, which had joined the Central Powers in 1914. At the same time, Shariff Hussein ibn Ali, head of the Hashemite family and the Ottoman-appointed leader of the Hijaz, had begun to chafe under Ottoman rule.[1] He feared that the traditional autonomy of the Hijaz was threatened by the centralizing reforms of the Young Turks who had taken power in Istanbul in 1908. One of these reforms was the extension of a railway from Damascus to Mecca. This railway, while vastly simplifying the annual pilgrimage to Mecca, would strengthen Ottoman administration of a region that previously enjoyed significant autonomy, weakening the Hashemites' primary source of authority: their administration of the *hajj*.

Further, Shariff Hussein harbored ambitions for the expansion of his own power not just the maintenance of his autonomy. To this end, Hussein approached the British high commissioner in Egypt, Henry McMahon, with an offer of Arab military support against the Ottomans in exchange for British support for an independent Arab kingdom under the leadership of Shariff Hussein or one of his sons, Faysal or Abdullah. Hussein's initial letter in July 1915 launched an exchange of letters that still "lie at the root of an immense controversy over whether Britain pledged to support an independent Arab state and then reneged on the pledge" (Cleveland 2004). Within the exchange, Hussein continually attempted to get Britain to agree to certain borders of said Arab state. Britain preferred to keep the proposed borders vague, allowing them through the course of the war to make other agreements with France and the Zionist movement regarding land Hussein believed promised to him.[2] In any event, this offer of support, as it was understood by Hussein, resulted in the Arab Revolt, launched in 1916, led by Faysal. Abdullah remained in the Hijaz to attack Ottoman outposts there. Although the Arab Revolt was only marginally important in the ultimate Allied victory over the Central Powers, it would prove essential in providing an early foundation for Jordanian national identity.

Shariff Hussein employed the language of nascent Arab nationalism in his communications with the British and with Arab elites who were increasingly attracted to this ideology. Arab nationalism provided both the legitimacy of purpose and a larger framework of endeavor to justify and ennoble Hussein's dynastic ambitions (Wilson 1987: 26). Up until that point,

Shariff Hussein had been willing to work within the Ottoman framework to expand his autonomy in the Hijaz and limit Ottoman authority there. Only when the option to constitute a new political framework based on a new justification – an Arab state founded on a unique and separate Arab identity – was presented by the British did the Hashemites begin to use the ideology of Arab nationalism (Wilson 1991).

Intellectually, Arab nationalism has its earliest roots in two trends beginning post-1850: first, a literary awakening (*al-Nahda*) promulgated by Christians in Syria and Lebanon who focused on the revival of the Arabic language and second, Islamic reform, led by Muslim scholars who attempted to revitalize Islam in order to confront the challenge of the West. *Al-Nahda* was primarily a cultural and scientific movement rather than a religious or overtly political one. It was embodied in the multitude of literary clubs and scientific societies throughout the Levant, but especially in Beirut. Arab Christians took the lead in this literary movement. The career of Butrus al-Bustani is instructive; a Maronite who converted to Protestantism, he produced a modern Arabic dictionary and encyclopedia, as well as editing Arabic periodicals, all of which "contributed to the creation of modern Arabic expository prose, of a language true to its past in grammar and idiom, but made capable of expressing simply, precisely and directly the concepts of modern thought" (Hourani 1983: 100).

During roughly the same time period, Muslim reformers, such as Jamal al-Din al-Afghani and Muhammad Abduh, also saw the need for cultural revitalization in their confrontation with the power of the West (Hourani 1983). They argued that an outdated interpretation of Islam and old-fashioned clergy played a large role (alongside colonialism) in weakening Muslim societies (Milton-Edwards 2000: 50). These thinkers observed that the strength of Europe lay in its commitment to free thought and reason. They argued that these principles were also central principles to an authentic Islam, but had been lost over time, leading the Muslim world to decline in power and wealth relative to Europe. They argued that Muslim societies could regain their strength by returning to Islam, but an Islam actively engaged with the modern world. As in most nationalist movements, the revival and modernization of the Arabic language played a central and relatively straightforward role in the development of Arab nationalism. The Muslim reformers, however, played a subtler but no less important role in transforming the traditional language of Islam into one that made Islam open to new ideas and innovation from outside, including the concept of modern nationalism.

These elements created the intellectual environment in which the Arab provinces of the declining Ottoman Empire would formulate their response to changes in Ottoman governance and ideology in the early twentieth century (Dawn 1991). Turkish nationalism had been growing in strength in the heart of the Ottoman Empire, but still competed with a sense of Ottomanism, the belief that the variety of peoples in the Empire could remain together as one political unit. As an identity, Ottomanism was seen by its proponents as a means of holding the Empire together against the tide of particularistic nationalism that had eroded the Empire's holdings in southeastern Europe. Reflecting these competing tendencies, Istanbul implemented centralizing reform aimed at holding intact what was left of the Empire. These centralizing reforms displaced the local (Arab) notables in the Arab provinces, notables who had long considered posts in the government an inherited right in exchange for their loyalty and service to the Empire. These disgruntled notables, along with other Arabs inspired by their travels to Europe, formed the nuclei of the early Arab literary societies that would prove the seedbed of Arab nationalism (Khoury 1983). Initially, the Arab regions under Ottoman rule only desired more cultural autonomy within the Empire, not independence. However, as Turkish nationalism gained ascendancy over the idea of Ottomanism in Istanbul, Arab elites in the Fertile Crescent responded with their own version of Arab nationalism that called for independence from the Ottoman Empire.

Although the Hashemites relied upon the rhetoric of Arab nationalism, the true degree of their commitment to its actual tenets is hard to gauge. Hussein employed the ideology exclusively in his communications with the British. Abdullah, Hussein's son and the future first King of Jordan, had never been a member of any of the early Arab cultural societies (Wilson 1987: 20–1). Only a few years earlier, Shariff Hussein and his sons had crushed a revolt against Ottoman authority very much like their own by Arabs in Asir, a region near the Hijaz.

Although Shariff Hussein used the emerging ideology of Arab nationalism to gain the external support of the powerful British, he employed Islam to rally the bulk of the troops who actually fought the Arab Revolt. Since he needed to justify an uprising by Muslims against a Muslim Empire, he claimed that infidel Turks were secularizing and abandoning Islam in favor of Turkish nationalism.[3] This call proved particularly convincing due to Shariff Hussein's Hashemite lineage. "Hashemite" refers to the Bani Hashem, a clan of the Quraysh tribe of Mecca, to which the Prophet Muhammad had belonged. This lineage conferred on Shariff Hussein and his sons, Faysal and Abdullah, the title of *shariff*. Although sharifian status "can be and (has) been forged, falsified and bought," the genealogies in the Hijaz were generally well preserved, adding legitimacy to the call to arms in 1916 and Abdullah's later claim for leadership (Wilson 1987: 6). Traditionally, the Hashemite lineage also confers the traditional role of protector of the holy Islamic places, including Mecca, Medina and Jerusalem, together with responsibility for administration of the annual pilgrimage.[4]

However, Hashemite leadership was not "Islamic" leadership in the contemporary sense of the word, as reflected in the call for Islamic law by Islamist movements. At the turn of the twentieth century, Islamic law was already the law of the land in the Ottoman Empire. Hashemite Islamic credentials were not based on religious learning or personal piety, but on noble status. Islam in this sense had little to do with the Islam representing the whole host of institutions, art and literature, spiritual and religious scholarship and daily practices that comprised the fabric of people's lives. The Hashemites invoked defense of Islam, based on their inherited Islamic status, to motivate participants in the Arab Revolt. In short, the Hashemites employed both Islam *and* Arab nationalism to justify their territorial ambitions and their opposition to the Ottoman regime.

The third aspect of the Arab Revolt that continues to play a key role in contemporary Jordanian national identity revolves around the tribes. Unlike Islam and Arab nationalism, which supplied pliable cultural material to the Hashemites, the tribal aspect was apparent simply in how the Revolt was fought. Some committed Arab nationalists, inspired by the call for an independent Arab state, served as Faysal's advisors. The majority of the troops, however, were tribes loyal to the family of the Hashemites and incited by the rhetoric of defending Islam. As the Arab Revolt moved up from the Hijaz and on to its ultimate destination, Damascus, some tribal groups, inspired by the call to defend Islam, joined in. Sections of the Huwaytat, Bani Atiya and Bili tribes in the south and sections of the Bani Sakhr tribe in the central region, closer to Amman, were the tribes that participated on Faysal's side. Most tribes did not follow the Hashemite call to rebel against the Empire and either stayed aloof or fought with the Ottoman army. During the early state-building period of the 1920s and 1930s, the tribes that had joined Faysal would become key supporters of the new regime.

There is little agreement among academics about the actual definition of tribes and tribalism, as tribal organization varies across regions. Richard Tapper suggests a workable definition of tribe as: "a localized group in which kinship is the dominant idiom of organization, and whose members consider themselves culturally distinct (in terms of customs, dialect or language, and origins) (quoted in Khoury and Kostiner 1990: 5). Tribes maintain their social solidarity through "a myth of common ancestry." Tribes and tribalism can also be described through their social and political relationships: the relationships between the tribe and the state, between the tribe and other tribes and within the tribe itself. Traditionally, tribes are defined in terms of their opposition to the state, their constantly shifting alliances with other tribes and the fluidity of their leadership structures within the tribe.

The leadership structure within the tribe had a Weberian patrimonial logic: *shaykhs* maintained their position only as long as they maintained the trust and loyalty of their followers. Their role and status was secured primarily by ensuring the continuous flow of goods and services to tribal members. If the leader failed in his duties, he was no longer seen as fit to lead and was replaced by a leader who could better see to the interests of his tribesmen. Alliances between tribes (chiefdoms, also called chieftaincies) were similarly fluid. Often created for the limited purposes of enduring existential hardships or minor territorial expansion, tribes felt little compunction about leaving alliances or contesting the leadership. Tribes easily entered and left alliances as suited their changing needs. The formation and management of coalitions (and their constant dissolution and occasional descent into lasting rivalries) lay at the heart of tribal politics in the area that became Transjordan. Abdullah would exploit these relations to his benefit and eventually freeze them, as he became the paramount *shaykh*, in a "tribal alliance" called the Jordanian state, but without the traditional tribal check on power: ability to exit freely.

Opposition to central authority is also a defining feature of tribal identity and social organization. As ideal-types, tribes and states are often seen as inherently incompatible social structures; "tribes represent large kin groups organized and regulated according to ties of blood or family lineage; states, by contrast, are structures that exercise the ultimate monopoly of power in a given territory" (Khoury and Kostiner 1990: 4). Tribal structures emerge and are strengthened in areas in which the power of the centralized state is weak.[5] In a sense, tribes and states are competing security rackets, with the state offering security in exchange for taxes collected through bureaucratic means, and tribes offering security in exchange for the *ikhwa*, the "brotherly tax", collected through raiding. Periodic raiding formed a central feature of the tribal socioeconomic system. Nomadic people would raid settled people to collect the goods their nomadic lifestyle could not provide them. In exchange, they offered "security" to the settled people from "taxation" by other groups. There were understood rules regarding when raiding was appropriate and who could be a target. But, like any other "protection racket," the settled population had little protection against arbitrary taxation from tribal raids.

Although complementary, "nomadism" and "tribalism" are not necessarily the same system. Pastoral nomadism refers to the practice of seasonal migrations to follow water sources in an arid environment not conducive to sedentary agriculture. Tribalism refers to the social and political relationships described above: opposition to the state, shifting alliances, etc. Nomadism, as an economic mode, tends to rely on tribalism as a political mode, but tribalism, as a political and cultural system, can exist without nomadism. Instead, the term "tribe" is better understood as referring to a category of identity, since many of the settled people in early Jordan considered themselves members of a particular tribe, and the tribe could include nomadic, semi-nomadic and sedentary branches (Fathi 1994: 35). Tribal lines intersected the prominent division between settled and nomadic people in early Transjordan. Even though there are virtually no people practicing a nomadic way of life in Jordan today, the issue of tribe as an *identity* continues to be a central one to which we will return in the final section of this chapter (Layne 1994; Shryock 1997).

The tribes that were convinced to join the Arab Revolt rallied to the cause of Islam, but they also shared the Hashemite grievance against the extension of the railway to Mecca. The railway, by offering pilgrims a secure route to the holy cities, would deprive the tribes of the Hijaz of the "protection" money they depended on for their livelihood. Since some tribes also rented their camels to pilgrims, the railway would deprive them of their camel transport profits as well (Wilson 1987: 23). Tribes had already attacked the rail system in 1908 (Oschenwald 1991: 195). In short, the tribesmen of the Hijaz had material grievances against the Empire, and could be easily convinced to join a rebellion, particularly under the leadership of the regional, governing family entrusted to protect Islam's holy sites. The men who fought the Arab Revolt were not nationalists, but rather tribesmen from the Hijaz, who were inspired by personal interest, their actions legitimated by defense of Islam. In Jordanian nationalist rhetoric, after the establishment of the state, they would be transformed symbolically into defenders of the Arab nation.

The Arab Revolt did not create Jordanian national identity. It provided the building blocks that the new Jordanian state would carry forth as its national identity: Islam, Arab nationalism and the tribes. The Arab Revolt drew from pre-state identities and forms the bridge to the nation-building efforts after the state was established. By stressing *Hashemite* leadership of the *Arab* Revolt fought by loyal tribesmen, Jordan's early leaders connected Jordanian nationalism to Islam, a larger Arab national identity *and* the tribes. In sum, the Arab Revolt would become the new Jordanian government's constitutive myth (Smith 1986: 15) and an enduring feature of contemporary Jordanian nationalism. The Jordanian state would attach that myth symbol to political power.

A new state, an identity solidifies

The area that became Transjordan[6] in 1921 was one of the more unlikely places for the formation of a modern state: it had no significant urban areas and a very small population of approximately 225,000 people (Wilson 1987: 55). In the words of a prominent historian, Jordan "had no reason to be a state on its own rather than a part of Syria, or of Palestine, or of Saudi Arabia, or of Iraq, except that it better served Britain's interests to be so" (Wilson 1987: 3). These origins in imperial interest rather than any preexisting national longing for a state place Jordan squarely in Smith's definition of a colonial state:

> [where] a modern, rational state is imposed from above on populations which are divided into many different ethnic communities and categories, who band together to achieve independent statehood under the aegis of a state-wide nationalism, and then try to use this territorial state and its "nationalism" to create a unified nation out of these divergent *ethnie*.
>
> (Smith 1989: 242)

However, the case of Jordan diverges from this description in that the region that became Jordan was characterized by localized power groupings (tribes) within a single Arab *ethnie*, a "named human population(s) with shared ancestry, myths, histories and cultures, having an association with a specific territory and a sense of solidarity" (Smith 1989: 32) not "different ethnic communities and categories."[7] Furthermore, these power groupings did not "band together to achieve independent statehood under the aegis of a state-wide nationalism," but rather were melded into a national group through compulsion and persuasion by the colonial state with indigenous help. These key features of state-building are the historical determinants of Jordanian nationalism.

The Arab Revolt failed to create a United Arab Kingdom under the leadership of Shariff Hussein or either of his sons. Although Faysal, his tribal troops and a coterie of Arab nationalist advisors had reached Damascus and set up an independent Arab government by July 1919, the British demurred to wartime promises to the French regarding French dominance of Syria, embodied in the Sykes–Picot Agreement. Faysal's regime in Damascus fell after five months when French troops marched in to eject him and Britain declined to intervene.[8] In 1920, the League of Nations imposed the Mandate system on the Arab lands of the defeated Ottoman Empire. France would govern Syria and Lebanon; Britain would govern Palestine and Iraq. Transjordan, originally part of the Palestine Mandate, was made a separate governance in 1921. The terms of the Mandate outlined a "supervisory" role for the European powers until the new states could govern themselves. In practice, the Mandate was simply another form of colonial control.

The British, like the Ottomans before them, considered Transjordan a place between other places, an expanse of territory that need only be governed to the extent that it cause no trouble to the governing body. After fighting a grueling war in Europe and facing rebellions throughout its overseas Empire, Britain could not dedicate significant resources to Transjordan. Abdullah, Faysal's older brother by four years, stepped directly into this flux. Abdullah had spent most of the Revolt laying siege to Ottoman garrisons in the Hijaz. After the fall of the Arab government in Syria, he began a march on Damascus to recover the family "inheritance" taken by the French, but stopped his troops to camp in Ma'an, a small town north of Aqaba, to await a British response. This was a shrewd political maneuver, calculated to "bring himself back to the attention of the British" (Robins 2004: 17). Through due diligence, his ploy worked.

At his camp in Ma'an, Abdullah received delegations and visits from two crucial bases of support: tribal *shaykhs* and nationalists. Tribal *shaykhs* came as a matter of course to pay their respects to a member of the Hashemite family and to create alliances that formed the heart of tribal politics. Arab nationalists, recently expelled from Damascus, sought leadership for their cause of regaining the Arab state. Through these relationships, Abdullah informally made himself a center of power where no center had previously existed, and therefore useful to the British who sought an expedient means to control an unruly territory. By the time he resumed his "march on Damascus" northward towards Amman, Abdullah had created a "slow-moving *fait accompli*" (Robins 2004: 19). In Amman, he presented himself as the Arab leader capable of serving as Britain's local governor and the conduit between the British and the local population. Governance in Transjordan under the British Mandate would be based on the British governing Abdullah, and Abdullah governing the tribes (Aruri 1972).

Furthermore, through these visits from tribal *shaykhs* and nationalists, the foundations of Jordanian nationalism laid by the Arab Revolt took further shape and were forged into another enduring myth symbol of contemporary Jordanian nationalism: the requests by the tribes and nationalists for Abdullah to be their king. While these individuals sought Abdullah out in pursuit of their own interests, contemporary Jordanian nationalists now view this period as one in which the people of the region voluntarily requested and submitted to Abdullah's rule, and thus forged the Jordanian nation: "on November 23, 1920, Amir Abdullah arrived in Ma'an, and the majority of the *shaykhs* visited him and Jordan turned to declare their allegiance and loyalty to him. Yes, this is how the Jordanian people proclaimed Abdullah their prince before the state (was established)" (Abu Nuwaar 1999). This rendering links state (Abdullah) and society (Arab nationalists and tribal leaders), legitimating Hashemite leadership of Jordan *before* the creation of the Jordanian state.

Abdullah needed both the nationalists and the tribal *shaykhs*. Since his brother Faysal had been installed as King of Iraq, a respectably large and prosperous territory, Abdullah harbored ambitions to claim the remainder of the Arab territories lost by the Ottomans and "promised" to his father by the British in the Hussein–McMahon correspondence. He viewed Transjordan as a stepping stone for greater territorial gains, namely Syria. In order to maintain his nationalist credentials, and hence some shred of legitimacy for his ambitions for territorial expansion, he maintained a collection of Arab nationalists as advisors. Abdullah's first cabinet, after he was made the *amir* (Prince) of Transjordan, was entirely made up of nationalists who had served with Faysal in Syria.

In addition to their ideological appeal, the Arab nationalists also served Abdullah on a more mundane level: as civil servants in the new bureaucracy. As Transjordan's local population provided few educated individuals able to fill those roles, Arab nationalists, who tended to be well educated, staffed the Mandatory government's offices. The early Transjordanian state also employed many Palestinian Arabs seconded from the Palestine administration based in Jerusalem. This appeared to exclude "native sons" and hence stimulated the formation of the Transjordanian National Congress in 1928 (Abu Odeh 1999: 22–3). This organization held six national conferences between 1928 and 1933, attended by urban and rural elites. The first conference, attended by "150 prominent personalities and *shaykhs*," called for

Transjordan to be "an independent sovereign Arab country," for the establishment of constitutional government and the reduction of British involvement to merely technical assistance (Massad 2001: 30). Subsequent conferences demanded "Transjordan for Transjordanians," a thinly veiled call to expel non-Transjordanians from the administration and replace them with "sons of the soil." Only one conference, in 1930, expressed support for pan-Arab unity. A number of trends emerged through these conferences: the formation of Transjordan as a unit of identity, the centrality of state employment in Transjordanian identity and tension between regime use of Arab nationalism and the emerging demand for a state-centered nationalism on the ground.

These tensions are well captured by Smith in one of his few references to inter-Arab politics. According to Smith, pan-Arab nationalism presented a "dual difficulty" for the people and states in the Arab Middle East:

> Geographical extent and separate political histories, both before and after the Ottoman conquest, presented a dual difficulty for any attempt at forming an Arab nation: on the one hand, application of a Western-style territorial concept of the nation inevitably spelt the permanent fragmentation of the Arab ethnic community, and on the other hand, the project of realizing an ethnic concept of the Arab nation encountered all the geographical, economic and political problems of any "Pan" movement.
>
> (Smith 1986: 143–4)

This dilemma for Jordan, and for other Arab states, would only be resolved by the decline of pan-Arabism in the aftermath of the 1967 war.

These Transjordanian National Conferences represent an important precursor to state-centered Transjordanian nationalism, but pan-Arabism, which called for unification of all Arabs under one state, was still the dominant form of nationalism at the time. Like Abdullah, the Arab nationalists saw Transjordan as a way station towards the greater prize of Syria. To that end, they conducted raids into French-controlled Syria. These raids created tension between France and Britain particularly after one raid that killed a French army officer in Syria. The British pressured Abdullah to rein in and eventually expel the nationalists.

Expelling the Arab nationalists on British colonial bidding made it more difficult for Abdullah to use Arab nationalism as a legitimating tool. Furthermore, as it became increasingly clear that the French would remain in control of Syria, Abdullah began to apply himself more diligently to expanding state control over the territory allotted to him, small as it was. To build his state, Abdullah turned to the local tribes as an alternate source of legitimacy, one rooted in the realities of Jordan rather than in ambitions to control Syria.

The Mandatory government faced the daunting challenges of compelling the tribes to submit to the state and melding a unified national identity out of these social forces defined by their competition with each other. Abdullah and the British used formal and informal means to integrate the tribes into the state. First, they needed to neutralize tribal opposition to the state and compel them to submit to the central authority. Early on, Abdullah's regime faced several tribal uprisings, including one from Shaykh al-Sharida in 1921 and one from the Adwan tribe in 1923. These rebellions would often be couched in the rhetoric of demands for a representative assembly and increased Transjordanian employment in the civil service; however, the root causes were often unequal taxation and tribal jealousies (Wilson 1987: 78). These rebellions were quelled relatively easily by superior British military power and technology, namely the Royal Air Force.

Putting down revolts was a necessary, but not sufficient condition for creating a viable state. Building legitimacy, and hence voluntary compliance with the state, is the only path to the long-term sustainability of state power. To accomplish this, the state also pursued policies of accommodation, transforming the tribes into the "bedrock of the regime" (Jureidini and McLaurin 1984). These policies did not disrupt traditional tribal hierarchies, but rather melded them to state-building purposes. The formal aspect of this integration was the creation of the Jordanian army and the recruitment of tribal members as soldiers; the informal aspect was embodied in Abdullah's extensive visiting with the tribes, cementing personal connections between state and society.

The creation of the Desert Mobile Force, which eventually became the Arab Legion, Jordan's national army, was a crucial formal means by which the state integrated the tribes (Vatikiotis 1967). Through the 1920s, British mandatory leaders had recruited a small military force from the settled, agricultural population of the north, viewing the nomadic tribes of the central and southern regions of the country as the enemy of stable, centralized rule. The settled population tended to be less resistant to centralized authority. As the frequent victims of tribal raids, they were willing to serve in armed forces to protect their property and livelihoods. However, the force was not sufficient to quell tribal opposition to the regime.

In 1930, Major John Bagot Glubb arrived from Iraq and created the Desert Mobile Force, which recruited primarily from the tribes, employing a technique that had been successful in Iraq during his tenure there. Glubb encouraged the Transjordanian tribes to join by enlisting approximately 20–30 percent of the fighting force from outside Transjordan, namely from Iraq. This way, "If the Huwaitat (a tribe in southern Jordan) did not enlist, the result would be that their country would be policed by men of other tribes, not, as they hoped, that it would not be policed at all" (Glubb 1946: 93). This nascent army channeled traditional tribal warrior values into a state institution that was used to pursue state aims, namely the quelling of inter-tribal raiding within Transjordan and cross-border raiding from tribes in Saudi Arabia. As a corollary to this policy, Glubb also instituted courts based on tribal law for the mediation of inter-tribal disputes. These courts existed alongside the central judicial system, which was based on an amalgam of European codes. Both the tribal courts and the army exerted the power of the central state by employing tribal structures and identities. Thus, the state's traditional antagonists, the tribes, were coopted to become its social base.

In addition to the formal institutions, such as the army, Abdullah relied on active patrimonialism, a more informal method to legitimate his claim to leadership (Alon 1998). Through personal visits to tribal leaders, Abdullah used tribal structures and identity to build his new state. He affirmed the tribal pattern of personalistic leadership, but also enlarged patrimonial authority by becoming the overall "shaykh of shaykhs," with all the tribes being forged into one Jordanian "tribe." Since the British viewed the region as ungovernable, internal tribal politics remained Abdullah's domain. In short, "Abdullah adopted the tribal ethos and turned it into the ethos of the whole nation, thus facilitating the tribal society's acceptance of the state" (Alon 1998: 12). The state became the tribe writ large. These identity patterns remain strong in Jordan, as many Jordanians consider their national Jordanian identity intertwined with their tribal identity, and an inherent aspect of being a "true" Jordanian citizen (Layne 1994).

In short, the regime created support for its rule from the dominant social organization, the "tribe," and the tribes came to depend on the state for their livelihood and also for protection against raiding by other tribes (Khoury and Kostiner 1990). These processes laid the groundwork for contemporary Jordanian identity where most tribesmen see no contradiction between loyalty to their tribe and loyalty to their state (Layne 1994).

Although "the tribes," have become the primary symbolic piece of Jordanian identity, the regime never abandoned either Islam or Arabness entirely. Abdullah continued to stress his Hashemite lineage and to harbor ambitions for an expanded Arab kingdom, ambitions that would find some gratification in the acquisition of the West Bank in 1948. By 1948, the foundations of a Transjordanian national identity were firmly in place.

Transjordanian nationalism today: persistent themes and continuing challenges

The bulk of this chapter has focused on the formative years of the Jordanian nation and state. Although the formation of the nation was strongly conditioned by the formation of the state, contemporary Jordanian national identity has its own trajectory, no longer dictated by the demands of state-building. Its early foundations have been remarkably durable and remain the parameters in which national identity is discussed today. While this concluding section is by no means a complete survey of current expressions and manifestations of Jordanian nationalism, it touches on the continuity of its primary elements: Arab nationalism, Islam and the tribes.

The war over Palestine in 1948 permanently altered Jordan's political development. Jordan "acquired" approximately 900,000 Palestinian refugees, some 450,000 who fled their homes in what had become the state of Israel and between 400,000 and 450,000 residents of the West Bank, now under Jordanian control. The dramatic influx of Palestinian refugees remains the most prominent issue affecting national identity in Jordan today (Nanes 2003: 16; Massad 2001). Almost immediately, Jordan granted citizenship to all Palestinians who fell under its rule, both refugees and residents of the West Bank.[9] For the years 1950–67, official Jordanian rhetoric stressed that Jordanians were "one Jordanian family, with Jordanian and Palestinian branches," and that "Jordanians come from all origins and birthplaces." Given the large numbers of Palestinians, and Abdullah's flickering but not entirely dead hope of a larger Arab kingdom, this rhetoric was the logical path for the regime to take, dictated both by the regional ascendance of pan-Arab nationalism in the 1950s and 1960s and the regime's desire to incorporate its new citizens. Despite its rhetoric, however, the regime never abandoned its commitment to the tribes, as evidenced by the reservation of sensitive, high-level posts for Transjordanians and the preference for the East Bank in economic subsidies, even during the period of unity of the two banks.

After Israel's capture of the West Bank in 1967, this outwardly accommodating language and policy began to be challenged in the 1970s and 1980s by a more strident, assertive cry of "Jordan for Jordanians" from Transjordanians themselves. The transformation towards state-centered nationalism resulted in large part from the battle between the PLO and the Jordanian army in 1970–1.[10] Radical Palestinian factions attempted to topple the Jordanian state as a step towards the liberation of Palestine west of the Jordan River. The Jordanian army, in a series of battles, ejected the PLO and all of its factions from Jordan. Although the majority of the Palestinian citizens of Jordan remained aloof from the actual fighting and the majority of Palestinian Jordanians serving in the Jordanian army did not desert (Gubser 1988), the aftermath of the civil war has seen the increasing "Jordanization" of the Jordanian regime (Abu Odeh 1999). Palestinian Jordanians who had served in the civil service and in the universities were systematically rooted out (Fathi 1994). Palestinian Jordanians still find it virtually impossible to gain employment in the bureaucracy today. Their political clout is systematically decreased by electoral rules that heavily overrepresent Transjordanian districts (Abu Odeh 1999). Rather than a complete rupture, the civil conflict can be seen as a tilt away from the delicate balancing act of accommodating Palestinian-origin citizens while nurturing the original social basis of the state practiced by the Jordanian government from 1950 through 1970, towards relaying on an exclusive Transjordanian identity after the civil conflict.

Of the three foundational strands of Jordanian identity, commitment to the tribes remains the strongest. There are currently two understandings of contemporary Jordanian nationalism: state-centered and society-centered (Lynch 1998). Reliance on the tribes for continued state legitimacy plays a key role in both. The state-centered trend is strongly pro-regime, stressing a tight linkage between the tribes, the state, the military and the Hashemite dynasty (Lynch 1998: 23). Tribes are important, but primarily through their service in the army and loyalty to the king. Conversely, the state and the king are crucial in holding the Jordanian nation (of tribes) together. In contrast, the society-centered view of Jordanian nationalism takes tribes as both the starting and ending point of Jordanian nationalism (Lynch 1998; Shryock 1997). For them, Jordan is a unique historical entity in its own right, dating back to the ancient civilization of the Nabateans who built Petra. The Jordanian state is an expression of that preexisting, independent identity. Jordanian identity is emphatically not a product of state forces. Needless to say, the society-centered view is the more radical of the two; however, both approaches to Jordanian nationalism include a central place for tribes.[11]

In the absence of genuine democratic reform, the regime depends on tribal support.[12] The tribes remain "the backbone of the regime" (Jureidini and McLaurin 1984). Most Jordanians see no contradiction between their tribal and Jordanian identities (Layne 1994). The term "tribes" in contemporary Jordanian discourse refers to a form of identity based on family or clan membership, particularly those families that were in Jordan before 1948, and therefore "true Jordanians." All "tribes" have well-educated members who participate in modern sectors of the economy, but are still well aware of their family background, hence tribal identity.

Basing the identity of a centralized state on tribalism, a decentralized system, however, has its perils. Tribal identity is no longer simply a tool in the hands of the regime. Tribal historians have begun to participate themselves in the construction of Jordanian national identity (Shryock 1997). The arrival of the Hashemites brought the extension of centralized rule and the end of tribal autonomy, a defining feature of tribal life. Thus, "the tribes" are in the strange position of being compelled to celebrate the institution (the Jordanian state) that meant the end of their independent tribal identity as the highest expression of that very tribal identity. In a remarkable anthropological work, Andrew Shryock shows the instability of the regime's reliance on "subdued" societal groups through his study of Transjordanian nationalists who use Jordan's tribal heritage to contradict the regime's discourse of unity and challenge the legitimacy of Hashemite rule (Shryock 1997).

Although Arab nationalism has clearly lost out to tribalism for hegemony in contemporary Jordanian nationalism, the Arab Revolt continues to play an essential role in representing Arab identity in the triumvirate of Jordanian nationalist symbols. In this way, the Revolt still plays an important, but now contested, role as a myth symbol in contemporary Jordan. For Ma'an Abu Nuwaar, a Jordanian historian, "the Great Arab Revolt (was) a Jordanian revolt in regards to the Jordanian nation," and the Arab Revolt has not failed but "remains burning in the mind and heart of every honorable and sincere Arab" (Abu Nuwaar 1999). For others, the Revolt's legacy is a heavy burden to bear because it compromises the citizens of Jordan's ability to discuss the state's own unique Transjordanian national identity. Fahd al-Fanek, a well-known Transjordanian nationalist columnist for the state-owned newspaper *al-Rai*, argued that the inheritance of the Great Arab Revolt distances the government of Jordan from its people and simply earns "Arab enmity" for Jordan (al-Fanek 1999). The Great Arab Revolt continues to be stressed in Jordanian textbooks as a formative event for the nation and the state. The Jordanian Monument to the Unknown Soldier, Jordan's primary military museum, features extensive coverage of the Arab Revolt. Its displays emphasize the Hashemite leadership of the uprising and the Arab Legion's defense of Jerusalem during the 1948 war as proof of Jordan's steadfastness in service to the Arab cause.

The regime still relies heavily on the Revolt for legitimation purposes, particularly when making decisions that may prove unpopular. For example, the Jordanian regime repeatedly reminded the public of the Arab Revolt in the period leading up to and immediately following the disengagement decision in July 1988, when King Hussein renounced Jordan's claim to the West Bank (Layne 1994: 27). Even after the disengagement, King Hussein continued to invoke the Arab Revolt in various highly public settings, from the thirty-sixth anniversary of King Hussein's accession to the throne in August 1988 to the establishment of the Arab Cooperation Council in February 1989. The leadership of the Palestinian Intifada on the West Bank had just rejected King Hussein's claim to represent their cause in December 1987. Hussein was concerned that Jordan's disengagement would leave him open to accusations of abandoning the Palestinians in their hour of struggle, but he knew he could no longer sustain Jordanian administrative ties to the West Bank. As his grandfather before him, Arab nationalism served as a useful cover for the pursuit of state interests.

References to the protection of Islam, however, are notably absent from the mainstream discourse about Jordanian national identity. Given the strength of the Islamist movement in Jordan and the region as a whole, the Jordanian regime does not want to stress its Islamic legitimacy too strongly, lest it be called on to implement Islamic law. Such a transformation would be anathema to the royal family, which strongly seeks to project a modern and moderate image for Jordan internationally. This image, incidentally, is crucial to retaining the American aid that sustains the Jordanian economy. References to the Hashemite lineage of the monarchy represent the extent to which the current regime incorporates Islam into Jordanian national identity.

Conclusion

The case of Jordan shows that nations cannot be created out of thin air, as Smith's work shows, and that even the most obviously arbitrary states must use preexisting cultural material to construct their nations. Jordanian national identity contains three features – Arabism, Islam and the tribes – which were certainly present in some form in the region that became Transjordan prior to the creation of the Jordanian state. These elements were combined together and transformed into modern nationalism only with the creation of the Transjordanian state over the 1920s and 1930s. Several decades later, those elements have materialized into a full-fledged national identity, with the tribal element currently taking precedent.

During the mid-1980s, the issue of tribalism came up for intense debate when Parliament proposed abolishing the tribal law instituted by Glubb in the 1930s. After a flurry of public discussion, where tribes were accused of being "backward," King Hussein rose to their defense. In doing so, he deftly wove together the tribes, Arab identity and Islam:

> I would like to repeat to you what I have told a meeting of tribal heads recently that "I am al-Hussein from Hashem and Quraish the noblest Arab tribe of Mecca which was honored by God and into which was born the Arab Prophet Mohammad." Therefore, whatever harms our tribes in Jordan is considered harmful to us, as this has been the case all along, and it will continue to be so forever.
>
> (*Jordan Times*, January 28, 1985, quoted in Layne 1994: 105)

The three elements of Jordanian national identity – the tribes with Hashemite religious legitimacy and Arab national identity – are all manifest in the person of King Hussein. It is also notable that this reference was given before a meeting of tribal leaders, emphasizing the traditional means by which the Jordanian monarch still retains his power and legitimacy.

Although the tribal feature of contemporary Jordanian national identity has come to be the most prominent, King Abdullah II, the current king, has attempted to dampen some of the overt shows of tribal support. For example, he called on tribal leaders to cease taking out large ads in newspapers to honor the king and assert their loyalty on the occasion of the king's birthday.[13] He has focused his attention on bringing foreign investment to Jordan and integrating Jordan into the world market through a free trade agreement with the United States. However, the Jordanian nation, and its "tribal character," is still relevant because the identity is ultimately connected to state power. Jordanian nationalism remains remarkably durable precisely because it absorbed the local tribes, Arab nationalism and Islam in order to legitimate the fledgling territorial Jordanian state. Despite its recent vintage, it now boasts a full-fledged national identity, which several million Transjordanians believe is the *raison d'être* for their state.

Notes

1 The Hijaz is the Western section of today's Saudi Arabia containing the Muslim holy cities of Mecca and Medina.
2 These territories include present-day Syria and Lebanon, promised to France in the Sykes–Picot Agreement, and Palestine, in which Britain pledged support for "a Jewish home" in the Balfour Declaration.
3 Given that secular Turkish nationalism had taken the reins of power in 1908 with the Young Turk Revolution, this analysis was not altogether incorrect.
4 The Hashemites lost control of Mecca and Medina to the Saudis after the battle of Turaba in 1919, but they maintained their claim to Jerusalem to bolster their religious credentials and Abdullah's ambition for Palestine. To this day, Jordan maintains a "special role" in the administration of Muslim holy sites in Jerusalem.
5 Counterfactual evidence for this process can be found in the subsequent weakening of tribal confederacies in Transjordan once the centralized colonial state began to improve individual security (Alon 2005).
6 "Transjordan" is the pre-1946 name for today's Jordan. It refers to the East Bank of the Jordan River. Transjordan became the Hashemite Kingdom of Jordan, or simply Jordan, with independence in 1946.
7 There are small communities of Circassians and Chechens in Jordan, who are not Arab. They have been loyal to the Hashemites from the establishment of the state.
8 Faysal was then installed as the King of newly formed Iraq.
9 By granting citizenship to Palestinians, the regime made them legally Jordanian. Today, the term "Jordanian" refers to one with Jordanian citizenship; however, the terms "Palestinian Jordanian" and "Transjordanian" have become more common usage in academic treatments of the subject of Jordanian national identity in order to identify Jordanians by their national origin. Often, there is slippage between the usage of the terms "Jordanian" and "Transjordanian," in real life and in this chapter, reflecting the ongoing debate as to whether or not Palestinian Jordanians are "truly Jordanian."
10 The massive defeat of the Arab armies in 1967 by Israel also vastly deflated pan-Arab ideology.
11 A key point of contention between these two strands is their relative approach to the issue of Jordanians of Palestinian origin; moderates believe they can assimilate and become Jordanian, radicals do not (Lynch 1998; Abu Odeh 1999; Nanes 2003).
12 The picture is more complicated, as the regime also relies on the compliance of the Jordanian business elite, many of whom are of Palestinian origin. However, the compliance of the business elite can be achieved quietly by the regime maintaining a secure investment environment, while Jordanian nationalists require more open assurances of their interests being met. It is widely observed that the regime continues to carefully nurture its support in rural Jordanian areas and of the leaders of prominent tribal families.
13 Personal observation during fieldwork, November 1999–November 2000.

References

Abu Nuwaar, M. (1999) "Muhawalat Mukhlisa lil-fahm . . . Fi al-Wataniyya al-Urduniyya [An Honest Attempt to Understand . . . About Jordanian Nationalism]," al-Rai, 4 December.
Abu Odeh, A. (1999) *Jordanians, Palestinians and the Hashemite Kingdom of Jordan in*

the Middle East Peace Process, Washington, DC: United States Institute of Peace Press.

al-Fanek, F. (1999) "Al-wataniyya al-Urduniyya" [Jordanian patriotism], *al-Rai*, 30 November 1999.

Alon, Y. (1998) "State, Tribe and Mandate: Transjordan's Shaykhs and the Creation of the Emirate," paper presented at the annual meeting of the Middle East Studies Association, Chicago.

—— (2005) "The Tribal System in the Face of the State-Formation Process: Mandatory Transjordan, 1921–1946," *International Journal of Middle East Studies*, 37: 213–40.

Aruri, N. (1972) *Jordan: A Study in Political Development, 1921–1965*, The Hague: Martinus Nijhoff.

Cleveland, W. (2004) *A History of the Modern Middle East*, 3rd edn, Boulder: Westview Press.

Dawn, C.E. (1991) "The Origins of Arab Nationalism," in R. Khalidi, L. Anderson, M. Muslih and R.S. Simon (eds) *The Origins of Arab Nationalism*, New York: Columbia University Press.

Fathi, S.H. (1994) *Jordan – An Invented Nation?: Tribe–State Dynamics and the Formation of National Identity*, Hamburg: Deutsches Orient-Institut.

Glubb, J.B. (1946) *The Story of the Arab Legion*, London: Hodder and Stoughton.

Gubser, P. (1988) "Jordan: Balancing Pluralism and Authoritarianism," in P.J. Chelkowski and R.J. Pranger (eds) *Ideology and Power in the Middle East: Studies in Honor of George Lenczowski*, Durham: Duke University Press.

Hourani, A. (1983) *Arabic Thought in the Liberal Age: 1798–1939*, Cambridge: Cambridge University Press.

Jureidini, P. and McLaurin, R.D. (1984) *Jordan: The Impact of Social Change on the Role of the Tribes*, Washington, DC: Praeger.

Khoury, P.S. (1983) *Urban Notables and Arab Nationalism: The Politics of Damascus 1880–1920*, Princeton: Princeton University Press.

Khoury, P.S. and Kostiner, J. (eds) (1990) *Tribes and State Formation in the Middle East*, Berkeley: University of California Press.

Layne, L. (1994) *Home and Homeland: The Dialogics of Tribal and National Identities in Jordan*, Princeton: Princeton University Press.

Lynch, M. (1998) "Jordan's Competing Nationalisms: Deliberation, Transition and Theories of Ethnic Conflict," paper presented at the annual meeting of the Middle East Studies Association, Chicago.

Massad, J. (2001) *Colonial Effects: The Making of National Identity in Jordan*. New York: Columbia University Press.

Milton-Edwards, B. (2000) *Contemporary Politics in the Middle East*, Oxford: Blackwell.

Nanes, S. (2003) *Citizenship and National Identity: A National Dialogue*, Ph.D. dissertation: University of Wisconsin-Madison.

Ochsenwald, W. (1991) "Ironic Origins: Arab Nationalism in the Hijaz, 1882–1914," in R. Khalidi, L. Anderson, M. Muslih and R.S. Simon (eds) *The Origins of Arab Nationalism*, New York: Columbia University Press.

Robins, P. (2004) *A History of Jordan*, Cambridge: Cambridge University Press.

Shryock, A. (1997) *Nationalism and the Genealogical Imagination: Oral History and Textual Authority in Tribal Jordan*, Berkeley: University of California Press.

Smith, A.D. (1986) "State-making and Nation-building," in J. Hall (ed.) *States in History*, Oxford: Basil Blackwell.

—— (1989) *Ethnic Origins of Nations*, New York: Blackwell.

Vatikiotis, P.J. (1967) *Politics and the Military in Jordan*, London: Frank Cass & Co.

Wilson, M.C. (1987) *King Abdullah, Britain and the Making of Jordan.* Cambridge: Cambridge University Press.

—— (1991) "The Hashemites, the Arab Revolt, and Arab Nationalism," in R. Khalidi, L. Anderson, M. Muslih and R.S. Simon (eds) *The Origins of Arab Nationalism*, New York: Columbia University Press.

Index